The Tragic Art of
ERNEST
HEMINGWAY

The Tragic Art of

ERNEST

HEMINGWAY

WIRT WILLIAMS

Louisiana State University Press
Baton Rouge and London

Copyright © 1981 by Louisiana State University Press
All rights reserved
Manufactured in the United States of America
Design: Albert Crochet
Typeface: Linotype Garamond
Composition: Service Typesetters
Printing and binding: Thomson-Shore, Inc.

LIBRARY OF CONGRESS CATALOGING IN PUBLICATION DATA
Williams, Wirt.
  The tragic art of Ernest Hemingway.

  Includes index.
    1. Hemingway, Ernest, 1899–1961—Criticism and
interpretation. 2. Tragic, The. I. Title.
PS3515.E37Z952   813'.52   81-4740
ISBN 0-8071-0884-7   AACR2

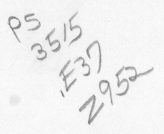

For Ann

Contents

Acknowledgments

I wish to thank the editors of the Louisiana State University Press for their dedicated and energetic sponsorship of this book; the Department of English of California State University at Los Angeles for providing valuable resource assistance; staff members of the Carlsbad City Library for their unfailing help; various professional readers who were indispensable mentors and guides; many friends and colleagues for their warm and steady encouragement; and most particularly Mrs. Kathleen Moore, for her priceless aid in every aspect of the preparation of the manuscript.

The Tragic Art of
ERNEST
HEMINGWAY

INTRODUCTION

The Tragic Field and
Ernest Hemingway

I

In 1927, Ernest Hemingway wrote a poem to certain reviewers called "Valentine." Smarting under attacks on his earliest published work, he mocked them by apparent quotation: "sordid small catastrophes / stack the cards on fate."[1] A little later, he declared, "*The Sun Also Rises* is a damn tragedy with the earth as hero abiding forever."[2] And he called *A Farewell to Arms* "my Romeo and Juliet."[3] More at the heart of things, perhaps, is his remark to the Old Lady in one of those marvelous conversations in *Death in the Afternoon*: "Madame, all stories, if continued far enough, end in death, and he is no true story-teller who would keep that from you."[4] How much do these and other often oblique invocations of the tragic mean in suggesting he saw himself clearly as a writer of tragedy? Maybe nothing, maybe everything. Certainly the ultimate identification of him as a writer of tragedy or of anything else is and must be in his work. But it is significant that a great many of his interpreters have strenuously urged that identification.

In 1952, Carlos Baker declared unequivocally that since *The Sun Also*

1. Ernest Hemingway, "Valentine," *Little Review*, XII (May, 1929), 42.
2. Ernest Hemingway to Maxwell Perkins, November 19, 1926, quoted in Carlos Baker, *Ernest Hemingway: The Writer as Artist* (Princeton: Princeton University Press, 1972), 91.
3. Quoted in Edmund Wilson, "Ernest Hemingway: Bourdon Gauge of Morale," reprinted in J. K. M. McCaffery (ed.), *Ernest Hemingway: The Man and His Work* (Cleveland and New York: World, 1950), 236–57.
4. Ernest Hemingway, *Death in the Afternoon* (New York: Scribner's, 1932).

Rises "all of Hemingway's novels have been tragedies." The same year, Philip Young wrote that the great achievement of *The Old Man and the Sea* was as a tragedy in the Greek mold, and comparable views were expressed at the time or developed subsequently by others. Some psychological explorations of author and work produced conclusions completely compatible with this perception of Hemingway as tragedy-maker. Young's view that the author's protagonists, like the author, are seeking to regain wholeness after the trauma of severe wounds of body and mind closely parallels the tragic design—where the hero seeks reconciliation and harmony after the great blow of catastrophe. Later, J. J. Benson saw tragedy as Hemingway's resource for resolving his deep inner divisions. Thus, there seems to be a critical consensus that Hemingway wrote tragedy consistently or on occasion, and many appear to hold with Baker that his residual and enduring statement is that of the tragic.[5]

What does this mean? Certainly it means that Hemingway saw man as born to lose for one reason or another—because he is fated to do so in unequal battle with some force in the universe, or because he always carries something in himself that brings the universe crashing down upon him, or both. It might mean, too, that the battle he loses in the flesh can be one he wins in the spirit, and he thus gives himself the only patent of nobility and heroism a mortal may truly possess. This is the highest emotional effect and philosophical statement of tragedy; in one sense, it may be both beginning and end of the tragic idea.

But there is much more inside the circle. If we are to think about Ernest Hemingway as a writer of tragedy, we ought to have a reasonably full understanding of what tragedy is. And arriving at such an understanding is an undertaking of some complexity.

Most recent critics have been concerned with the philosophical nature of the tragic attitude, its ultimate emotional and epistemological communication. Broadly, they seem to share the conviction that the tragic protagonist must wrest from an external disaster some triumph of the

---

5. Baker, *Hemingway: The Writer as Artist*, 152. Philip Young, *Ernest Hemingway: A Reconsideration* (State College: Pennsylvania State University Press, 1966), 129. This is a revised edition of Young's *Ernest Hemingway* (New York: Rinehart, 1952), and unless otherwise specified, quotations will be from it rather than the 1952 book. J. J. Benson, *Hemingway: The Writer's Art of Self-Defense* (Minneapolis: University of Minnesota Press, 1969), 102.

spirit, an awareness of the nature of the universe that reconciles him to it. Joseph Krutch writes, "We accept gladly the outward defeats which (tragedy) describes for the sake of the inward victories which it reveals . . . the idea of nobility is inseparable from the idea of tragedy." And Robert Corrigan says, "Man's tragic condition is that he is doomed by Fate to defeat. The affirmation of tragedy is that it celebrates a kind of victory of man's spirit over his fate." Among many others, Richard Sewell, Karl Jaspers, Herbert Weisinger, and Max Scheler suggest the same conception. Tragedy assumes that it is impossible to win except through total defeat and even destruction; such a victory is itself transcendental.[6]

Indeed, "transcendence" is the term usually given to this inner victory through outer defeat. It is closely related to "reconciliation," that acceptance of the world whole, and all its injustice, that the tragic protagonist may attain through his catastrophe. This reconciliation carries with it inalienably a final sense of universal harmony and even serenity, such as notably concludes *Oedipus at Colonus* and *The Old Man and the Sea*. Many see this as a necessity of tragedy: Murray Krieger insists upon "the need in tragedy to have dissonance exploded, leaving only the harmony of serenity behind."[7]

However, these concepts essentially explore the ultimate transmissions of tragedy, the very nature of the vision; also needed is some formulation of the inner workings of its projections. Looking for these has been a pastime of some popularity since Aristotle, and lately the popularity has been high. As we examine the systems of dramaturgy or architecture that various students have proposed, and as we look closely at a reasonable number of tragic works themselves, we are apt to conclude that there are several different branches of tragedy. Yet they all have a way of coming together, of getting in the end to the same place.

6. Joseph Krutch, "The Tragic Fallacy," reprinted in Mark Schorer, Josephine Miles, and Gordon McKenzie (eds.), *Criticism: The Foundations of Modern Literary Judgement* (New York: Harcourt, Brace, 1958), 79; Robert Corrigan, *Sophocles* (New York: Dell, 1965), 15; Richard Sewell, *The Vision of Tragedy* (New Haven: Yale University Press, 1959), 1–8; Karl Jaspers, *Tragedy Is Not Enough* (Boston: Beacon Press, 1952), 41–56; Herbert Weisinger, *Tragedy and the Paradox of the Fortunate Fall* (East Lansing: Michigan State University Press, 1953); Max Scheler, "On the Tragic," trans. Bernard Stambler, reprinted in Robert Corrigan (ed.), *Tragedy: Vision and Form* (San Francisco: Chandler, 1965), 3–18.
7. Murray Krieger, *The Tragic Vision* (New York: Holt, Rinehart, and Winston, 1960), 4.

Aristotle's basic, that tragedy is "an action that is serious, complete, and of a certain magnitude,"[8] seems simplistic at a glance but is not so at all; its usefulness is apt to be felt increasingly as one broods on it, particularly its requirement of magnitude. Yet the heart of Aristotelian tragedy as we speak of it today is the "fatal flaw": a quality in or even an action by the protagonist which brings catastrophe down upon him. Reducing still more, Aristotelian tragedy is tragedy in which the character himself brings about his catastrophe.

Friedrich Hegel, the other "classic" writer on tragedy, sees tragedy as a collision between opposite ethical absolutes or states of being—between characters or forces of any kind that must in the nature of things collide with the opposite, opposing quality.[9] Both should be "good." Thus in *Antigone*, Antigone as family loyalty must collide with Creon, the personification of loyalty to the state, with foreseeable catastrophe resulting. Friedrich Nietzsche's conflict of the Apollonian and Dionysian is, fundamentally, a case of this Hegelian collision.[10] It should be remembered constantly that both Hegel and Aristotle were attempting to generalize empirically from the example of Greek tragedies, Aristotle's chief specimen being Sophocles' *Oedipus Rex* and Hegel's being the same poet's *Antigone*.

Closely related to this species is the tragedy of division and choice, suggested briefly by A. C. Bradley in his essay on Hegel and developed by Robert Heilman into a thorough and sophisticated system.[11] Thus Antigone herself is presumably divided between family loyalty and civic duty: the conflict is *inside* herself, and she must make the fateful, tragedy-creating choice. So must John Dryden's protagonists in his love versus honor heroic tragedies.

Arthur Miller has seen tragic catastrophe as the result of an individual asserting the inviolability of his personality against a universe

8. Aristotle, *The Poetics*, trans. S. H. Butcher, reprinted in Schorer *et al.*, *Criticism: The Foundations of Modern Literary Judgement*, 202.
9. Friedrich Hegel, *The Philosophy of Fine Art*, trans. F. P. B. Osmaston, reprinted in part in Corrigan (ed.), *Tragedy: Vision and Form*, 428–42.
10. Friedrich Nietzsche, *The Birth of Tragedy and the Genealogy of Morals*, trans. Francis Golping, excerpt reprinted in Corrigan (ed.), *Tragedy: Vision and Form*, 443–50.
11. A. C. Bradley, "Hegel's Theory of Tragedy," reprinted in Schorer *et al.*, *Criticism: The Foundations of Modern Literary Judgment*, 55–56; Robert Bechtold Heilman, *Tragedy and Melodrama* (Seattle: University of Washington Press, 1968). See particularly "Tragedy and Disaster," 3–31.

determined to break it:[12] his own *The Crucible* is an impressive example of his theory. This kind of tragedy is, perhaps, a case of a supreme
moral virtue become a pragmatic, operating flaw, finally a fatal one and
hence, permissively viewed, an Aristotelian one. Generically, the subspecies might be seen also as Hegelian—the assertion of individuality is
one absolute and society's or the cosmos' insistence on the abandonment
of that individuality is another. The last may not be "good," so the subspecies may not be a perfect collision tragedy. Yet the example shows
how different kinds of tragedy seem to merge, to coalesce. The difference is really one of stress, of which aspect is the heaviest in the work.

It may be that the most consistently encountered quality in tragedy
from the Greeks on is that of *hubris*. This we once experienced as a flaw
of mad vanity, or megalomania. Now we know better. As Corrigan and
others have pointed out, we read *hubris* now as an attempt to transcend
the human possibilities, to take more from life than life has to give.
This noble attempt is always overpunished, but the principle of overpunishment, and gigantic overpunishment, is one of the immutables of
tragedy. The tragic hero steps on the toes of tragic necessity; necessity
bashes his brains out with a mace.

In some tragedies the hero need not even tread the toes of his cosmic adversary. The adversary bashes him *anyway*. This seems the very
antithesis of the fatal flaw, but perhaps the fact of being human, of
being born, is in these tragedies the flaw, and flaw enough for the great
enemy.

What is that enemy? It is in the very nature of things, certainly, a
mysterious X that assaults men and either thwarts or destroys them;
inevitably, the destruction is more evident in the literary work than in
literality, but it must be to show its power. Is the X irony? No. Irony
may be part of that X, or it may be a loose agent descending where it
will, or it may simply be one view of the X in action. Irony is a wanton
violation of probability, what ought not to be, and it is much easier to
see than to define satisfactorily. Examples arise: the unforeseeable de-
taining of the priest in *Romeo and Juliet*, as he carries the message that
would save the lovers; the circumstance that Oedipus should meet and
kill his real father on the road when he is fleeing Corinth to avoid kill-

ing the man he thinks is father; the fact so obvious to Thomas Hudson, that his death and the death of the men he is pursuing will result from their massacre of the villagers—a stupid and wasteful mistake they have committed in trying to *save* their own lives. Tragic irony is most powerful when it embodies waste and misunderstanding.

Is it finally, then, simple bad luck? It is much more. It is the universe in action in a way that cannot be fully understood or explained. It changes and smashes the lives of men, like its senior, fate; it is felt, yet never truly comprehended.

The paradoxes and differences among types of tragedy have brought many to the view that it is impossible to reach a single satisfactory definition for tragedy—and their tantalizing closeness has kept students of the form trying. Nowhere has the dilemma been more directly posed, nor a more satisfactory solution to it suggested, than by Northrop Frye in "The Mythos of Autumn." Frye writes, "There are two reductive formulas which have often been used to explain tragedy. Neither is quite good enough, but each is almost good enough, and as they are contradictory, they must represent extreme or limiting views of tragedy. One of these is the theory that all tragedy exhibits the omnipotence of an external fate. . . . The other . . . is that the act which sets the tragic process going must be primarily a violation of *moral* law, whether human or divine; in short, that Aristotle's hamartia or 'flaw' must have an essential connection with sin or wrongdoing."[13]

This insistence that the first cause of the tragedy of flaw be a *moral* transgression does narrow the field, for what we might term the tragic transgression may be an affirmation of moral value even as it violates a social norm (*The Crucible*), or even another moral principle (*Antigone*); it might simply be an error in judgment. Yet if we accept what seems to be the heart of his definition of that wing of tragedy—that it originates and has its cause in a quality or an action of the protagonist himself—then Frye's boundaries indeed contain all tragedy between them.

Rephrased, at one edge tragedy originates in fate and shows the helplessness of man against that fate; at the other tragedy originates in man himself and demonstrates that he is the ultimate author of his own downfall.

13. Northrop Frye, "The Mythos of Autumn," in *The Anatomy of Criticism* (Princeton: Princeton University Press, 1957), 209–10.

A single tragedy may demonstrate one extreme, or the other, or both. Overwhelmingly, most tragedies partake of both.[14]

It will be noted that this definition is philosophic. It is in its way complete, for it is not for the moment concerned with the possible transcendent triumph. However, for a working view of tragedy in action—achieved tragedy—certain dramaturgic postulates must be added. One concerns its structure; the other involves its effect.

First, the tragic protagonist must sustain a catastrophe that is irreversible and irremediable *on its own plane of being*.

Second, tragedy must have a sufficient impact upon the beholder to move his emotions very powerfully.

The first of these considerations is clearly objective; equally clearly, the second is subjective.

Catastrophe: As we understand and use the word today, it is more than Aristotle's Scene of Suffering: it is the *ultimate blow* the protagonist receives, whether from fate, the gods, or tragic necessity and his own actions. It is also rock bottom in the trajectory of the tragic hero: it represents the final destruction of those hopes and desires that have motivated him from the beginning—and the final ordeal or punishment of the hero himself.

In his valuable and unjustly forgotten *Form in Literature*, Harold Weston designates as catastrophe that phase of the dramatic action in which the protagonist falls the greatest distance from the putative attainment of his objective, his "intention."[15] This is, it would seem, simply the traditional catastrophe viewed in another perspective: when the final blow is being received, the protagonist is manifestly the greatest distance from his objective.

Obviously, catastrophe, so viewed, occurs in forms other than tragedy. But in these, the protagonist may rebound from it to achieve his desire. The absolute necessity for the tragic catastrophe is that it be final: *on its own plane of being* it may not be reversed or remedied. The protagonist may rise from this absolute defeat, usually material or physical, to a

14. Cleanth Brooks (ed.), *Tragic Themes in Western Literature* (New Haven: Yale University Press, 1955). Brooks takes an apparently opposite view (p. 5): "On the tragic hero, suffering is never imposed; he incurs it by his own decision."
15. Harold Weston, *Form in Literature* (London: Chatto and Windus, 1936), 5–31.

triumph *on another plane*. Out of the material, outward defeat, he may achieve that spiritual, inward triumph described by so many, but this triumph is manifestly in a different dimension from the catastrophe. It is again transcendence; he transcends catastrophe and, in doing so, perhaps may achieve a larger awareness and the reconciliation to the universe and to life in their totality. Transcendence and reconciliation are, jointly, the distinguishing property of the most elevated, the "noblest" tragedies. But they are not indispensable to all tragedy.[16] The irreversible catastrophe is.

Impact: We are almost confronting again Aristotle's catharsis—his arousing of pity and fear in order to purge them. Yet "catharsis" in its long currency has accreted about itself so many conceptions and counter-conceptions, so many psychic biases, that it is probably better to move on to an equivalent, to avoid "pity and fear." Emotional impact is clear enough; as a term it is incomplete, of course, but it will serve. Tragedy must move the emotions of the beholder very powerfully; the work must have a sufficiently powerful impact upon the beholder, or it is not tragedy. Even though the work's theme is clearly in the tragic field, even though the protagonist sustains the irreversible catastrophe, it is not tragedy if it is short of the requisite impact.

What is the measure of the "requisite impact"? How powerful is "sufficiently powerful"? These are unanswerable questions, in the absolute sense. Impact will not be exactly the same for any two communicants, and the subjective character of this necessity simply cannot be altered. It is nonetheless a necessity. Works that do not affect the emotions of a beholder strongly enough are not tragedies so far as that

16. Louis L. Martz, "The Saint as Tragic Hero. Saint Joan and Murder in the Cathedral," in Brooks (ed.), *Tragic Themes in Western Literature*, 150–53; Charles L. Glicksburg, *The Tragic Vision in Twentieth Century Literature* (New York: Dell, 1970), 4, 70, 148. It is on precisely this point that some of the most acute interpreters of tragedy divide. Martz, who otherwise expresses a considerable admiration for the book, rejects *A Farewell to Arms* as tragedy because it offers no such clear triumph of psyche. Glicksburg gives an excellent example of the counter view: "Though the modern tragic vision affirms no principle of moral or spiritual transcendence, it does exhibit the drama of unjustified and unrelieved suffering. Though the tragic visionary catches no glimpse of significance that would redeem his suffering, he is not without a measure of greatness when he is brought face to face with disaster." Hemingway's Frederic Henry, he feels, is an example of this modern "unheroic" tragic hero and says that Hemingway's heroes, presumably thus typical of the modern tragic hero, refuse to submit meekly to the absurd and its tyranny.

beholder is concerned. Most of Hemingway's short fiction exemplifies this. Although the stories in question at least approach the tragic philosophy and their protagonists sustain the irreversible catastrophe, their author has deliberately kept them short of the tragic impact for most readers: thus for most readers they are outside the condition of tragedy. These not-quite-tragic stories demonstrate, too, that magnitude is indeed a modulation of tragic impact, and thus of the tragic condition itself. Thus we again acknowledge Aristotle. Those who insist on his importance do not err if they do not stop with him—if they do not take the view, as a surprising number of nonspecialists do, that he described tragedy once and for all.

In a working approach to tragedy, then, and this is somewhat more than a definition, the critic assumes a tragic philosophy that sees man as born to suffer and to sustain a massive defeat, either through the nature of the universe, or his own actions, or both. He assumes as an absolute dramaturgic necessity a protagonist who sustains a catastrophe that is irreversible on its own terms, whether or not it is transcended in another dimension. And he assumes a work that effects a profound emotional impact on its beholder, though he is aware that this impact will be different for each beholder. When all are fused in one work—the tragic philosophy, the irreversible catastrophe, the stunning impact—tragedy is fully achieved.

One must routinely ask, and try to answer, the question, "is tragedy possible in our age?" Krutch and later George Steiner have said that it is not, citing chiefly a paucity of spirit on our part. It is an entertaining hypothesis and both make it brilliantly, but the best refutation of it is the simple recalling of works of tragic stature—in drama, film, and fiction. We all have our own lists. It is not that the tragic spirit has left us; it is, rather, that its forms have changed. Corrigan aptly declares that it is necessary "to distinguish between the form of tragedy, which constantly changes . . . and *the tragic*, which is a way of looking at experience that has persisted more or less unchanged in the western world from the time of Homer to the present."[17]

It has been frequently said that the chief preoccupation of our mid-

17. Krutch, "The Tragic Fallacy"; George Steiner, *The Death of Tragedy* (London: Faber and Faber, 1961); Corrigan, *Sophocles*, 12–13.

century's literature is the confrontation of a universe without apparent meaning, one that is, consequently, hostile in aspect and function. This need not produce tragedy, but it sometimes produces splendid tragedy—there is no better example than Jean-Paul Sartre's own, *The Flies.* The existential man encounters the void as the tragic hero encounters catastrophe, and both define themselves by their response and action. But they are not the same, though sometimes they coincide. The tragic situation virtually always contains the existential situation, but the existential situation need not even approach tragedy. If it does enter tragedy, however, it is likely to do so at a point very near Frye's boundary of hostile fate.

It is about here that Hemingway enters. But he continues to move, to progress inside the field, and his later work is located where most great tragedy is located—approximately midway between the boundaries, where the universe and the man are jointly responsible for his fall, but where his transcendence depends upon himself.

II

Hemingway's first book, *In Our Time*, is not tragic and its author is not yet functioning with a fully tragic view of life; yet the stories approach tragedy even if the author keeps them short of it. All depict protagonists in confrontation with an overpowering universe, the protagonists sustain an irreversible catastrophe, and many achieve a spiritual transcendence of it in another dimension. Yet the requisite impact is not there, and the author does not wish it to be there: by ellipsis, understatement, and what might be called the miniaturization of his material, he has made his statement in minor key. The stories, with one exception, and the larger chronicle of which they are a part thus meet all the conditions of tragedy except impact, but not meeting that, they are not tragic. Quite unilaterally, this study calls them subtragic, perhaps a useful word for any work that has the form and something of the attitude of tragedy but not its impact, its capacity for Krieger's "exploding dissonance." Their primary statement, both individually and in aggregate, might be put, "The world is hard; one must be hard to survive it." This is not yet the equation of tragedy.

A case can be made for *The Sun Also Rises* as Hemingway's first major projection of the tragic. Certainly the case is not unchallengeable;

yet it has its persuasions. As protagonist, Jake Barnes suffers a catastrophe that is indeed irreversible on its own grounds, and it is possible to see in the symbolic ambiguity of its end a transcendent, spiritual triumph for him. The overriding question as to its tragic status is, "Does it have the tragic impact?" and the answer must be subjective. Baker goes straight to that question and gives a negative answer,[18] and few critics since have put the book forward as tragedy. The view here is that it is indeed Hemingway's first big tragedy, though it insists that the only way to confront catastrophe is with heroic passivity, to triumph by accepting with grace.

A Farewell to Arms stresses the immutable, total destruction of catastrophe and does not really suggest the possibility of even the psychic victory over it. Yet its stunning impact makes it a clear tragedy for most; it may be one of the most convincing examples in literature of a powerful tragedy without transcendence or reconciliation. There is another way of reading it, in which the triumph over catastrophe precedes catastrophe, but all the elements of the end seem to urge unrelieved doom.

Like those of *In Our Time*, the author's stories in his next two collections, *Men Without Women* and *Winner Take Nothing*, are virtually all subtragic. Only one in the two volumes, "The Undefeated," seems authentic tragedy. Its protagonist, the matador Manuel Garcia, brings himself to catastrophe by persevering in his attempt to define himself by bullfighting despite the limitations of age and physical equipment: his resolution to continue to death is unaltered by a goring. Of the four stories of the late thirties included in *The Fifth Column and the First 49*, however, at least three approach closely or even attain full tragic stature. "The Short Happy Life of Francis Macomber" shows its protagonist breaking out of his life-long fear into freedom and self-esteem, deliberately risking and ironically receiving death in his psychic victory. "The Snows of Kilimanjaro" has a protagonist come to the finish of his life partly from "bad luck" but more from the long operation of his moral weakness. It offers a unique, even bizarre transcendence. "The Capital of the World" presents a romantic busboy who brings about his death when he tries to prove his bravery in a simulated bullfight in

18. Baker, *Hemingway: The Writer as Artist*, 96.

his cafe. Its status as tragedy may be ambiguous, one depending again on that subjective response, but the case for it is a good one.

All three of these later stories show the protagonists as at least equally responsible with the universe for their catastrophes, and they suggest that Hemingway has moved a considerable distance from Frye's omnipotence of fate boundary which he approached so closely in the first two novels. As, in fact, he has. *To Have and Have Not* (1937), Hemingway's third novel, is his first one in which Aristotelian flaw is invoked:[19] Harry Morgan brings himself to catastrophe, in part, by his misapprehension of the nature of reality, his fatal determination to wrest a life from the universe on something like his own terms. But the nature of the universe, and the overpunishment it administers, make the novel partake of both tragic extremes and lie between them, though clearly closer to the boundary of the flaw. In *Green Hills of Africa*, the author gives both tragic design and tragic theme an *allegro* treatment: the unfairness—and the incongruity—of the universe are demonstrated, yet the tone of the book is light hearted and the very antithesis of tragic gravity. The author hunts the greater kudu desperately, through three-hundred-odd pages, and after killing one he finds that his friend, a bad hunter, has killed a bigger one. This is presented unflinchingly as catastrophe, and the author-protagonist reacts with catastrophic anguish—though he treats it, fortunately and effectively, as comic. This and the attendant self-deprecation preserve some proportion. But though the book is far from tragic, its postulation is a postulation of tragedy: catastrophe is inevitable; one may palliate it only by the rewards of consolation.

Death in the Afternoon, of course, has no unified dramatic narrative, but incidents, tales, and authorial judgments saturate it with a tragic perspective. Matadors come to grief through their own shortcomings—and their "bad luck"; a young man succumbs to homosexuality (in 1930 a considerably bleaker destiny than at present) through a conjunction of circumstance and personal weakness. Often ironically, but sometimes gravely, the author enunciates tragic inevitability with great frequency.

---

19. Jerry Brenner, "*To Have and Have Not* as Classical Tragedy: Reconsidering Hemingway's Neglected Novel," in Richard Astro and J. J. Benson (eds.), *Hemingway In Our Time* (Corvallis: Oregon State University Press, 1972). Brenner offers a different interpretation from that projected here.

And against all these instances runs steadily the melody of the noble bulls, ultimate tragic heroes born both for the catastrophe of violent death and for the transcendent triumph of meeting it bravely.

For Whom the Bell Tolls represents another shift in emphasis in Hemingway's equation: the protagonist brings himself to the catastrophe of death with full foreknowledge that his choices and acts can have no other result. This marks, indeed, an intensely significant breakthrough in the author's operating conception of tragedy, and the protagonists of all his subsequent novels so far published act with essentially the same knowledge. When Robert Jordan chooses to accept a bridge-blowing mission that he knows may be fatal, he has made his first fateful choice, and he makes a second when he insists that the guerrillas leave him, wounded, to hold off the fascists and die. Pragmatically, his dedication is a "flaw"—yet it is the noble flaw and defines him. Two states of being, two abstractions—love and duty—war inside him, and the abstractions of republicanism and fascism, of self-preservation and duty, contend outside. And the novel lies between Frye's two boundaries of operations, thus intersecting several varieties of tragedy, and here, too, casting a mold for most of Hemingway's later major work.

Across the River and Into the Trees might appear to be a sharp movement back, toward *The Sun Also Rises*, the omnipotence of fate, and acceptance with grace the only dignification possible in facing that fate. Certainly Colonel Cantwell faces a sure death. But his choices and the actions resulting from them are more than positive; they are aggressive, defiant; they are a total commitment of energy in a *battle* against catastrophe, and he fights his way to transcendence.

The Old Man and the Sea may be the richest of the author's novels-as-tragedies. Not only is it, at least, a three-tiered drama, but it also functions as tragedy on each of its levels; as tragedy, it fuses several subspecies and many different conceptions of the form. Although it is located very close to halfway between the tragic boundaries, it draws sustenance from each. Even more emphatically than *For Whom the Bell Tolls*, it places man's responsibility for both his fate and his identity upon himself. Its theme, directly counter to the helplessness expressed by *A Farewell to Arms* and the style-hammered stoicism at the heart of *The Sun Also Rises*, can be put: "Life is tragic; man defines himself by the action he takes against the inevitable catastrophe." As tragedy, the work is first of all the tragedy of noble *hubris*: in staying with and trying to catch a fish so big that it is pulling *him* far to sea, Santiago tries to surpass the limits of human possibility and thus brings himself to catastrophe; he transgresses against the physical order of the universe, and as a consequence the universe recoils against him. His great resolution thus becomes, in the pragmatic perspective, a "flaw," and that "flaw" is also his supreme virtue. Also, he and the fish are each obeying the Hegelian imperatives of their existence as they move toward reciprocal destruction. Santiago is exercising the fateful choice every instant he stays on the line and refuses to cut it. Thus the great stress of the novel, in all its modes, is upon the interior triumph he wins from physical defeat: his transcendence becomes not only a reconciliation but a resurrection.

This thrust continues, if less sharply, in the significant final section of *Islands in the Stream*; it is in this last third, "At Sea," that the book comes into focus, declares itself, and achieves its theme. Captain Thomas Hudson understands completely the relative insignificance of his search for the escaped German submariners; he equally understands his obligations of action in this insignificance and upholds them with total fidelity, to bring himself to catastrophe and death. His action is existential in the precise definitions of Sartre. It is tragic, too, *if* it exerts a powerful enough effect on the individual witness. It repeats the primary theme of *The Old Man and the Sea*: one defines himself by his action against the inevitable catastrophe for the existential void. Like that book, it too is a tragedy of the fateful choice, of conflicting imperatives, and of the noble flaw.

Although *A Movable Feast* appears between the last two books, much of it by report was composed earlier. It is a strange and elliptical as well as a beautiful book; the reader is scarcely aware that he is witness to a complete personal drama, much less one of tragic possibilities, until he is suddenly confronted with its catastrophe—the author's love affair with his wife's friend and the resulting destruction of his marriage. The story of the marriage is such a carefully muted counterpoint to the sketches apparently about other characters that few would even suggest it as a fully developed tragedy; equally few, perhaps, would deny the cathartic power of the last few pages, or that they have the impact of tragedy. Its statement is clear enough; it implies that fate and flaw join

14

to produce catastrophe, and it is moot which is the more potent agent.

Tragic irony is a potent and mysterious element working with flaw and fate, though some might not wish to divorce it from the last. Irony is at the source of the mistake that cuts Frederic Henry off from the Italian army and drives the lovers into their isolation: having been an exemplary officer in crisis for a foreign nation, he is ordered shot for his accent, which earlier underlined his semiheroism and got him a medal. This fundamental irony has its metaphor in Lt. Henry's firing at two runaway soldiers—and a little later running away from soldiers firing at him. A bizarre and unpredictable snowstorm in May dooms El Sordo's guerrillas, a forecast of a more important irony: Robert Jordan gets his ultimately fatal wound after the greatest danger at the bridge seems over. Harry Morgan's boat is returning to Key West after its escape from the Cuban Coast Guard when it is unanticipatably spotted by a neurotic federal bureaucrat. Later, the Coast Guard finds it in concealment by an equally unpredictable accident. In the writing, all of these emerge as tragic irony and are profoundly important in bringing the action to catastrophe.

Hemingway apparently tried to use irony less markedly as an agent of action in *The Old Man and the Sea*, wishing to make every phase of the story follow the one before it in a completely understandable and predictable chain of cause and effect. Yet he cannot remove irony from the prime cause, Santiago's hooking of so huge a fish when he is alone. Nor can it be really explained literally by the old man's declaration that he went out too far. The almost final, overpowering image of the tourists confusing the fish with the sharks who destroyed it is pure irony, even though it is an irony of emotional effect rather than of cause. It seems fair to say that tragic irony is one of the author's most powerful and most naturally employed tools in his creation of tragedy.

As this is written, other novels Hemingway wrote before his death have not yet been published. They might move in a sharply different direction from his other work, of course. But the example of work already published posthumously, *A Movable Feast* and *Islands in the Stream*, suggests otherwise. In the canon of the work we have, Hemingway's view of the world is clear, and the changes in it are not great. He always declares that life is tragic and catastrophe inevitable; almost always, he suggests that one defines himself by the manner in which he meets that catastrophe. At the beginning he believes that fate or the universe is the primary maker of catastrophe, with the individual playing a far lesser part. Later, he implies that fate and man are coequals in responsibility. In his earliest work, the response to catastrophe available to his protagonists is essentially one of enduring and of acceptance, though that acceptance may require a powerful act of will. In the later works, the protagonist almost always takes positive action *against* catastrophe, defining himself not only by style but also by struggle—by something like Goethe's striving, the unending struggle of the human will not only against the universe but against its own mistakes. Chiefly there is a clear shift in position: finally he has come to see man as at least coauthor of his fate. The distance his tragic vision has moved is short, but it is long enough to take him to that place where, perhaps, the greatest tragedies are located.

III

The magnitude of any writer is in part a function of the magnitude of his statement, of his most deeply held view as to what the world is and human life is. But only in part: it is a critical commonplace that small themes well expressed are infinitely better than large ones badly expressed. Hemingway's primary theme is both grand and simple, for it is the abiding theme of tragedy; what makes his work count for us is that this theme is projected in compelling works of art. Once his deeply intuitive and profoundly felt world view is understood, there remains the task of perceiving how he fashioned the works that project it.

To do this totally is, and ought to be, an impossible task. The deepest mysteries of the artist's temperament are not only a collective partner with his most self-conscious strategies, they are the senior partner, the unquestionable dominant force. Yet without those strategies to liberate them, to permit them to function, these mysteries of the deepest self could not come into play. The strategies, at least, can be analyzed, and certain of Hemingway's more important strategies are ultimately more visible, more deliberate than those of any other major fictionist since Flaubert. Most of them, too, have been more thoroughly defined, but it should be useful to codify them again and see how they serve the author's tragic perception of things. Also, a more extensive consideration than we have had so far is needed of Hemingway's musical training as a source for his organization of fiction.

Actually, his techniques would also serve other attitudes toward life than the tragic. But since most of them are directed toward a concentration of effect, they are uniquely effective in projecting tragedy, the emotions of which are traditionally the most intense in literature. The most prominent of these strategies appear to be the following: (1) the conceptions of Imagist poetry, as enunciated and exemplified by Ezra Pound, (2) those of Impressionist and post-Impressionist painters, (3) those of musical composition, notably melody-counterpoint-harmony, as expressed particularly in fugue and sonata-allegro, and (4) the example of antecedent fiction writers.

The master-apprentice relationship between Pound and Hemingway is copiously documented.[20] Hemingway once said, "Nobody taught me as much about writing as Ezra," and on winning the Nobel Prize, he told Malcolm Cowley, "If I could have gone and talked, I would have talked about Ezra."[21] Hemingway writes in *A Movable Feast* that Pound forced him through a discipline of French novelists when he would rather have been reading Russians, and Gustave Flaubert, naturally, is presumed to be a chief item.[22] On the *prima facie* evidence of the writing itself, however, the great gift that Pound gave Hemingway was the doctrine and the example of Imagist poetry, and one of Hemingway's greatest literary significances was his transmission of the Imagist principles into fiction. Put simply, the center of the practice of the Imagist poets was to try to show a thing exactly and to convey an emotion and an attitude by that concentration of image-picture: Pound said, "An image is that which conveys an intellectual and emotional complex in an instant of time."[23]

The influence of the Imagist poets may be the most pervasive of any

20. Harold Hurwitz, "Hemingway's Tutor, Ezra Pound," reprinted in Linda W. Wagner (ed.), *Hemingway: Five Decades of Literary Criticism* (East Lansing: Michigan State University Press, 1974), 8–20.

21. Malcolm Cowley, "A Portrait of Mr. Papa," reprinted in McCaffery (ed.), *Ernest Hemingway: The Man and His Work*, 34–56.

22. Ernest Hemingway, *A Movable Feast* (New York: Scribner's, 1963), 131–32.

23. William Pratt, *The Imagist Poem* (New York: Dutton, 1963), 18.

systematically organized group in recent literature; its doctrine moved directly into poetry through Pound, for a critical period its chief propagandist as well as exemplar, and from Pound through his protégé Hemingway into fiction. But the fascinating history of the group is available elsewhere: a particularly good examination of history, principles, and examples is William Pratt's *The Imagist Poem*.[24] Here, the great thing to remember is that Imagism deals with pictures so concentrated they are themselves both idea and emotion—ideally. In Hemingway, the best of these are indeed compactions of the tragic idea and the tragic emotion: Frederic Henry alone in the rain that is catastrophe's signature; the man's coffin vanishing in windblown grain and the bull's ear lost in cigarette stubs; Jake and Brett helpless before the "deity" with the baton; the old man looking at the crucified fish as he begins the last act of his own Calvary, the climb up the hill.

But the novelist, obviously, can seldom approach the concentration of the poem, except in a very few lines at a time—when he is, in effect, writing something like a short poem of his own. So with the images of Hemingway's fiction: at their most intense, they will indeed reveal the author's truths, but much more frequently they will simply reveal the physical truth of the passing instant, showing what the eye sees, or the ear hears, or other senses feel. This less intense function is itself indispensable to the art of the novel, building the physical universe of the work, serving in Conrad's dictum, "to make you see." Yet even when the Hemingway image appears to be purely literal and naturalistic, it is imbued to some degree with those most profoundly held attitudes of the author that culminate in the theme of the work (Baker and Young cited this Imagist aspect in 1952; Richard Hasbany examines it in detail as it appears in *In Our Time*[25]).

An analogy might be helpful. Consider a Hemingway work as a long narrow chamber with a searchlight beaming powerfully through it. In the chamber, skillfully arranged, are a series of mirrors of varying sizes and shapes. These catch the light and bounce it off, increasing its intensity and illumination. Some do so far more strongly than others,

24. *Ibid.*, 11–39.
25. Baker, *Hemingway: The Writer as Artist*, 50–58; Young, *Hemingway: A Reconsideration*, 184; Richard Hasbany, "The Shock of Vision: The Imagist Principle in *In Our Time*," in Wagner (ed.), *Hemingway: Five Decades of Literary Criticism*, 224–40.

depending on their construction, but all catch the light one way or another. The searchlight is his tragic attitude; the mirrors are these images which reflect it and intensify its power. To be sure, the analogy is effective for almost any good novel or poem or film and its primal attitude; Hemingway's uniqueness lies in the force of the attitude, and the concentrated power of those images that reflect and reveal it. Hemingway must have been speaking of his role as Imagist when he told Samuel Putnam that he wished to "strip language clean, to lay it bare to the bone."[26] It is extremely useful to read the first chapter of *A Farewell to Arms* and passages cited in that and other novels alongside key poems in the movement, by Pound and H. D. Some may find the conclusion irresistible that in these passages, at least, he is himself one of the best Imagist poets.

Since the visual principle of imagism and those of the seriously intended film are so close, it is impossible not to see a close kinship between Hemingway's fiction and the film. But judging from all accounts and various memoirs, he owes nothing directly to film technique—any more than manifestly discernible parallels between Flaubert and the film can be attributed to the film's influence on Flaubert. It seems rather a case of the camera following the course of a methodical human eye. The progression of Hemingway visuals does follow frequently that long-medium-close pattern, the pans and quick cuts, and other designs that the camera was once expected to observe; a good example of the first is the snow on the mountain / snow in the trenches sequence early in *A Farewell to Arms*. This would seem to be a case of the similar operations of natural aesthetic laws taking place in overtly different mediums. Still, anyone as attuned to the intellectual currents of Paris in the 1920s as was Hemingway could scarcely fail to be aware of the works of Sergei Eisenstein, V. Pudovkin, Carl Dreyer, and the other great European film makers.

Not speculative at all is Hemingway's very heavy debt to the Impressionist and post-Impressionist painters, one acquired through careful assimilation and adaption. Impressionist painting is blood brother, in fact, to Imagist poetry—a kinship its first spokesman, T. E. Hulme,

26. Samuel Putnam, *Paris Was Our Mistress* (New York: Viking, 1947), 128.

and Pratt both insisted upon.[27] Hulme's remarks appear to be more concerned with the emotional springs of both movements; Pratt writes that "poetic techniques should become subtle enough to record exactly the momentary impressions—the *images* . . . which were the real substance of experience." He stresses the closeness of the Impressionist to the French symbolist poets and the novels of Henry James, Joseph Conrad, and Flaubert. Emily Watts, too, stresses the relationship.[28]

Hemingway's deep interest in all painting makes a copious record (that article by Lillian Ross is a fun-house mirror to his expertise in modern movements[29]), and the reader who is only an amateur student of painting is apt to be most forcefully impressed by his affinities with the Impressionists and post-Impressionists. It is hard to find an explicit definition of the method of impressionism, but it seeks to present a picture that can be perceived instantly in its totality; it strikes heavy contrast in mass, color, and line and forgets ornament and most detail; above all, it is a reduction to the pattern—the impression and image—made at a stroke by its primary elements. It fulfills Pound's decree for the image—a complex of truth in a flash of time—with total fidelity. And Hemingway's visuals, whether landscapes, street scenes, or portraits, are built upon that absolute reduction to the primary.

At their most compressed, the visuals naturally are thematic in Hemingway's own dimension, an epiphany of one of his truths in themselves. But often they simply show his love for making the picture, for seeking that single impression. Baker's example of Hemingway as Impressionist (from *The Sun Also Rises*) is as good as any available, and it also is an excellent specimen of the verbal painting executed for pure pleasure. A word or phrase gives each primary element its single dominant quality (italics mine): "It was a beech wood and the trees were

27. T. E. Hulme, "A Lecture on Further Speculations," in Sam Hynes (ed.), *Further Speculations* (Minneapolis: University of Minnesota Press, 1955), 68; Pratt, *The Imagist Poem*, 24–25.

28. Emily Watts, *Ernest Hemingway and the Arts* (Champaign: University of Illinois Press, 1971), 14–28. Watts cites Hemingway's familiarity with Impressionists and post-Impressionists and sees strong links between Imagist poetry, cubism, and surrealism. She implies that Hemingway wished to create a landscape like Cezanne, "to embody the world of dreams like the surrealists, to create a poetic image in an extended prose work . . . (in) a single art" (28).

29. Lillian Ross, "How Do You Like It Now, Gentlemen?" *New Yorker*, May 13, 1950, pp. 36–62.

very old. Their *roots* hulked above the ground and the *branches* were *twisted*. We walked on the road between the thick trunks of the old beeches and the *sunlight* came *through the leaves* in *light patches* on the grass."[30]

Hemingway declared Cézanne his chief mentor among painters—"I wanted to do with the country what Cezanne did" and, later, "I can make a landscape like Paul Cezanne"—and Robert Lair and Watts have been deeply concerned with this relationship, the first exclusively.[31] Watts sees Hemingway's transference of the principle of Cézanne's "planes" to be the dominant feature in his construction of landscapes —the geometry of which has been irresistible to so many.

Judging how the methods of one art work in another is always chancy and probably never better than approximate. We have Hemingway's own pronouncements, of course, and since they reinforce his texts so directly, they are useful. But it is the work itself that is important, both in its relationship to painting and to music, the art that perhaps ultimately produced an even greater intensity and unity in the work.

Music, fiction, and drama all exist primarily in time rather than space, all involve contrast and conflict between interior elements, and all proceed through this conflict to some kind of resolution. Consequently, the parallels between them are heavy and discernible; the dramatist and the novelist may execute designs that strongly suggest musical forms while having no knowledge whatever of musical composition. To consider that excellence in this execution is due to the use of such forms as models may be ludicrously unjustified. There must be more than generic parallels between works in the two different arts to see the example of one influencing the other. What underwrites such a study in the case of Hemingway is that he spent a long period in his youth in the enforced study of music, that he himself has avowed the force of its ex-

---

30. Baker, *Hemingway: The Writer as Artist*, 117.
31. Robert L. Lair, "Hemingway and Cezanne: An Indebtedness," *Modern Fiction Studies*, VI (Summer, 1960), 165–68; Watts, *Hemingway and the Arts*, 14–37. Watts cites Hemingway's letter to Gertrude Stein, August 15, 1924, "I'm trying to do the country like Cezanne (etc.)" and points to Hemingway's effect of planes, of color as a component of form, and of the firmness of backgrounds, particularly the mountains, as deriving directly from Cézanne. See Raymond F. Wilson, *Hemingway: Artist-Expressionist* (Ames: Iowa State University Press, 1979), for a different view.

amples in his fiction, and that the parallels are so intricate and close. Given the intrinsic evidence of his work *and* the biographical data *and* the authorial pronouncements, there seems no question of the decisive influence of music on the fiction of Ernest Hemingway. It should be an article of assessment, however, that whereas the last two factors corroborate the apparent debts found in the first, they rank far behind it in importance; without the illustrative example of the text, they are, indeed, without importance.

That musical education is described at great length by Hemingway's sister, Marcelline Hemingway Sanford, who shared it. Their mother had given up a promising concert singing career—she was well reviewed in her one appearance at Carnegie Hall—to marry Dr. Hemingway; the training she enforced upon the household and particularly upon her older children was a consequence of that career. As described by Mrs. Sanford, it would seem to be a fair equivalent of a baccalaureate in musicology: "Mother gave Ernest and me . . . a wonderful background in the appreciation of music. . . . [We] had season tickets to the Columbia Opera Company in 1915. . . . Mother took us to symphony concerts and operas in Chicago . . . and saw that we had music lessons all our growing-up years. I was started on the piano when I was five years old and Ernest began the next year. . . . Ernest [later] worked hard on his cello [and in] . . . the family orchestra played hymns, Gilbert and Sullivan, and the simpler parts of the great sonatas."[32]

A particularly striking aspect of the program is the constant exposure to the sonata that the sessions of the family string group gave Hemingway. The melody-counterpoint-harmony contrasts are the foundation of the sonata, and that contrast was to become one of the foundations of his own art. He told George Plimpton that it "should be obvious" what a writer could learn from a study of counterpoint, and in 1952 he wrote a correspondent that he thought he had the harmony and counterpoint just right in *Across the River and Into the Trees.*[33] It is the evidence of the works themselves that really counts, however, and an aware scrutiny of these reveals that all the novels and most of the

32. Marcelline Hemingway Sanford, *At the Hemingways* (Boston: Little Brown, 1962), 123, 125.

33. George Plimpton, "An Interview with Ernest Hemingway," reprinted in Carlos Baker (ed.), *Hemingway and His Critics* (New York: Hill and Wang, 1961), 19–29; Ernest Hemingway to Wirt Williams, December 7, 1952.

stories are carefully suspended upon the tension between large opposing emotional forces (the sonata) or between lines alternating in variation of a commonalty (the fugue). On more than one occasion, in the
novels, it is a fair conclusion that Hemingway aspired to the compounded form of the symphony. The broadest common conception in
all of these is a mounting tension between oppositions or variations,
meticulously developed by alternation.

This tension between opposing forces is an invariable foundation of
all drama and fiction, certainly, but Hemingway builds it with a pre-
cision, an attention to form, that attests an aware and sophisticated
knowledge of models. His movement back and forth between inclusive
forces may be seen as suggesting the movement between opposing key
areas; the shift from one character to another as exfoliation of literary
theme is like the shift between voices or lines inside those areas; the
miniature projection of idea through imagistic passage and incident may
be seen very roughly as a "vertical" development, a kind of literary
parallel to harmony; the contrast and variety of tempo in his longer
works suggests that same variety in any long musical form. It cannot
be labored too heavily that such manifestations may be found in any
number of novelists without musical sources; it is the awareness and
self-consciousness with which they are employed, and the tightness of
the compositional structure to which they contribute, that are the internal signatures of a clear influence.[34]

This idea accepted, one must next ask: need the employment of these
models, transferred to fiction or drama, be confined to producing the
tragic emotion? Obviously not: it is not in most of the author's short
stories. But it is singularly useful for producing that emotion, once the
imperfect conversion between arts is made. Just as the imagistic principle produces such an intensity and compactness in the individual passage, so this complex and yet tight musical organization can produce
great intensity and compactness in the fictional whole. And once more,
the Hemingway strategy is singularly adapted to the creation of that
emotional intensity and impact that is one of the few indispensables
of tragedy.

In this connection, it is useful to consider how musical examples

34. Sheldon Grebstein, *Hemingway's Craft* (Carbondale: Southern Illinois University
Press, 1972), 35, 169.

appear not only to help organize the novels but to urge them toward the tragic concentration. And a more detailed analysis of the first two novels may help establish principles for all. A look at *The Sun Also Rises* ought to begin with a description of the fugue; Joseph Machlis writes of it:

> A fugue is a contrapuntal composition, generally in three or four voices, in which a theme or subject of strongly marked character pervades the entire fabric, entering now in one voice; now in another.... The subject or theme is stated alone at the outset in one of the voices.... It is then imitated in another voice—this is the *answer* ... [and] the subject will then appear in a third voice and be answered in a fourth, while the first two weave a free contrapuntal texture against these....
>
> When the theme has appeared in each voice once ... the first section, the Exposition, is at an end.... As the fugue unfolds, there must be ... the sense of mounting urgency.... Especially effective in the *stretto*, with the subject entering in one voice before it has been completed in another. The effect is one of voices crowding upon each other, creating the heightening of tension that brings the fugue to its climax. There follows the final statement of subject, generally in triumphal mood.[35]

In the novel, the "voices"—Jake, Robert Cohn, Brett Ashley, and Mike Campbell—are set forth in the Exposition as evocations of the basic thematic consideration—making meaning in a void—and are developed more urgently in the various "episodes" of the Pamplona pilgrimage. The voices beat against each other in swift alternation, briefly resting in the pastoral interlude of the mountain fishing, and finally coming to a climax, like the *stretto* of the fugue, in the fist fight and the last bull fight. At the end, Jake comes home to the spiritual triumph of tragic transcendence: though he has suffered the outer defeat, he has achieved reconciliation.

Machlis describes, in part, sonata form or sonata-allegro: "We may regard sonata-form as a drama between two contrasting key areas. The plot, the action, and the tension derive from this contrast. Sonata-allegro ... is an artistic embodiment of the principles underlying the major-minor system ... home key- (opposing) key are associated with two contrasting themes. In this way, the opposition between the two key areas is sharpened—dramatized, as it were—and presented to the lis-

35. Joseph Machlis, *The Enjoyment of Music* (New York: Norton, 1963), 297.

24

tener as a conflict between two ideas."[36] And *A Farewell to Arms* can certainly be seen as a fictional conversion of this sonata form. The contending keys are those of love and war (which becomes death), with the characters functioning as lines or voices inside the key areas. The melodic line of Frederic Henry functions in both keys; it is in effect transposed frequently from one to the other. In paralleling the entire novel with the sonata-allegro, one sees the love-war conflict introduced in the Exposition (Book I), expanded and heightened in the Development (Books II, III, IV), and resolved (though not in triumph) in Recapitulation (Book V).

But though the novel scans as sonata-allegro, it is large in its development, and thus the larger symphony, with its multimovement involving the sonata cycle, may offer a closer correspondence in form. The five books in the novel match reasonably either the movements of the unusual five-movement symphony, or the conventional four-movement symphony with an unconventionally long coda added. The first chapter is a symbolic overview of the entire work, functioning as the prelude to the total organization.

To Have and Have Not also builds on sonata form, with Harry's will to survival and freedom functioning as home key, and the forces, economic and cosmic, that would take it away as the other, the dominant key. The dominant again triumphs in Harry's death, and whether his final awareness is triumph for the subject is extremely moot.

Love and war are again probably the conflicting keys in *For Whom the Bell Tolls*; though a case can be made for love and duty, duty is probably a component of the key area of war. And though the dominant war key is the inevitable physical victor, Jordan's act of abnegation at his death is a transcendental triumph for himself and for home key. As with *A Farewell to Arms*, the novel scans as sonata-allegro, but its length and complexity of development suggest the more massive symphony as model.

In the author's work, sonata form is nowhere more evident as source, or more important in development, than in *Across the River and Into the Trees*. The conflict is between Cantwell's approaching death and his will to meet it with grace and dignity; it is developed by an elaborate

36. *Ibid.*, 197–205.

alternation of these keys and the imagery inside them. And unless this formal balancing and contrast succeeds, nothing succeeds. As always, the death key demonstrates its dominance, but the colonel wins a spiritual triumph for his tonic key by dying on his own terms. Catastrophe is once more transcended, and tragedy achieved.

In *The Old Man and the Sea*, Santiago's resolution and nobility is the tonic, home key, and the hostile universe and the ordeals it imposes upon him are the other. In the loftiest, and tragic, Hemingway finish, the home key achieves its own appropriate triumph in the face of the heavier overt victory by the dominant.

Stripped of that fourth part, *Islands in the Stream* has a clear analogy with the three-part symphony, in which each section follows an unusually distinct sonata structure. Broadly, the keys are Thomas Hudson's quest for identity, selfhood, and even happiness, and the fate that would keep him from these. The quest changes its modulations from part to part: in the first, he wants only to hold the stasis and balance he has won; in the second, he wants to conquer his grief and find happiness for a moment; in the third, he wants to perform his duty at whatever cost. The hostile force that has beaten down his thrust in the first two parts does not do so in the end; it kills him but he achieves his duty exactly as he wished: with the price willingly paid, the transcendent triumph of Hudson, and of the tonic, home key, is virtually perfect.

The last novels show perhaps an even greater absorption with musical example and melody-counterpoint-harmony principle than the earlier, but from beginning to end it has been one of the strongest elements in Hemingway's art. It is a pervasive force, and he calls it up easily and intuitively, varying the pattern of the models to meet his own needs. Like Machlis' ideal composer, he "allows the content to shape the form, so that what looks on paper like a fixed plan becomes, when transformed into living sound, a supple framework of infinite variety."[37]

Like every other human being, a writer is part of all that he has met, and among those persons and things a writer has met—particularly on the printed page—are inevitably a large number of other writers. A real examination of Hemingway's literary sources is completely outside the

37. *Ibid.*, 199–200.

scope of this study, and a great deal of what might be said about this fascinating subject has already been written anyway. In the early books, Baker cites Turgenev, Chekhov, Tolstoi, Dostoievski, Stendhal, Balzac, Flaubert, Hudson, Twain, Crane, James, Mann, Conrad, and Joyce as influences; Young points to most of these and writes on the influence of Twain and particularly of Stephen Crane.[38] In 1972, Baker made discoveries of Conrad as source in *Islands in the Stream* and early stressed the admiration, approaching adulation, that Hemingway felt for Joyce.[39] Hurwitz, in describing the syllabus of informal study through which Pound led the author, cites Flaubert as a prominent item.[40] Baker recounts Hemingway's friendships, most of them now well known or even notorious, with other living writers: Joyce of course, Fitzgerald, Anderson, Stein, MacLeish, Ford, Dos Passos, Cowley, Stewart, William Carlos Williams, and others.[41]

The details of his debts to Flaubert and Joyce might be examined a little more closely. The last relates quite directly to the subject at hand, for *Dubliners* may have served to some degree as a model for *In Our Time*, not only in the close thematic relationship between its stories, but, perhaps more importantly, in the architecture of the stories themselves. Almost all of them offer the equation of tragedy but not its tragic impact. Neither, it should be observed, do they slip into pathos. The main character sustains his irreversible catastrophe, but irony, miniaturization, and a general *diminuendo* tonality restrain the effect, so that it becomes something quite different from the tragic. This is exactly what happens in most of Hemingway's stories, not only in *In Our Time* but in his next two volumes, and this aspect of the Joycean example has not been widely commented upon.

Flaubert is still one of the great encyclopedias of fictional technique; Hemingway certainly is now another, and many of the basic strategies Flaubert imparted to all fiction came from him to Hemingway, directly as well as through the intermediaries of a century. These would include the principles of rendering, of dramatizing the vital moments; the care-

38. Baker, *Hemingway: The Writer as Artist*, 25–47, 48–74; Young, *Hemingway: A Reconsideration*, 191–98, 211–41.

39. Baker, *Hemingway: The Writer as Artist*, 70–74, 405–407.

40. Hurwitz, "Hemingway's Tutor," 8–20.

41. Carlos Baker, *Ernest Hemingway: A Life Story* (New York: Scribner's, 1969). References are too numerous to itemize here; see index, 673–97.

ful alternation of scene and summary; the methodic, step-by-step movement of aim of the point-of-view camera; the foreshadowing of Pound's principle of the image (in passages like that of Emma straining to drain the glass); the controlled movement into deeper and deeper layers of the conscious. These obviously have served all fiction, but Hemingway's methodical use of them is very close indeed to Flaubert's.

Baker concludes, "Hemingway had a proud prejudice against being a sedulous ape, yet he was undoubtedly sedulous."[42] It is a good description: Hemingway's search for and assimilation of source approaches in system the similar quest of Ezra Pound, who learned difficult and then-obscure languages so that he might be instructed by their poets. But as with Pound, all the lessons Hemingway learned from other arts and other writers he shaped into instrumentalities uniquely and intimately his own. These two fashioned a body of work in which—even more than with most other writers—the thing said and the manner of saying it are one. And that thing said is a constant, though its silhouette varies according to the immediate perspective in which it is viewed. It is that life is tragedy, in the face of which men must measure and define themselves.

42. Baker, *Hemingway: The Writer as Artist*, 29.

1

In Our Time
Ranging Shots on the Near Side

In Paris, the author of *In Our Time* came to convictions about blows received and given in remembered places: Michigan, Chicago, Kansas City, Italy, the Near East. Wound by wound, shock by shock, Hemingway's first book does indeed show a vulnerable boy becoming an aware man. But it is also the shadowy self-portrait of a writer drawing closer and closer to a highly personal vision of tragedy—and stopping just short of it. Through some fear of what an acceptance of tragedy as the world's way might mean to him as man and artist? There are lines in "Big Two-Hearted River," the story of summation, that—if they are pulled out of context—strongly suggest this might be the case. But it seems much more reasonable to suppose that the author's attitudes are simply in an early stage of development, that *In Our Time* shows where he was emotionally when he wrote it. Whether or not the author shied away from his deepest intuitions is interesting, even fascinating; it does not make the book less an achievement or less a personal statement. Whatever the exact relationship of Nick Adams, or Krebs, or the nameless one to Ernest Hemingway, none who knew him ever doubted that the core stories of the work are extracted one way or another from the writer's life, and his reflections on it.

The examiners have agreed on that from the beginning (Wilson in 1930, Baker and Young in 1952[1]). Baker's critical study and later his

1. Edmund Wilson, Introduction to Ernest Hemingway's *In Our Time* (New York: Scribner's, 1930), ix–xv; Carlos Baker, *Ernest Hemingway: The Writer as Artist* (Princeton: Princeton University Press, 1972), 117–43; Philip Young, *Ernest Hemingway: A Reconsideration* (State College: Pennsylvania State University Press, 1966), 29–55.

biography related incidents in most of the stories to the author's life; Young's trauma theory and his psychological examination of the author through his protagonists are rooted in this work. Like the majority of Hemingway's later novels, *In Our Time* is a textbook example of the reduction of experience to essence and its recasting into art—in shapes still much like those of the originals.

The casting was interestingly evolutionary; it might be useful to trace it yet once more. The first book of the title was *in our time*, the words uncapitalized, and was printed by William Bird Press in 1924. Only 170 copies came undamaged from the press. The book contained eighteen short chapters, or "miniatures," which became the italicized interchapters of the next version. Two exceptions were elevated to full story status in that version: these became "A Very Short Story" and "The Revolutionist." Acquiring capitals in the title, the next *In Our Time* was published in 1925 and was a considerably enlarged book: it presented fifteen stories, with the interchapters making a slender line of harmony and counterpoint between them. The 1930 version added "On the Quai at Smyrna" as an introductory unit, thus spoiling a rather neat symmetry that had seen the work start and end with an interchapter.[2] And the Edmund Wilson introduction admirably explained aspects of the work.[3] But by 1930 Hemingway was a world figure; it was the 1925 edition with which early reviewers were immediately concerned. That version had an extraordinary effect on a discerning few, who—even if they did not perceive the layered complexity of the book—nevertheless were moved by its strong sense of life, its exciting and elusive mystery.[4] Nor was the writer's absorption with catastrophe and an overpowering universe unnoted. Still, it is the 1930, enlarged edition that stands now as *In Our Time*, complete and, presumably, beyond further change.

It has long been recognized that the book has considerably more unity of subject matter and theme than most other collections of short

2. Carlos Baker, *Ernest Hemingway: A Life Story* (New York, Scribner's, 1969), 124–40.

3. Wilson, Introduction to *In Our Time*, ix-xv. One aspect of the book Wilson cites is its conviction that pleasure and pain are inextricable.

4. Audre Hanneman, *Ernest Hemingway: A Comprehensive Bibliography* (Princeton: Princeton University Press, 1967), 346–48. Some key reviews of *In Our Time* are abstracted.

stories. Baker and Young pointed out early—as did Joseph De Falco and others subsequently—that the chronological narrative developed by the larger number of stories in the book make it more of a *bildungs-roman*, a novel of the maturing of a young man, than a story collection with a recurring character. Clinton Burhans has delineated a much more complex unity, in which theme and chronology and placement closely fuse stories and interchapters: he sees the result as "a literary hybrid . . . neither anthology nor novel but a new form."[5]

Another unity involves Hemingway's inevitable melody-counterpoint architecture, both in the work as a whole and in its parts. But more important—and permeating the others—is the unity of a world view and a matching dramaturgy that is almost, but not quite, tragic and re-sides both in the work entire and in the individual stories.

In the book considered as a unified narrative, the melody, and prin-cipal line, is the chronicle of the boy-into-young-man adventures of the character known most of the time, but not always, as Nick Adams. The stories that do not involve this character nevertheless have a close the-matic relationship to those that do: as lines of counterpoint intensify and develop the melody in certain musical *genres*, these stories outside the young-man chronicle focus and illuminate those within it. So, of course, do the interchapters.

Why is the book not tragic? Both the chronicle and most of the stories do follow roughly one of the most basic of tragic designs: the protagonist thrusts toward his goal, however dimly perceived it is; he suffers a blow that destroys his thrust in catastrophe however small it might be; from the wreckage he rises to some kind of psychic triumph over, or reconciliation with, the forces that have knocked him down. Sometimes after catastrophe no reconciliation is made. Sometimes the stories present a double catastrophe—one that is observed by the prin-cipal, and one experienced by him as a result of that observation. In "Indian Camp," Nick witnesses the suicide of the Indian husband; this inflicts a substantial shock upon him and momentarily shatters his own quest for experience. But he rallies from that blow to reach a recon-

5. Baker, *Hemingway: The Writer as Artist*, 125–31; Young, *Hemingway: A Recon-sideration*, 30–31, 47–48; Joseph De Falco, *The Hero in Hemingway's Short Stories* (Pittsburgh: University of Pittsburgh Press, 1963), 14–20; Clinton S. Burhans, Jr., "The Complex Unity of *In Our Time*," *Modern Fiction Studies*, XIV (Autumn, 1968), 313–28.

ciliation and larger understanding. At the center of "The Doctor and the Doctor's Wife" is father's humiliation by the big Indian, the observed catastrophe; it hurts Nick more than it does his father, for he has seen an idol exposed as mortal and must reconcile himself to the lesson of that loss. The relationship between the two catastrophes may sometimes simply be parallel and not that of emotional cause and effect, as with the disappointment of the fishing guide Peduzzi and that of the young husband in "Out of Season"; a further subtlety is present in that story when its apparent focus on Peduzzi's defeat ultimately points to the slow failure of the young man's marriage. One way or another, the stories meet the first test of tragedy even though they are patently far from tragic: consistently they offer a protagonist who has sustained what is to him a major blow or defeat, which is irreversible on its own terms.

It is the test of impact that they do not meet, and, again, the author clearly does not wish them to meet it—"My Old Man" excepted. He has deliberately held them far short of the necessary emotional intensity —the necessary, incontestable effect. They have the requisite dramaturgic pattern but not the requisite emotional result to qualify as tragedy, either in their individual existences or their aggregate existence as chronicle.

It will be useful to review again this often-described chronicle. The adventures of a young man account for eleven of the fifteen stories in the volume. In seven he is called Nick or Nick Adams; in one, "Cat in the Rain," he is called George (once); in another, "Soldier's Home," he is called Krebs and the external circumstances of his life are made significantly different from Nick's. In "A Very Short Story" and "Out of Season" he is never named.

This giving of different names to the young man creates a problem for the critic. Young admits to the Nick sequence only those stories in which that name is actually used; Baker accepts those in which the young man is given no other name and says two ("Soldier's Home" and "Cat in the Rain") might have been about Nick, except for the names.[6] Actually, to apprehend fully the sequence as the young-man sequence, do we not have to go still further? Must we not accept the paradox quite frankly and consider that *all* the young-man stories are

6. Philip Young (ed.), *The Nick Adams Stories* (New York: Scribner's, 1972); Baker, *Hemingway: The Writer as Artist*, 128–30.

about a single protagonist—whatever his name? And must we not consider that sequence a single narrative?

For the eleven stories show a clear continuity—an odyssey of revelation and discovery of one man from boyhood to young maturity. As the boy Nick Adams, the hero makes certain discoveries about the nature of life and death ("Indian Camp," "The Doctor and the Doctor's Wife"). As a late adolescent, still in Michigan, he reinforces and enlarges these discoveries ("The End of Something," "The Three Day Blow," "The Battler"). As a young soldier on the Italian Front in World War I, he undergoes the catastrophe of a severe wound and an ill-fated love affair ("A Very Short Story"). After the war, as Krebs in "Soldier's Home," he is an alien in his own home and country and finds himself no longer suited for either. Returned to Europe with a wife, he discovers in marriage a subtle frustration and sense of loss; in wandering, he feels the vacancy of alienation ("Cat in the Rain," "Out of Season," "Cross Country Snow"). Finally, having been witness to an unending montage of violence, absurdity, and suffering, he returns alone to the Michigan woods. There, at the roots of his life, he renews it again ("Big Two-Hearted River").

So the book has a continuing, unified narrative about what is demonstrably a single character, and it thus emerges as essentially novelistic in structure. Although its episodes are completely finished stories, even when viewed in isolation, they are far stronger inside the continuity of the chronicle. The summation story, "Big Two-Hearted River," would be severely impoverished and almost uninterpretable if withdrawn from sequence.

The four stories outside the chronicle develop the same themes and present the same elements, in different situations with different characters. Three—"On the Quai at Smyrna," "The Revolutionist," and "Mr. and Mrs. Elliott"—are not much longer than the italicized interchapters between the stories; two were included in the preliminary *In Our Time*. "My Old Man" is the longest story, the only incontestable tragedy, and the *tonal* catastrophe of the book.

In sum, and with a single exception, the individual stories, like the whole book, are not tragedies though they have gone a significant distance toward the tragic. The catastrophes and responses are so understated, so miniaturized, that they seldom have the force necessary to produce real catharsis, or impact, and the author does not intend that they should: his attention—and ours—is fixed primarily upon the discoveries that illuminate the life of the continuing character, and these, finally, coalesce into a system.

Most of all, the never-completely-to-be-defined tragic spirit is simply not in most of the stories; they are art of a high order but they are not tragic art, a circumstance that certainly need not diminish them. The author's emotional center here says, "Life is hard, and one must be hard to survive in it." In this collection, catastrophe as it occurs is not a decisive test of spirit by ordeal: it is, rather, one more jolt on the road to awareness.

This process of instruction is continued by the interchapters, though they impinge directly upon the reader rather than using a character as intermediary. Each is a synecdochical instant of experience pressed down to the smallest possible displacement: Pound's image, "a fragment of truth expressed in an instant of time."[7] Thus they offer at its most concentrated the chief technique and achievement of the language of the work: a stark visual imagery based upon the Imagist theories of Hemingway's mentor Ezra Pound, set forth earlier. Hasbany, in fact, sees the Imagist principle as the dominant force in the whole work.[8] Hemingway has not yet attained either the intensity of pictorial visualization of *The Sun Also Rises* and *A Farewell to Arms*, or the fusing of the visual with a rough metric, as he was to do in the latter book. But his landscapes are so spare and precisely arranged as to suggest geometric equations; his selectivity is such that his visualizations are very nearly irreducible.

The interchapters are part of the book's intricate melody-harmony-counterpoint schema: they are harmony and counterpoint to the main line the stories represent, and within their own sequence they show several smaller melody-harmony-counterpoint arrangements. The first interchapter points the course of the book; the last serves to summarize it. The first suggests that life is a journey in the dark; the last declares that the great necessity is to survive. Those in between chiefly dramatize

7. William Pratt, *The Imagist Poem* (New York: Dutton, 1963), 18.
8. Richard Hasbany, "The Shock of Vision: The Imagist Principle in *In Our Time*," in Linda W. Wagner (ed.), *Hemingway: Five Decades of Literary Criticism* (East Lansing: Michigan State University Press, 1974), 224–40.

the harshness that Hemingway then saw as the core of life, and the inextricability of pleasure and pain.[9] Together, the stories and the interchapters present this firm and programmatic view of life, whether it was reached awarely or intuitively: (1) Violence, brutality, and disappointment are the larger part of the substance of life. (2) In this harsh universe, pleasure and pain are interwoven and inseparable. (3) No matter what, life goes on. (4) The first and final duty is to survive. (5) Man attains his largest stature when he meets the hostile element with style and control.

The function of the introductory "On the Quai at Smyrna," clearly, is to suggest through its specifics the kind of universe the book and its protagonist must deal with. That world is cruel, purposeless, sometimes ridiculous, and always capricious; life and death occur in it randomly but simultaneously after a fashion; pleasure coexists with pain—and humor with horror, though the humor is essentially gallows humor. The mass screaming on the pier at midnight suggests that pain and irrationality are at the center of the universe; the Turkish officer's delight at the promised punishment of the British sailor dramatizes the fused relationship of pleasure and pain; the fact that the sailor is both innocent and not really to be punished intimates an element of incongruity and ridiculousness in the universe.

The next jump is to women who refuse to give up newborn babies who have died, a focused example of the closeness of life and death and the irrationality that is part of the life process. An old woman who dies and has instant rigor mortis demonstrates again the omnipresence of death and the universal incongruity (instant rigor mortis is supposed to be impossible). An exchange of gunfire between the narrator's warship and the Turkish shore batteries is barely averted; it would have had its cause in a trifling order from the Turk and would have resulted in a bloodbath, another suggestion of incongruous violence always ready to erupt. Emblems of destruction and death are always present, yet joined to those concomitants of death are those of life continuing: "You didn't mind the women who were having babies as you did those with the dead ones. They had them all right. Surprising how few of them died. You just covered them over with something and let them go to

---

9. Wilson, Introduction to *In Our Time*, ix-xv.

it."[10] The harsh portrait of a harsh world is completed in a final image of cruelty, death, and absurdity: the Greeks kill their mules by breaking their legs and pushing them into the sea. Thus is sketched the picture of the world that the young man chiefly known as Nick Adams must confront.

Catastrophe by catastrophe, he learns his lessons in it. In "Indian Camp," he is present when an Indian cuts his own throat because he cannot stand his wife's childbirth agony; he is instructed by this and other circumstances that life and death, pleasure and pain, are part of the same process, and most of all, that life goes on, no matter what. He must witness the humiliation of his father in "The Doctor and the Doctor's Wife," learn that there are no demigods, and that he must accept those he cares for in all the fallibility of their mortality. "The Battler" again presses home to him that catastrophe is the human condition and that meeting it may demand resourcefulness as well as courage: he sees a mentally damaged old boxing champion and a vagrant making a life for themselves in which kindness and necessary brutality —pleasure and pain—together make the foundation. He not only experiences one of the most universal catastrophes, the death of love, in "The End of Something," but learns that sometimes life demands that he be inflictor as well as receiver of pain. "The Three Day Blow," one of the most vibrant stories in the collection, shows him rallying from the return of the love-death grief with the overwhelming revelation that nothing in life is as important as life itself. In his wounding on the Italian front and his heartbreak at his "betrayal" in his first real love affair—in "A Very Short Story"—he sustains the great catastrophe of his own life and, throughout the remainder of the book, tries to rebound from it.

We must accept paradox to accept Krebs as Nick in "Soldier's Home," and George as Nick in "Cat in the Rain," but the logic of the chronicle insists upon it. In the first story, he loses the stasis he has achieved by choosing disengagement in his parents' home after the war; the sad learning from this catastrophe is that there is no separate peace, no withdrawal from combat. In "Cat in the Rain" and in "Out of Season," he finds, observing the catastrophes of others, that he is as displaced, as

10. Ernest Hemingway, *In Our Time* (New York: Scribner's, 1955), 11. All quotes are from this uniform edition.

alienated in marriage as out. We learn of his discovery only after the third of three stories in what might be called the young-man-married group, "Cross Country Snow." There, he is reminded again that life is loss and catastrophe and that significance can be seized only in an instant of willed transcendence, concentrated here into a downhill rush on a ski slope.

With a significant omission of narrative tissue, Nick does not appear again until the two-part story, "Big Two-Hearted River." This is not only the last story in the book, it is the cumulative statement of the young-man chronicle, and it is thus crucial within the apparatus of *In Our Time.* An imagistic parable of a spiritual journey from desolation to renewal, it rises from the thematic and tonal low of "My Old Man" to a reconciliation between man and the world. And since renewal is developed in a deliberate parallel to Christian ritual, the story presents several modes simultaneously: it is the literal account of a fishing trip; it is a communion fable of reaffirmation of personal faith in life; it is the provisional ordering of the demi-tragic experience of the book.

The reaffirmation and ordering are presented in such an elliptical manner, relying almost completely on imagistic implication, that the story's thematic significance is apt to evade even the most patient critic who reads it out of sequence. To an even greater degree than the other stories, it is much larger as a part of a whole than as an isolated entity: indeed—as Cowley[11] and virtually every subsequent writer on it has pointed out—separated from the whole it loses most of its meaning. It brings the book full cycle—not only back to Nick but back to the Michigan woods as a paradigm of the universe. It dramatizes Nick's achieved recovery from personal catastrophe to a reunion with the life force and a renewal of his own life, and it thus completes his chronicle and is, in a real if unique sense, his and the book's reconciliation to experience that, at the least, has elements of tragedy in it.

One of Nick's reflections may bear directly upon the author's gathering view of tragedy. Looking into the swamp as he fishes in the stream running into it, Nick thinks, "in the fast deep water, in the half light, the fishing would be *tragic*. In the swamp fishing would be a *tragic* adventure. Nick did not want it. He did not want to go down the stream

11. Malcolm Cowley, Introduction to *The Portable Hemingway* (New York: Viking, 1944), xix-xx.

any further today" (211, italics added). The reasonable inference is that Nick wants to defer an immediate return into experience that has been painful and stamped with some aspects of tragedy. But might not the author also be indicating subliminally that he was reluctant to take the final step toward an acceptance of his own tragic vision—to assume his robes as priest of tragedy?

The four other stories in the book not part of the young-man sequence still reflect its philosophical themes. The introductory "On the Quai at Smyrna" was added in the second edition, as noted, to give a fragmented, imagistic view of what was to come. "The Revolutionist" shows its protagonist caught in permanent catastrophe, apparently by incurable idealism; in "Mr. and Mrs. Elliott," the principal is kept in the same condition through his weakness. Of the four, the most impressive in its own right is "My Old Man."

"My Old Man" is well advertised as derivative of Sherwood Anderson; it is also the first fully, conventionally, and only incontestable tragedy in the book. No irony plays against the tragic structure: the catastrophe—the violent death of the storyteller's father—is in major rather than minor key, its impact direct and jarring rather than tangential. And quite simply, the tragic spirit is there and is felt: necessity moves directly against the protagonist and wrings from him an undisguised cry of grief—this time unrelieved by any transcendence or reconciliation.

The protagonist is a boy, Joe Butler, who idolizes his jockey father; his tragedy is the loss of his father through disillusionment as well as death. Joe suffers a great sense of loss and sadness when he learns his father is corrupt. This corruption finds its objective correlative when the father loses a race on a great horse, Kzar, and the horse then becomes for Joe a concomitant of the good, the beautiful; in thwarting Kzar's natural triumph, his father has allied himself with the bad. But he forgives his father when the older man buys and races his own horses; rapport is restored; Joe feels again he is touching what he seeks. He is thus at that high point of fulfillment or near fulfillment that precedes catastrophe; that comes when the father, honest at last, is killed in a steeplechase race. As he leaves the track, Joe hears a judgment pronounced that destroys his father in memory as well as fact: his old man was a "crook" who "had it coming to him." "And George Gardner looked at me to see if I'd heard and I had all right and he said, 'Don't you listen to what those bums said, Joe. Your old man was one swell guy.' But I don't know. Seems like when they get started they don't leave a guy nothing" (173). The prime motivation of Joe's life—to preserve his father as the king of his universe—has crashed. And there is no transcendence or victory of spirit—only loss.

Within the structure of the collection of stories, "My Old Man" occupies a unique position. Although it is unrelated in subject matter to the other stories, it is tightly joined to them in tonal progression. Not only is it the only conventional tragedy among the stories, and the only one that ends in catastrophe unrelieved by any kind of reconciliation, it is also the emotional nadir of the collection, and the fullest expression of the central component of the tragic view of life: that something in the universe defeats us all. It is the next-to-the-last story and stands in close relation to the last, "Big Two-Hearted River." For "Big Two-Hearted River" offers a statement of reconciliation by Nick Adams and moves to that statement in a swift, steep ascent from "My Old Man." Consequently, "My Old Man" occupies the position of catastrophe in the *emotional* progress of the volume: one might conveniently and accurately call it the *tonal catastrophe*—as distinguished from the narrative catastrophe of Nick's wound and love affair.

So seen, the position of "My Old Man" in sequence is both strategic and effective, and with "Big Two-Hearted River" it completes a unified pattern for the book. Finally, of course, the book is not tragic, but it is moving toward tragedy. It has parts that are touched with the tragic emotion, and almost all the stories have the requisite dramatic scaffolding on which tragedy could be built. In retrospect, with hindsight made keen by the novels that followed, it is hard to resist the conviction that the author's tragic vision is beginning to assume its shape here—incomplete as it may be for the time being.

2

The Sun Also Rises
Passivity as a Tragic Response

Almost the only way in which *The Sun Also Rises* has not been widely considered is as a fictional tragedy. Astute critical views have put it forward as a sturdy morality play, as a fable of a contemporary waste-land, as a projection of Sartrism before Sartre, and in various other intriguing perspectives. But for a long time the only reader who saw it as tragic was the author himself, and his astonishing identification of the hero as "the earth" had to produce a certain discounting. Aren't writers notoriously the worst judges of their own work, after all? Yet if the novel meets the subjective test of impact, it is indeed tragic, for it meets the other tests. And for those who do experience it as tragedy, it is the first major revelation of Hemingway's tragic vision.

So accepted, then, it is one of the key works in that vision. But it is a key book in other respects, too; some might be profitably recalled. One of the most fascinating of these is the process by which its source experience was converted into art. Another is the explosive effect it had on Hemingway's literary fortunes. For *The Sun Also Rises* was the book that brought Hemingway's reputation out of the closet and into the world. We are told it set fashions for manners for sophisticates and those who wanted to be, that it created a small sensation in Paris as a roman à clef, nobody having any doubt who was who, and that it made Gertrude Stein angry because the dialogue was so good.[1] Certainly it evoked imitations, and imitations, and imitations; an emulation still

1. Ernest Hemingway, *Green Hills of Africa* (New York: Scribner's, 1935), 65–66.

40

crops up now and then. And it established the author at once as one of the very best of American novelists.

Harold Loeb's thirty-year-postponed rebuttal, *The Way It Was*, gives an account of the adventure that became the novel from the lacerated consciousness of the man who was sure he "was" Robert Cohn, and the Baker biography enlarges our knowledge of the event from other perspectives.[2] One finishes both with no doubt at all that this *was* the way it was—Loeb's dignified control of an understandable and too-long-suppressed indignation is a little awesome—and with no doubt whatever that the novel represents one of the great triumphs in literature of the conversion of event to art. In its refinement and reconstitution, the structuralists have one of their best examples. It is one of the best examples, too, of what should be a truism: that a work of the imagination should never, ever, be confused with its literal antecedents. Such confusion does violence to feelings and reputations and actuality: it should be desperately avoided: it will not be.

For a full understanding of the differences between the novel and the trip to Pamplona by Ernest and Hadley Hemingway, Bill Smith, Donald Ogden Stewart, Harold Loeb, Lady Duff Twysden, and Pat Guthrie, the reader not already familiar with them is referred to the sources.[3] For quick examples of what happened in the novel's elevation: Smith and Stewart are combined in Bill Gorton; an admiration that the matador Cayetano Ordoñez felt for Hadley Hemingway becomes a full-fledged affair between Pedro Romero and Lady Brett Ashley, with no Hadley-inspired characters otherwise appearing; the big scene in which Robert knocks out Mike Campbell and Jake Barnes stems from a ludicrous "trip outside" a cafe by Hemingway and Loeb that ended in absurd comedy. And one believes Loeb absolutely when he says he tried to leave at the outset of the bickering with Guthrie-Campbell, but was restrained by Duff Twysden, the Brett prototype.

To know this is interesting and, in its way, valuable. It is finally only incidental to the novel as novel, and to the novel as tragedy. The author called his story "a damn tragedy with the earth as hero abiding for-

---

2. Harold Loeb, *The Way It Was* (New York: Criterion, 1959), 285–98; Carlos Baker, *Ernest Hemingway: A Life Story* (New York: Scribner's, 1969), 144–57.

3. Bertram P. Sarason, *Hemingway and the Sun Set* (Washington, D.C.: WCRI Microcard, 1972).

ever."[4] It was a fanciful assessment, and one suspects its romantic quality made it irresistible to him. But he does seem convinced that the novel was a tragedy, and in its way a formal one, even if he nominated a bizarre protagonist.

There is almost no endorsement of the work's tragic stature by his critics. Baker declared early and unequivocally that Hemingway's novels were among the great fictional tragedies—but *The Sun Also Rises* was his exception.[5] Young focuses on the novel as Hemingway's *Wasteland*, though he sees real strength in some of the characters; coping with wound and trauma, Jake, he suggests, grows "strong at the broken places." Young's view of the archetypal Hemingway hero as overcoming his disasters to achieve wholeness, indeed, is more than a parallel to the conception of him as rising from the ruins of catastrophe to the spiritual triumph of tragic transcendence. It is the same victory seen in a different perspective and described in a different laboratory vocabulary.[6] Baker's description of Jake as "Beat up, not lost" is trenchant and points toward the Sartrean as well as the tragic core of the book; so does his conclusion that Jake displays resolute strength against a background of waste and debilitation to give the novel "a sturdy moral backbone."[7] Yet neither perceives the novel as tragic, nor do R. P. Adams, Sheldon Grebstein, Earl Rovit, Arthur Waldhorn, or most other comparatively recent assessors.[8] Burhans, an acute analyst of the tragic in *The Old Man and the Sea*, has not directed his approach there to this book.[9] Mark Spilka appears to feel that the novel has the possibility

4. Ernest Hemingway to Maxwell Perkins, November 19, 1926, quoted in Carlos Baker, *Ernest Hemingway: The Writer as Artist* (Princeton: Princeton University Press, 1972), 91.

5. Baker, *Hemingway: The Writer as Artist*, 96.

6. Philip Young, *Ernest Hemingway: A Reconsideration* (State College: Pennsylvania State University Press, 1966), 82–88.

7. Baker, *Hemingway: The Writer as Artist*, 75–93.

8. R. P. Adams, "Sunrise out of the Wasteland," *Tulane Studies in English*, IX (1959), 119–31; Sheldon Grebstein, *Hemingway's Craft* (Carbondale: Southern Illinois University Press, 1973); Earl Rovit, "*The Sun Also Rises*: An Essay in Applied Principles," in *Ernest Hemingway* (New York: Twayne, 1963), 147–62. Rovit's position is essentially Sartrean: the novel, he finds, declares that "individual man is the puny maker of meanings in his life" (161). Arthur Waldhorn, "Artist and Adventurer: A Biographical Sketch," in *Ernest Hemingway: A Collection of Criticism* (New York: McGraw Hill, 1973), 1–17.

9. Clinton S. Burhans, Jr., "*The Old Man and the Sea*: Hemingway's Tragic Vision of Man," *American Literature*, XXXI (January, 1960), 446–55.

of tragedy, but that its protagonist never attains it, that Jake is finally only pathetic.[10] John Killinger's assessment of the work as a powerful existential fable is incipiently, perhaps, an acceptance of it as tragic, but he does not pronounce it.[11] Thus an insistence that the novel is fictional tragedy, and tragedy of a high order, is well outside the received wisdom. Yet the position here is that the author was right: for some, the book *is* tragic, and powerfully so.

The two necessities of tragedy that have been proposed are that the protagonist suffer a catastrophe which is irreversible on its own terms, and that the work have a sufficiently powerful impact. If one accepts them, the operational question here quickly is seen as the subjective one —is the novel's impact profound enough or not? Since it is a subjective question, it can properly be answered either yes or no: if the book moves the reader sufficiently, it is tragic for him; if he is less moved, it is not. The response here is, simply, that its impact *is* that of tragedy.

If the novel is tragic, it is certainly irregularly so. The circumstance that keeps it carefully life-sized, in no way "larger than life," does not annoy the student of tragedy at this point, but the absence of a conventionally rigid dramaturgy and of a heavily underscored scene of catastrophe might well confuse him. Also, some initial disagreement as to the identity of the protagonist is understandable. It seems not unreasonable to take the view that the protagonist is collective—a unity made of those characters who gather in Paris, make the emotion-charged pilgrimage to Pamplona, and then disperse, not outwardly too different from what they had been. But a closer consideration leaves no doubt that Jake is protagonist as well as central intelligence; for those to whom the work is tragic, he is also tragic hero. The individual dramas of the other characters are contrapuntal to his own and reinforce it; in a pattern that appears deliberately modeled on the musical form of the fugue, he is "home" key and the others are the "foreign" keys, all sounding the same theme differently. Tension mounts as the action alternates from one to another. Put simply, they are different instruments playing the same tune, differently scored in each case.

10. Mark Spilka, "Hemingway and the Death of Love in *The Sun Also Rises*," reprinted in Carlos Baker (ed.), *Hemingway and His Critics* (New York: Hill and Wang, 1961), 80–90.

11. John Killinger, *Hemingway and the Dead Gods: A Study in Existentialism* (Lexington: University of Kentucky Press, 1960).

Yet it is Jake who is the main character and it should be remembered that his total story is far advanced when we meet him. The novel demonstrates one of Hemingway's most frequently used and artful strategies, that of beginning not simply in the middle of things but well toward their end—often, in fact, at the onset of catastrophe itself. So here: in Jake's *whole* story, the part that appears in the novel is virtually all catastrophe, capped finally by his transcendence of it. Readers of Greek tragedy will note a generic parallel and possibly a source.

Where is Jake when we find him? What is he seeking? After receiving the war wound that left him incapable of conventional sexual expression, he has been simply trying to come to terms with life, to achieve a stasis. His short retrospectives indicate that he had been moderately successful until Brett reentered his life. It has been her return, or rather his surrender to the emotions her return evokes, that has knocked him off his achieved and precarious balance; when we meet him, he has already entered catastrophe. It turns out to be a long drop; the entire novel is devoted to his experience of it, and finally his spiritual triumph over it.

The Sun Also Rises is located far closer to Frye's omnipotence-of-the-crushing-universe boundary of tragedy than to the other, that of the personal flaw. But it touches both. Jake seems almost an archetype of the hero overwhelmed by circumstances not of his making; yet he also commits a subtle *hubris*. His allowing himself to "fall in love" with Brett is an overreaching, an attempt, however involuntary, to take more from life than it has let him know it means to allow him, and it is this that has set in motion his catastrophe—classically enough. We are within our rights, even, in deducing an earlier *hubris*: Jake's wound is the consequence of his flying in the Italian air arm, and it was patently a romanticism, a thrust toward the ineluctable, that caused him to enlist in a foreign force in the first place. So his romanticism, broadly speaking, both caused his wound and caused him to fall in love with Brett. We are justified, also, in seeing it, dramaturgically, as the fatal flaw. So as tragic hero, Jake sustains catastrophe both because of the operational hostility of the universe *and* because of a quality in himself.

Even as he confronts tragic catastrophe, Jake also confronts the existential void—perhaps even more visibly. In a perfectly Sartrean sense, his life *must* begin on the far side of despair: he must create meaning after his wound has denied him so many possibilities of meaning. He does make and act upon aware choices. These lead to the construction of a network of consolatory pleasures, and to the maintenance of a posture of confronting misfortune that is both esthetic and philosophical. He is an existential success because he works at it; he knows he must earn or pay for every consolation.

> I thought I had paid for everything. Not like the woman pays and pays and pays. No idea of retribution or punishment. Just exchange of values. You gave up something and got something else. Or you worked for something. You paid some way for everything that was any good. I paid my way into enough things so that I had a good time. Either you paid by learning about them, or by experience, or by taking chances, or by money. Enjoying living was learning to get your money's worth and knowing when you had it. You could get your money's worth. The world was a good place to buy in.[12]

However, Jake's identity as existential man is part of his identity as tragic hero, and his life of action may be examined as a tragic line. Just as *Oedipus Rex* represents the concluding phase of a total narrative and simultaneously contains a complete dramaturgy and unity within itself, so does *The Sun Also Rises*. In Jake's larger story, the novel as catastrophe renders his sufferings and continuing efforts to bear them with grace after his fall from stasis because of his emotional surrender to Brett; it culminates in his apparent transcendence of his griefs by a re-achieved and more profound acceptance of his condition, and the human condition of which it is a metaphor. But though it invokes Jake's earlier history, it is, like *Rex*, complete in itself. At the outset, Jake faces a task: to break from Brett and once again create a life that is at least endurable. The great barrier to his doing so is the intensity of the emotions that hold them together; it appears that it is she, rather than himself, who sets him on the way to apparent freedom by declaring the unconsummated affair ended. Shortly after this illusory "release," he most closely approaches his goal of serenity and balance on the fishing trip in the mountains with Bill. In the perspective of his quest, this is his highest point, the closest he comes to achievement of it, until the

12. Ernest Hemingway, *The Sun Also Rises* (New York: Scribner's, 1953), 148.

end of the novel. He thinks, indeed, that he has made it; he may even believe he is telling Bill the truth when he says he is no longer in love with Brett. But when he comes down from the mountain, he enters the familiar ordeal of pain again. Its climax is his personal nadir: when he debases himself in his own eyes by handing Brett to her bullfighter and taking a humiliating beating from his philosophical and tonal antagonist, Robert. This is the *novel's* catastrophe proper—the catastrophe within the larger catastrophe, so to speak.

What causes Jake's resurgence, transcendence, reconciliation, rendered with such symbolic and metaphorical brilliance in the two swimming scenes at San Sebastian, after the fiesta? We are not told; we are only given the elaborate, coded statement by ritual that it has taken place—that Jake has finally won through to acceptance. It may be that the absence of an explanation as to *how* he has done so is the most serious weakness of the book. On the other hand, it may be that the omission, the forcing of a deduction of internal processes by external images, is one of the author's most artful strokes; it should be noted that the principle was the very foundation of the art of certain French novelists of the fifties and sixties—most celebratedly, Alain Robbe-Grillet. Whatever, we accept the declaration: Jake has won the psychic triumph. The dinner scene with Brett in Madrid is more than coda: it affirms both the spirit's victory and the unchanging character of material defeat. And the culminating image is one of human traffic obeying the commands of a policeman "deity" with a baton, an aspect of the primary, tragic theme: man is finally helpless before the dictates of an indifferent but punishing universe; he can only dignify himself by the manner in which he *accepts* the inescapable catastrophe.

This theme, most powerfully and directly produced by the drama of Jake, is reinforced and restated through the lines of the other characters —who play against Jake as foreign keys play against home key in the fugue. Their condition is held in common, and the author makes us accept it as the human condition: all have suffered loss and pain of overpoweringly traumatic proportions; all are trying to work clear of their personal wreckage and fashion or find a viable life; all face the universal catastrophe as a kind of moral examination they will pass or fail.

Robert Cohn, of course, is the chief of these other lines; he is the opposing key in the fugal structure, and he is both Jake's opposite and semblable. Where Jake hides emotion, gracefully, Robert expresses it awkwardly; where Jake is tightly disciplined, he is uncontrolled; where Jake is stoic, he is sentimental; where Jake stands for the new coolness, he is apotheosis of an archaic overstatement. Yet at core the two are not only alike but nearly identical: they are both incurable romantics. They are not twins but mirror images; the romanticism that has produced one configuration in Jake has produced its reverse in Robert. This produces a special unity in the very opposition of the two keys and contributes substantially to the tightness of the pattern. Like Jake, Robert's romanticism has propelled him to his present: he is, and always has been, trying to fulfill a romantic self-image.

Neglected at Princeton, he has worked hard to assert his dignity by becoming middleweight champion. Humiliated in marriage, he has sought to regain his self-esteem in the relationship with Frances. But he feels trapped in his own colorlessness until he becomes infatuated with Brett and finally gets to spend a weekend with her. Although for her it is a careless, one-time diversion, for him it is the great reversal, the too-long delayed leap over that invisible barrier that has stood between him and the fulfillment of his destined—*i.e.*, romantic—estate of self-hood. Once he has entered "his affair with a lady of title" (178), he can see himself clearly as romantic hero; it is an adolescent vision, but he has made it come true, at least in his own consciousness. He thinks he has achieved his intention; the drop from that pinnacle is his catastrophe, and like Jake, he must see the woman he loves in the arms of other men. It is more than ironic that in the case of all three male characters with fully developed lines—Jake, Robert, Mike—the pain of catastrophe comes from romantic love for the same woman, Brett. Not only is the fugal unity thus drawn still tighter, but a commentary on the inevitable outcome of such love is supplied as well, and in the perspective of the Hemingway canon it is the author's prevailing view: romantic love destroys itself, and often its communicants with it.[13]

For Mike Campbell, too, the shape of catastrophe is essentially the same as was Jake's and Robert's. His bankruptcy in business is presented as a concomitancy of a personal bankruptcy; out of it, he has somehow managed a handhold on a tenable existence by his relationship

13. Spilka, "Hemingway and the Death of Love in *The Sun Also Rises*," 80–90.

with Brett. The novel witnesses its disintegration and his own—his fall from his unsafe perch.

The involuntary agent of suffering of these others, Brett has not and does not escape it herself, of course. In the exhausted, annihilated state to which the death of her lover and two destructive marriages have reduced her, promiscuity has been her anodyne and sexual conquest her avenue to brief self-esteem. She has pulled herself upward to brief self-respect by her love for Jake, but is pushed off that shaky sanctuary by the tensions created by Jake's impotence. Her weekend with Robert marks her return by choice to her old ways, though her catastrophe had already begun with the agonies of her unfulfilled love affair with Jake. Like Jake's, it lasts through most of the novel; however, her catastrophe is characterized chiefly by self-loathing—until her relinquishment of the young matador provides the act of transcendence that reconciles her, somewhat, to herself.

One finds no approach to the tragic in the development of two other important characters, Bill Gorton and Pedro Romero. For Gorton there seems to be no *dramatic* line at all: he does function on occasion as chorus and commentator, and sometimes perhaps as preacher, as M. L. Ross holds;[14] his chief use may be simply as contrast to these characters who have complete personal dramas. He remains a constant, not *visibly* experiencing catastrophe or confronting the void at all and thus escaping the moral examination that accompanies both. He goes through the book unchanged—and untested. Quite different is the case of Romero. He has a dramatic line of development, if an embryonic one, and he survives his catastrophe—the beating by the distraught Robert—rising from it to a triumph that is psychic *and* material. He is thus outside tragedy altogether. He passes the imposed examination totally, but one never really expects him *not* to pass it: on his own terms, he has done so every time he went into the ring. His key, so to speak, is that of the achieved ideal, and it affords both example and contrast to that of the others, who struggle and flounder. He thus joins Jake and Brett among the successes of the book—those who pass—whereas Robert and Mike are the failures.

It would be grossly overreaching to see the characters as representing

14. Morton L. Ross, "Bill Gorton, the Preacher in *The Sun Also Rises*," *Modern Fiction Studies*, XVIII (Winter, 1972–73), 517–27.

ideational abstractions after, say, the manner of *The Magic Mountain*; however, their personalities are carefully orchestrated. The four principals are all paradigms of the smashed human being, but they are finely differentiated and arranged in a surprisingly delicate balance. Jake has a clear inner discipline as well as outward style. Brett has style but no discipline—until she summons it at the final testing and makes the style stronger. Mike has style but never discipline, and without discipline the style erodes to nothing under stress. As the others see it, Robert has neither style nor discipline, but does have awkward manners that have become nonfunctional and sometimes ridiculous and fail him in a crisis. As an entity, too, they all have another concomitancy: disordered themselves, they are emblems of the new and disordered world that has come out of the first great upheaval of the twentieth century. Hence the perhaps excessively advertised keynote quotation from Gertrude Stein.[15] Still they are all trying, and even the failures arouse our sympathy. Yet from the doomed struggle with necessity, only Jake and Brett wrest a meaning and a significance; only they attain or approach tragic stature. Failing, the other two are only pathetic, negatives in the novel's vision that finds its full tragic statement only in the story of Jake.

So the primary theme is a variant of the enduring tragic theme; as stressed here, it might read: man achieves such significance as he can by the fortitude and dignity with which he *accepts* the universal catastrophe; no other victory is possible. The lesser themes are corollaries to the greater, ribs to its spine: they are an indispensable part of the ethos of Hemingway, and they recur through the Hemingway canon. But they are always complementary to his vision of the tragic.

Of these corollary themes, some emerge as major. (1) Those who meet the universal catastrophe with style are aristocrats and valuable; those who meet it without style are nonaristocrats and not valuable. (2) What is "real" is good and is a concomitant of aristocracy; what is "fake" is bad and is a mark of the nonaristocrat. (3) Since catastrophe is universal, solace must be found in compensatory pleasures. (4) Such pleasures must be earned by commitment of one kind or another: one does not necessarily get what he pays for in the pursuit of consolation, but he *may*, if he is a tough bargainer. (5) God may exist and religion is one of the very best consolations—but both are beyond the

15. Ernest Hemingway, *A Movable Feast* (New York: Scribner's, 1963), 29.

reach of most. (6) Pleasure and pain form a unity. (7) Romantic love always destroys itself.

These secondary themes are presented by example, and often by the example of polarities or paired opposites. Aristocrat is posed against nonaristocrat; good style against bad; real against fake; achieved compensatory pleasures against the nonpleasures of apathy. The aristocrats, of course, are those who have good style and who emphasize in their various stances the real rather than the fake; the nonaristocrats have bad style and drift toward the fake. Good style is understated gaiety and courage; bad style is overstated sentimentality. The aristocrats know that all we get from life, aside from the dignity of acceptance of its tragedy, are the compensatory pleasures, and they cultivate these energetically; the nonaristocrats whine over the universal catastrophe and seldom learn to enjoy the compensations. The idea of aristocracy is defined early, in the scene between the Greek count and Jake and Brett. The count is "one of us," Brett proclaims, and he serves as an instant paradigm of the Hemingway aristocrat. He has suffered much but jokes about it; he has "values" that include food and wine, friendship and sex, courage and durability. But he is not interested in displaying them: he only wants to know how to get his fair value out of them—paralleling Jake's subsequent interior monologue. "You ought to write a book on wines, Count," Brett tells him and he answers, "My dear, all I want out of wines is to enjoy them." Joining him as the aristocrats of good style are Jake, Brett, and Romero; the nonaristocrats are Mike, whose apparently good style goes bad, and Robert, whose bad style turns worse (he cannot mask his anguish at any time, and after the debacle with Romero, he weeps unashamedly). The scene between Jake and Robert in the hotel room after the fight is another confrontation of polarities: Jake has "good" style and forgives, casually, the beating and insults Robert has given him; in weeping and asking forgiveness so embarrassingly, Robert has "bad" style. Which is, after all, the "good" style of an earlier, archaic time. Ray West has said that the grandmothers of the other characters would prefer Robert to their own descendants.[16] The aristocrats, finally, are those who are competent, and who *endure* catastrophe in a manner that dignifies their lives. Hemingway has not yet

16. Ray B. West, Jr., lecture at University of Iowa, October, 1951.

come to the place where his characters achieve their affirmation through an aware and *powerfully willed* positive action that at once redeems and defines, even if it destroys, them.

The concept of the real versus the fake is most directly drawn in the explication of Romero's excellence as a matador; it is suggested less explicitly elsewhere, including the early scene with the count where important definitions are made. The superb wine the count insists on drinking is a specific of the real—as opposed to the less excellent, therefore an imitation, therefore a partial fake. However, the definition is direct in the Romero sequences: "Montoya caught my eye and nodded his head. This was a real one. There had not been a real one for a long time." Romero counterpoints the great, declining Belmonte, who does not fake in the ring but fakes outside it by insisting upon and getting inferior, nondangerous, fake (after their fashion) bulls.

The idea of consolatory pleasures appears early in the novel and runs through it: it is dramatized lightly in that scene between Jake, Brett, and Count Mimipoppolus which is so concentrated in thematic suggestion. The careful, almost ritualistic, attention Jake gives to food, wine, personal relationships, the sports and arts he follows is not casual. His attitude toward these, clearly, deliberately, and self-consciously achieved, is directly defined in his interior monologue: "You could get your money's worth. The world was a good place to buy in." By learning, he has come to understand and enjoy many things. By spending money *carefully*, he is able to obtain the enjoyment of those that cost money. By commitment, he had developed several strong friendships. The novel does not show him overtly taking chances, though his relationship with Brett certainly has a strong element of risk, and one presumes his wartime flying was first undertaken for thrills.

Robert, Mike, Bill, and even Brett are less programmatic in their compensations, and they are clearly less fully developed personalities, less rewarded than Jake and the count, who have cultivated their consolations with complete awareness. Romero's mastery of his metier is won through commitment and hard study as well as talent: he gets his highest pleasure and fulfillment from taking great chances in the bull ring, and his Spanish knowledge of meaningful manners has contributed to his "good" style.

Jake's own easy but unshakably good manners are dramatized at least as well in the final scene with Brett as anywhere else. Rendered there, too, are other of the secondary themes: the value of compensatory pleasures and the unity of pleasure and pain, the destructive impact of romantic love. He hears Brett, whom he loves, describe her affair with another man and behaves with such casual grace that only one line of Brett's suggests his wound may be showing: "Jake, don't get drunk. You don't have to get drunk." As he conceals his suffering, he is determinedly taking the solace of food and wine, and pleasure and pain thus fuse for him as they do for Brett. Her pleasure comes from her tragedy-fulfilling act in giving up Romero, her pain from losing him. They both elliptically express the desire for, and the unattainability of, God. And immediately after leaving the table, they are to enter a taxi and confront the policeman with a baton, who imagistically and finally conveys the principal, tragic theme. This understated restaurant scene is one of the most thematically concentrated in the novel.

The submerged God search is intimated early in the dining car: Jake, a nominal Catholic, cannot get a seat—*i.e.*, he is denied communion—with the Catholics on pilgrimage. Later he and Brett try unsuccessfully to pray—Jake twice.

The pleasure-pain principle, which so dominates the stories and interchapters of *In Our Time*, moves to the background in *The Sun Also Rises*, but it appears occasionally and often powerfully, notably in the Jake-Brett scene just cited, and in what is perhaps the book's finest sustained image, that of the funeral of the man killed by the bulls. This unity is the heart of the bullfight sequences, where it is invested with its greatest complexities and deepest resonances. It is expressed more superficially, and often nastily, in several scenes where Robert, who has caused pain to others, is dealt it himself—the long monologue in which his mistress Frances taunts him, the deviling he takes more than once from Mike, the confrontation with Romero where each inflicts a different kind of injury on the other. He has pained Frances by leaving her, Jake and Mike by having sex with the woman both love, and Romero by a physical beating; he is wounded in turn by each.

These lesser, contrapuntal themes are so closely allied to the novel's central vision of tragedy that they form a close, ultimately indivisible unity with it. They intensify it, and some even suggest paths to tragic reconciliation. Others, of course, indicate only palliatives—but these, the novel tells us, are our greatest benisons.

The manner in which Hemingway's attitudes combust in symbol and metaphor is long since a matter of received wisdom; it is difficult to remember that once upon a time so many had difficulty grasping what has become the obvious. But consensus is fixed on a principle, not an exclusive reading of the individual images; like certain key scenes, these have an inviting ellipsis that will always admit one more interpretation, or two, or three. There is a rich variety of development in the symbol sequence of *The Sun Also Rises*, with the author's minor themes often exfoliating as interestingly as the major. And many symbolic passages are also metaphorical, in that they dramatize elements and relationships inside the work. But the firm central line in the symbolic composition is the proper reinforcement of the central thematic line—that the universe will exhibit its power through our suffering, and that we can dignify ourselves only by the manner in which we endure.

An extended network of image projects that permeating conviction. It may not be so marked as a comparable development in *A Farewell to Arms* or indeed, most subsequent Hemingway novels, where the prevailing attitude of tragedy invests the work more copiously and heavily. But it is marked and unmistakable: from beginning to end, the symbology is saturated with the idea of one tragic extreme, that of man facing the universe in doomed and unequal battle. The fate figure manipulating human toys, the cockroach casually crushed, the river barges running with no propulsive power and little steering control, the disposition of a man killed by a bull and that bull killed by a man—these are only a selection of such configurations. All culminate, of course, in the final view of the mounted policeman as fate, whom all must obey without recourse.

The building to tragic statement is steady and the effect is subliminal, for the symbolic and naturalistic levels are merged completely; the non-professional might read the book a dozen times without being aware it had a symbol in it. But if he *is* moved to something like catharsis by the novel, one reason will be the cumulative effect of those images that fuse in a tragic thrust and a final tragic impact. Their statement and the statement made by the action of the book ultimately become one.

It is worth noting every time the topic comes up that all visual and sensory depictions in Hemingway are not necessarily thematic. In fact, most are intended simply to give full physical dimension to his fictional cosmos or even to indulge his obvious pleasure in pictorial composition. In a series of such completely naturalistic specifics, theme may suddenly flare into one or two and then subside as suddenly. Or it may not appear at all. But in the most complex passages, all elements work simultaneously. There is an extraordinarily compelling unity, for example, in the first taxi sequence: in it merges the literal, metaphorical, and symbolic in one paragraph—and in key sentences, these modes are simultaneous.

> The taxi went up the hill, passed the lighted square, then on into the dark, still climbing, then levelled out onto a dark street behind St. Etienne du Mont, went smoothly down the asphalt, passed the trees and the standing bus at the Place de la Contrescarpe, then turned onto the cobbles of the Rue Mouffetard. There were lighted bars and late open shops on each side of the street. We were sitting apart and we jolted close together going down the old street. Brett's hat was off. Her head was back. I saw her face in the lights from the open shops, then it was dark, then I saw her face clearly as we came out on the Avenue des Gobelins. The street was torn up and men were working on the car-tracks by the light of acetylene flares. Brett's face was white and the long line of her neck showed in the bright light of the flares. The street was dark again and I kissed her. Our lips were tight together, and then she turned away and pressed against the corner of the seat, as far away as she could get. Her head was down.
> "Don't touch me," she said. "Please don't touch me."
> "What's the matter?" (25)

The passage is not only a highly effective juxtaposition of simple visuals, but it also projects many conceptions and emotions—and an overriding sense of catastrophe. In one incandescence, these show many faces of the book's truth. The "old street" points to the prewar world of older conventions and an even older thoroughfare: that of the sexual relationship. With the same multivalence, the "torn up" stretch into which the taxi passes is an equivalent of the world of twentieth-century upheavals, the disruption of those conventions, and the marring of sexual possibility for Jake and Brett. The acetylene torches—hard, bright, and unnatural—are both connotative, perhaps, of the harshness of the new external world and metaphorical of Jake's personal universe, which is also broken, also illuminated by the manufactured light of painfully acquired philosophy. More, the total image of shadows tailing in a dark lighted by strange fires suggests a hell; it urges at once that Jake and Brett are in hell and, less immediately, that hell may be the human condition. The hell that the two are passing through is the catastrophe for each, and it is possible to see in the passage a foreshadowing of an intensification of that catastrophe, a warning that even worse is to come. It is one of the most accomplished extended images in the novel, and it sounds, subtly but powerfully, the tone of tragedy very early in the book.

So declared, the tragic continues to increase its presence, almost imperceptibly, through that series of casual images cited earlier. Most of these, and others, function simultaneously on metaphorical and symbolic levels *inside the book*. The girl manipulating two toys in a boxing match as she looks indifferently away is of course fate, by whatever name. But three tourists are watching, and thus the number of actors is five male and one female—the exact number of principals in the Pamplona explosion. So the sidewalk drama forecasts the other to come. Which two men are the combatants, Jake and Robert or Robert and Romero? Perhaps a better reading is that Brett is simply to inspire combat among *all* the men who surround her, and the fighters are not specifically representational.

Jake sees a group of barges being towed down the Seine, the bargemen manning them having the most limited control over their movements. They are propelled by external forces, the tug and the current, as, in one equation of tragedy, all human lives are propelled by an external force, the omnipotence of the universe. At the same time, the barges are emblematic of the specific characters in this book, nearly helpless before a whole sweep of forces. The limited control exercised by the bargemen may equate with the narrow range of response to universal catastrophe stipulated by the novel: one has enough control to *accept* well or badly, and no more.

When Jake steps on the cockroach in the Bayonne Hotel lobby, one inevitably thinks of those lines from King Lear (IV, 1, 36–37): "As flies to wanton boys are we to the gods. They kill us for their sport." The idea that insects are to man as man is to a higher power is developed with far greater tragic impact in the image of Henry and the ants on the log in *A Farewell to Arms*, but in context, the tragic is suggested here too, masked as it is. So, of course, is the idea of Robert, another invader, being crushed by the group.

Fate, or tragic necessity, or X, is given a prophetic voice in the brilliant night club scene, the crescendoing finale of Part I. This is the dark drummer: he beats and chants at a rising tempo as the tempo of the scene mounts and the emotional voltage between Jake and Brett becomes clear. His only discernible words are, "you can't two-time," a clear warning that Jake and Brett face penalty for having tried to get something for nothing; in effect, they are undergoing the retribution imposed by necessity for having tried to push the universe off balance. The chanted line is a statement of the inevitable, and it has its sad resonances of tragedy and catastrophe. This warning, oracular motif is continued on the fishing trip to the mountains, for even as Jake reaches the closest approach to happiness he will make, he encounters mute reminders of doom: on the wall of his hotel room are panels of rabbits, pheasant, and duck—all dead.

In this book, with certain important exceptions, man's chief response to his overwhelmingly more powerful enemy is not to throw himself body and soul into unequal and foredoomed combat, as Santiago is to do much later, but to create for himself rituals of consolation, ceremonials of dignity. The implication is that these are not nearly enough but are all we have. One such expression of the frailty of the response is the incident of the stuffed dog. When Gorton urges Jake to buy a stuffed dog from a Paris taxidermist—"Simple exchange of values. You give them money. They give you a stuffed dog." (72)—he is being used to suggest that any deal with fate is a deception, one in which man is ultimately cheated. The money tendered is real; what is returned is finally counterfeit. And this general implication is fused with a specific in the book: Jake's carefully created body of consolatory values is useful, even handsome, but it has no vital power; it cannot hold back the natural force of catastrophe, can never be more than consolation.

One large comfort against the universal catastrophe is communion of various kinds: finding one kind of unity or another, men huddle together before the cold wind and make warmth for themselves. One such communion is formal religion. But though it is seriously offered as a possible mitigation of ordeal for some, it does not work for the principals. First, they are excluded from eating in the dining car with a group of religious pilgrims—a clear communion rite—even though Jake is himself a professed Catholic. Later, Jake and Brett attempt on different occasions to pray in the cathedral at Pamplona, but are unable to achieve communion, to establish a sense of unity with a deistic power. It is important to note that Jake does not discount religion, but only his present inadequacy for it: "I . . . regretted I was such a rotten Catholic, but realized there was nothing I could do about it, at least for awhile and maybe never, but that anyway it was a grand religion" (97). Brett says later, "(God) never worked very well with me" (245). Only Romero, in his visits to the chapel before his fights, shows a possible religious affinity, though one suspects this is a deep-grained formality, and that his real communion is in the ring with the bulls.

As a kind of homogenizing and emotion-making agent, the bulls create several unities and communions, and are, naturally, the foundation of the entire fiesta, which is a continuing communion for those who do not exclude themselves from its fusings and spirit. That communion finds its rituals in the unloading of the bulls, the running before the bulls in the streets, and the climaxing passion of crowd joining man in the confrontation with the bulls in the *corrida*. And there are sharp concentrations of self-exclusion: Robert goes to sleep, the British women remain shut tight in the big car, Belmonte shuts himself off from the possibility of either his own greatness or communion with his passion by handpicking limited and inferior adversaries.

In Pamplona, at the fiesta, the only gods are the bulls. When Brett presides over the chanting *riau-riau* dancers it is as easy to see her as a priestess of bull worship, of a celebration of the deep, and dark, emotions implied in that worship, as it is to see her as a transient fertility goddess. This inevitably calls to mind the author's own description of the bull fight, in *Death in the Afternoon*, not as sport but as tragedy. And though it is the matador who is our empathic hero, is it not the bull—the bull-god—who is the true tragic protagonist and uniting force of the drama? He may kill, but he must die. He is, of course, the force of putative catastrophe for the matador—the double tragic drama is always possible—but for him, catastrophe is inevitable. Thus worship of the bull-god at the *corrida* is a celebration of the tragic, a celebration rooted in an awareness and comprehension of its spirit that is deeper than cerebral. Those who see the *corrida* itself as the great objective correlative of the book are right in more ways than one. Its tragedy proclaims the novel as tragedy.

Interestingly, the controlling image of the bull tragedy, and one of the defining passages of the novel, is not the visualization of an instant in the ring at all, though it partakes of such an instant. This is the sequence of paired paragraphs that epiphanize the ultimate earthly destiny of a man killed by a bull, and the same bull killed by another man. The first paragraph begins with a careful, literal cataloging of facts about the man: his name, his manner of life, the bare statement that a funeral was held, and that a procession of dancing and drinking societies leads the coffin to the railway station, where it is loaded on the train under the escort of his wife and two children. The paragraph ascends slowly in tempo and then flares suddenly into its great culminating image: "The train started with a jerk, and then ran smoothly, going down grade around the edge of the plateau and out into the fields of grain that blew in the wind on the plain on the way to Tafalla" (198).

The next paragraph is shorter and rises more simply to its paralleling climax:

> The bull who killed Vicente Girones was named Bocanegra, was Number 118 of the bull-breeding establishment of Sanchez Taberno, and was killed by Pedro Romero as the third bull of that same afternoon. His ear was cut by popular acclamation and given to Pedro Romero, who, in turn, gave it to Brett, who wrapped it in a handkerchief belonging to myself, and left both ear and handkerchief, along with a number of Muratti cigarette-stubs, shoved far back in the drawer of the bed-table that stood beside her bed in the Hotel Montoya, in Pamplona. (199)

Thus each paragraph rises through lesser levels to the decisive and pure image of statement: everything mortal passes, and material remains vanish in the passing of time. The long passage is a clear invocation of the keynote verse from Ecclesiastes: all rivers run to the sea. But at least as importantly, the author has given us a configuration of double tragedy. In the passage's selective span the man killed has become the brief surrogate of the matador, and thus in the tragic drama of the bull, both man and bull die. By this doubling, the universal is fixed still more deeply: the ultimate catastrophe is inescapable and the same for all. Yet in the face of it both bull and man have dignified themselves as best they can—more positively, in fact, than the novel's stoic principals. This is all anyone can do, is the implication. The passage inevitably calls to mind a picture from *The Old Man and the Sea*: the skeleton of the heroic fish adrift with garbage, waiting to go out with the tide. There, the implication of the highest tragedy—that noble effort of spirit outlasts the death of the flesh—is clearer, though not necessarily stronger. And there, the fish and the man pair as do the bull and the man here.

Melvin Backman has written that the tension between the matador and the crucified—*i.e.*, the slayer and the slain—is one of the key patterns in the Hemingway canon; with equal perceptivity, he writes that in *The Old Man and the Sea* Santiago becomes both matador and crucified, slayer and slain.[17] One can go further, in fact, and see this identity, this fusion running through all the works. In "The End of Something" and "The Three Day Blow," Nick is inflictor of pain and sufferer from it; so are Frederic Henry, Harry Morgan, and Robert Jordan in their various ways. Thomas Hudson in *Islands in the Stream* is hunter and hunted, slayer and slain, in the ritual of battle and experiences a merging of identity in another ritual, that of love: "I'll be you and you be me," his former wife tells him in their consummation. In the biography, Baker describes an unpublished novel in which hero and heroine not only merge but reverse their identities, back and forth.[18]

In the tragic framework, image underlines the statement of action. Everything mortal is both dealer and receiver of catastrophe; there is nothing living that is not a player in the universal drama.

An indispensable part of tragedy is aspiration; without a climb, there can be no fall, without longing, no grief. Aspiration has a firm imagistic concomitant running through the novel—the mountains. Writing about another novel, *A Farewell to Arms*, Baker has exactly and exhaustively described Hemingway's recurring mountain phenomenon. He calls the mountain Home and the plain Not-Home. One may supply his own equivalents, but the polarity and the broad emotional objectifications are unchanging. The mountains are the romantic ideal, even a

17. Melvin Backman, "Hemingway: The Matador and the Crucified," reprinted in Baker (ed.), *Hemingway and His Critics*, 245–58.
18. Baker, *Hemingway: A Life Story*, 454–55.

Platonic ideal of the good, for which men yearn but which, in its absolute form, they are doomed never to reach. Thus the mountains make a perfect backdrop for the tragic action, bespeaking possibility, denying fulfillment. The low country, to the contrary, is anti-idealistic and emphasizes elements of the tragic only by contrast; it is quotidian, pragmatic, ordinary. Put simply, high is romantic, low is realistic. The higher one goes, the greater his feeling of intensity, awareness, and possibility, even if the possibility is to be smashed; if he descends too low, his perceptions and feelings are correspondingly reduced, to the literal and practical. Spain is high, France is low, and the entry into Spain from France is rendered almost as a passage from one dimension to another. Jake experiences increasing exaltation as he makes the ascent; when he completes it, he feels "then it was really Spain" (93). Much later, he feels a kind of relief when he goes back down into France: his emotions—and his pain—are soothed by the return to ordinariness; they are reduced as the intensity of the dimension is reduced.

On the two ascents into the mountains—the car ride into Spain and the bus ride to the fishing inn—mountains are the heart of the visual rendering, and the imagizing of them is extended and brilliant. No matter how high the travelers climb, they always see larger, stranger mountains in the distance—ultimate and unattainable. The monastery at Roncesvalles is situated where the last great battle of European chivalry was fought and where—perhaps—Roland blew his horn; it is itself a concentration of the romantic absolute which the mountains apotheosize. Pamplona is the place of the most intense perceptions and agonies, of climax and catastrophe; it is first seen on a high plateau, rising out of and well above the plain, backed and flanked by even higher mountains.

The mountains are used subsequently as a correlative of emotion, reflecting the degree of tension of the characters and in the narrative. As Jake and Bill begin their fishing, Jake's closest approach to fulfillment of his intention during the novel, there are no clouds on the mountains. The day before the start of the fiesta, and the great increase in tensions that it is to bring, high white clouds stand above them. The morning before Jake is to deliver Brett to Romero and the party is to explode in fistfights, a fog from the sea comes over the mountains and obscures them. The tragic core of the work finds a powerfully concrete evocation in one of the climactic mountain images. As the dramatic crisis approaches (the onset of the *stretto* in the fugue) and Brett asks Jake to take her to Romero, "There were the lights of a car on the road climbing the mountain. On top of the mountain one saw the lights of the fort" (183). The universal attempt to attain one's aspiration is compressed into the car ascending; the fort on top suggests that the goal, romantic happiness, is formidably defended—too well defended for any attempt to reach the top to succeed. Immediately, of course, the car is a metaphor of Brett in her latest, most desperate attempt; less obviously, it is an ironic opposite to the action Jake is about to take—the abandonment of his own principle to aid Brett in her quest. Later, when Jake comes back to Spain after a quick trip to France, his return from the lower to the higher reality is signaled by a view of a green mountainside over housetops. And in the second swimming scene at San Sebastian, the last mountain configuration—a green hill with a castle closing the harbor—suggests with casual subtlety that the ultimate promise of the mountains, the ultimate romantic fulfillment, may be death itself.

That green hill with the castle is the concluding visual of the two swimming scenes; considered jointly, they are among the novel's decisive sequences. Abstractly, they suggest Kenneth Burke's tragic rhythm of purpose, passion, perception—with perception widening and deepening into reconciliation. More narrowly, they are a synecdoche of Jake's total situation in the book: in terms of Jake's dramatic thrust, they are a declaration that he has achieved transcendence of catastrophe. In the first passage, the cold water he enters and the roller that comes at him are the ordeal produced by his wound; the roller forces him under for a moment (he has to swim out under water), but he accepts and adjusts to a degree—"all the chill [is] gone" (235). The raft he reaches, where a boy and girl sun and laugh, is the man-woman relationship, and though Jake rests upon it briefly he cannot really achieve it. He is excluded, an exclusion to which the gesture of the girl turning her back is signatory. His dive to the bottom is the nadir of his experience, handing the woman he loves to another man. But he maintains his awareness in his pain—keeping his eyes open in the "green and dark" water—as the unachievable man-woman unity, the raft, makes a dark shadow in that awareness. He touches that relationship, one last time, diving off the raft to swim to shore, his lonely stasis.

This sequence has been a symbolic summary of what Jake has experienced to this point; his next swim is both a reprise of his total experience and foreshadows his last meeting with Brett, which is still to come. Too, it epiphanizes his reconciliation.

Jake stays in stoic control of his pain and necessity most of the time ("Trying to swim through the rollers but having to dive sometimes") but periodically he succumbs briefly to it: "in the quiet water I turned and floated." He sometimes achieves serenity and stasis, as on the fishing trip. And refreshed by spells of rest, he tries to function in life and avoid singularly painful experiences ("[I] swam, trying to keep in the trough and not have a wave break over me"). When he swims to the raft, he is forecasting the last encounter with Brett, which is to occur shortly. The green hill is again the unreachable ideal of experience, perhaps death itself, and Jake's reflection, "I thought I would like to swim across the bay but I was afraid of cramp" expresses a biological fear of death which prevents him from following his impulse toward death, surcease. When Jake dives "cleanly and deeply" from the raft he knows he is leaving even the remnants of man-and-woman permanently; as he swims "slowly and steadily" to shore, he is returning to life, limited as it is, and metaphorically affirming his reconciliation (238). This time the act is presented more decisively, as a finality and assertion.

Why the *double* telegram from Brett, summoning Jake to her that last time? One copy is forwarded to him from his office in Paris, the other from Pamplona. The office is the locus of the lower reality, Pamplona the citadel of the higher; thus she calls to him in both dimensions of his existence. Their subsequent dinner scene in Madrid is more than a narrative coda; it is a compression of statement, one of the book's most telling dramatizations of theme. How one interprets the book depends to a considerable degree on how he interprets this scene. Spilka sees it as a demonstration that Jake has lost permanently his illusion that he and Brett might have been happy had it not been for his wound, that at last he understands her inability to live with a fine man without destroying him.[19] Another view can be maintained, and is central to a view of the book as tragedy. For is not the emphasis upon the quality of abnegation, of spiritual triumph, in Brett's action? And is not Jake's confrontation of her at the dinner table a compaction of what he has confronted throughout the book? She is quite simply one face of his ordeal, his own variant of the universal catastrophe. He meets this evocation of catastrophe face to face and *acccepts* it with grace and dignity and responsibility; in the face of it he programmatically devotes himself to the rewards of consolation that are available—food and wine. What he has is trivial compared to what he has lost, but it is what he has, and he makes the most of it. The thematic implication is underlined by their exchange: "You like to eat, don't you?" Brett asks (246), and he replies that he likes to do a lot of things. It is certainly defensible to see this as a final reduction of Jake to the pathetic, but it is far more consistent with the total structure of the book to see it as the final underlining of his transcendence, of his somber triumph over catastrophe—already transmitted symbolically in the swimming scenes. The ritualistic eating and drinking, indeed, becomes an act of communion, a reaffirmation of personal belief.

The tragic momentum of the novel comes to a single, final point of concentration in the concluding image:

> "Oh, Jake," Brett said, "we could have had such a damn good time together."
> Ahead was a mounted policeman in traffic. He raised his baton. The car slowed suddenly pressing Brett against me.
> "Yes," I said. "Isn't it pretty to think so?" (247)

The lesser, sexual implication is obvious and need not be labored. It is the larger one that really counts: the policeman is fate, the Absurd, tragic necessity, or whatever name one wishes to give to the force in the universe that exercises impersonal control over our lives. One comes and goes at its absolute decrees; it does not care.

Thus Hemingway completes his first major tragic statement. In it, he has placed himself fairly near one of the absolute boundaries of tragedy, the concept that man is inevitably destroyed by a force in the uni-

19. Spilka, "Hemingway and the Death of Love," 88–92.

verse that is abstractly indifferent but operationally hostile. Yet, more than one at first realizes, he does not acquit his humans from all responsibility for their plight; they have contributed to it in each case, even though the preponderant responsibility belongs to the order of things. And he gives them a chance for dignity and redemption through the possibility of a narrow kind of transcendence: they can accept bravely, and, at their best, gaily. Later in his work, he is to allow them the possibility of a more vigorous response, of an even stronger exercise and triumph of the spirit. But as a self-conscious, ordained *vates* of tragedy, he begins here.

3

A Farewell to Arms
Without Victory

Hemingway once called *A Farewell to Arms* "my *Romeo and Juliet.*"
It isn't. If one must pair it with an older tragedy of romantic love, it is
his *Troilus and Criseyde.*[1] The affinities—and paradoxes—that arc between the two works are as remarkable as they almost certainly are accidental.[2] In each, a tragedy of romantic love takes place in the back
areas of a massive war; not in the midst of a family feud. In each, the
instrument of contact between the man and woman is the benign and
worldly friend, so saturated with skepticism that he becomes an incarnation of it: Pandarus and Rinaldi. In each (though Criseyde is a widow
and Catherine a virgin), the woman has lost her man earlier in the war
and is emotionally propelled by the loss toward a new, and larger, love.
And both works present love and war as the great opposing forces, the
conflict between them building to catastrophe. Chaucer inveighs directly
against a Fortune that plays games with the lives of its characters; Hemingway symbolically indicts a universe that does the same. The endings,
certainly, are markedly different—but it is impossible to avoid the reflection that had the novel stayed with the author's earlier exploration
of the more direct source experience, "A Very Short Story," even these
would have made a real pairing. There, after the war has separated

1. Edmund Wilson, "Ernest Hemingway: Bourdon Gauge of Morale," reprinted in
J. K. M. McCaffery (ed.), *Ernest Hemingway: The Man and His Work* (Cleveland
and New York: World, 1950), 236–57.
2. Carlos Baker, *Ernest Hemingway: The Writer as Artist* (Princeton: Princeton University Press, 1972), 96. Baker intuits resemblances between Chaucer's *Troilus* and another Hemingway novel, *The Sun Also Rises*, but in tone and irony.

them the lieutenant loses his nurse to an officer in another army—a fair rough match for Troilus' loss of Criseyde to the Greek leader Diomede after *she* is ordered to another force. As the novel stands, the death of one principal actually constitutes the tragic impact; Troilus' death only underlines it in the older work.

The paradox is that Chaucer's poem is much more like the archetypal twentieth-century long fiction in the complexity of its psychological insights than is Hemingway's novel, and Hemingway's novel depends even more heavily on certain powers and instruments of poetry than does Chaucer's poem. A tempting epigram—that Chaucer's poem is the better novel and Hemingway's novel the better poem—may not be a violently unsound critical judgment.

In fact, Daniel Schneider has argued, effectively and at length, that the best way to read *A Farewell to Arms* is as a poem.[3] He urges that the concentration of character and consciousness to single and simple emotional essences is what gives the book sufficient compaction to permit it to ascend to the level of poetry; conversely, the tremendous complexity of insight and characterization in *Ulysses*, a great novel, keeps it from approaching that level. The point is central to a reading of *A Farewell to Arms*, and what Schneider says about *Ulysses* applies, if infinitely more moderately, to *Troilus*. Its superb, pioneering penetrations of psyche blur its thrust as poem.

Another paradox lies in the materials of the two works: drawn from vastly different sources, how could their narratives look very much alike? For Chaucer's source is one of the anecdotes of the Trojan War that Homer didn't tell—part of that war's apocrypha, so to speak. Hemingway's source is his own life—and not one but three of the women in it.

It has been widely believed that his principal model was a beautiful American Red Cross nurse named Agnes von Kurowsky of German descent. Hemingway met her in hospital after his Italian wounding, and their relationship resembled that of Frederic and Catherine—but only up to a point, as Michael Reynolds demonstrates.[4] It is clear

3. Daniel J. Schneider, "Hemingway's *A Farewell to Arms*: The Novel as Pure Poetry," reprinted in Linda W. Wagner (ed.), *Hemingway: Five Decades of Literary Criticism* (East Lansing: Michigan State University Press, 1974), 252–66.

4. Michael S. Reynolds, *Hemingway's First War* (Princeton: Princeton University Press, 1976). Reynolds' study is the most extended examination of the characters,

enough from both scholarship and *A Movable Feast* that the idyllic apogee of the Alps is drawn entirely from Hemingway's Austrian winters with his first wife, Hadley. And the childbirth sequence closely follows the confinement of his second wife, Pauline, in Kansas City, and her Caesarean. Not the least of the lessons the book offers young writers is, don't be afraid to mix your love affairs, including marriages —at least literarily. The fusion of the author's three great early loves in one woman, Catherine Barkley, is useful in more ways than concentrating experiences: it helps make the novel more than the story of one romance and contributes significantly to its elevation to apotheosis of all romantic love. This means, for Hemingway, that it must be tragic. And the tragedy is the starkest in all the Hemingway novels; Baker aptly calls it his "first study in doom."[5]

As an expression of the tragic, *A Farewell to Arms* differs quite visibly from *The Sun Also Rises*. It is less complicated, less a special case. And it is more concentrated. For this greater specified gravity there are many reasons: the clarity of its tragic design, the greater and more poetic compactness and concreteness in its images, a generally more intense employment of many of its artistic strategies. It also differs importantly from the earlier book in that no transcendence and subsequent reconciliation are achieved. Indeed, reconciliation is counter-suggested, in both the narrative and the statement of the two decisive symbolic-metaphorical sequences of the novel—Frederic Henry walking to the hotel

---

events, and personal experiences in which the novel had its beginnings. Although acknowledging the connection of Hemingway and Agnes von Kurowsky as at least partial source, he finds that the intrinsic nature of the fictional and actual relationships was vastly different.

> Agnes . . . was more sophisticated than most Red Cross nurses and a better linguist. She was older than Hemingway, and it was she who broke off their relationship. She was never devoted to anyone, nor was she ever war-weary. . . . In short, Agnes von Kurowsky contributed little to Catherine other than her presence and her physical beauty. . . . Agnes may or may not have had a sexual relationship with Hemingway. (She emphatically denies it in a taped interview with Reynolds.) Ultimately it does not matter, for whatever the relationship, it could not have been that of Frederic and Catherine . . . in its emotional essences. (219)

Reynolds also finds that Agnes, Hadley Hemingway, and Pauline Hemingway all contributed to Catherine's characterization (196), a conclusion reached earlier by Baker and Young. Yet Agnes signed some of her letters to Hemingway, Reynolds reports, as "Mrs. Kid" (133).

5. Baker, *Hemingway: The Writer as Artist*, 96.

in the rain alone and the ants being burned to death on a campfire log. At the end there is only catastrophe, only doom: Nada—nothing—prevails unchallenged. In Hemingway's tragic equation, the stress has shifted from the possibility of individual transcendence of catastrophe by acceptance to the inescapable *fact* of universal catastrophe. If the very highest species of tragedy is that in which "inner triumph is wrested from outer defeat," *A Farewell to Arms* fails of it. This circumstance does not diminish the stunning singleness of its impact; indeed, the novel demonstrates as well as any other work that tragedy, and powerful tragedy, may be achieved without the clear triumph of spirit, without transcendence.

In the structural pattern, it is reasonable to see the duality, Frederic-Catherine, as protagonist. But it is better, perhaps, to regard Frederic as functioning alone in that role: both the larger quantity of narrative and consciousness are his, even though he and Catherine are so closely joined, and are in nearly identical situations at the beginning. The author has told us by imagistic prophecy that we are destined for tragedy before we lay eyes on them, whether or not we immediately understand the coded transmission. They are also in as typical a Sartrean posture as that author's Orestes. They have appeared, come on the scene,[6] but have not yet made the choices and taken the actions that give them the full weight of existence. Before their meeting, Frederic has divided his time between work, drink, and whoring and has never made a profound choice or commitment in his life; Catherine has actually declined such a choice when presented with the opportunity of making it in an early, unrealized love affair. Both are waiting unknowingly for the choice and the action that will give definition. They play with the choice and touch but push away the defining action in the early stages of their relationship in Gorizia; it is not until after Frederic is wounded and under Catherine's care in hospital that the choice is made and the action entered. The choice is not only Sartrean; more importantly to the tragic design, it is that choice described by Bradley and Heilman as the necessary and inevitable beginning of tragedy, the turn that once taken irreversibly leads to catastrophe. The choice of Frederic and Catherine has been to love and both will be destroyed by it, though differently.

6. Jean-Paul Sartre, *Existentialism and Human Emotions* (New York: Wisdom Press, 1957), 15.

The choice made, both commit themselves totally: they move into a new dimension of sensibility and they seek to move even further. This is of course *hubris*; they are overreaching, in classic terms, trying to force more from life than it has to give, and in those same terms they are doomed. The tragedy is thus—at once and at least—Aristotelian and Heilmanic. And it also partakes of both of Frye's limiting definitions, though it expresses much more powerfully that of the omnipotent universe indifferently crushing puny humans.

That power is moving upon them unseen at the very time of their greatest happiness, their interlude in the mountains during Catherine's pregnancy. When the invisible assault culminates in catastrophe at the death of Catherine in childbirth, Henry is as destroyed as she. There appears no transcendence of reconciliation for him, only loss; his catastrophe is unredeemed and final. Thus the author's chief emphasis in this variant of his tragic equation is on the finality and inescapability of catastrophe. Life is tragic, Hemingway declares here, and nothing can alter or mitigate the fact that man is sentenced to destruction by an uncaring but functionally inimical universe.

Another view is tenable—that Frederic and Catherine have taken a triumph from their lives by their love, even though it destroys them. This implies, of course, a transcendence that precedes catastrophe, a mildly unusual but by no means unknown sequence. Yet the requisite communication of a sense of spiritual triumph is simply not in the novel. And an elaborate system of symbol, metaphor, and interior monologue insists upon the other view: that catastrophe is the ultimate end of life, and against it all attempts at amelioration are puny and futile.

This is the only Hemingway novel with this emphasis. In *The Sun Also Rises*, the stress is upon the spiritual triumph of strong and graceful *acceptance*; in final work, it is to be upon a positive, active *fighting back* against catastrophe. Clearly, *A Farewell to Arms* cuts away from the straight line of development that starts with *The Sun Also Rises* and ends in *The Old Man and the Sea* and *Islands in the Stream*. Its emphasis makes it the "saddest"—as most know the word—of Hemingway's novels; it offers a powerful rebuttal, too, to the conviction that all tragedies are, in the ultimate view, "happy."

In moving toward its stunning, tragic culmination, the author as always in his novels has given his composition much of its shape and its tension by patterning it upon a generic musical model, here the sonata-allegro. The sonata-allegro is a larger and more complex effort in counterpoint than the fugue; it is chiefly distinguished by the conflict between two powerful key areas. From this conflict the tension is generated, and in each key area various instrumental voices may appear. In this novel, a conflict between two powerful opposing forces, at once emotional and physical, immediately appears and intensifies as the book develops. Young describes them as love and war; Warren implies, without using the words, that they are the sacred and the profane. Both observations are accurate and judicious and clearly imply an assemblage of elements in each force that is larger than the simple appellation. Baker chooses terms which acknowledge even more directly that each force contains many quantities; citing the sacred and profane, he calls them Home and Not-Home.[7]

Whatever called, the two forces are shaped as the contending keys of the sonata-allegro. One key, the home key, is the key of life, love, and hope; the other, the opposing or dominant key, is that of death, war, and negation. It is no improvement on Home and Not-Home, but perhaps a rough approximation of that balance, to call one key the life key and the other the death key, or even more simply, one the positive and the other the negative. Within each key, the voices blend into a rich and powerful unity. But as the work progresses more and more of the complexity of the keys is stripped away, until each is invested almost completely with a single tonality. These tonalities are the great contraries of tragedy: the positive key is a development of the efforts of the protagonist—or protagonists—to achieve meaning against overwhelming odds; the negative emerges ever more clearly as that force in the universe which crushes humans indifferently, and it includes but is more than the old tragic necessity. The tremendous conflict between these primal tragic forces is the source of the novel's power; now one key, now the other predominates. But when the dominant, death key finally overpowers the home, life key, the finality is catastrophe and the tone, shape, and statement of the work is finally tragic.

7. Philip Young, *Ernest Hemingway: A Reconsideration* (State College: Pennsylvania State University Press, 1966), 92–93; Robert Penn Warren, Introduction to *A Farewell to Arms* in *Three Novels of Ernest Hemingway* (New York: Scribner's, 1962), iii–xii; Baker, *Hemingway: The Writer as Artist*, 101–109.

The alternation of the keys is extremely skillful, and its tempo superbly controlled; it is useful to look from a sufficient distance at the broad movements, the advances and retreats, in the conflict. At the outset, both are sounded in a sequence so close that they appear almost simultaneously. In the first sentence of the first paragraph in the first, overture chapter,[8] the positive key quickly comes on in the idyllic image of house-river-plain-mountain, the mountain triumphing over all. But it is immediately supplanted in the paragraph's last line by the negative images of troops on the road on the plain, falling leaves, and dust. Both keys having declared themselves, there is now throughout the chapter an alternation between them. The second paragraph is devoted to home key—the fruitful orchards and mountains—with phrases of the negative—gunfire and fighting—being just audible. In the third paragraph the opposing key crescendoes, with powerful evocations of war and death projected by guns and soldiers. There is a relaxation of tempo in the fourth paragraph, as the king drives through ruined battlefields, but the intimation of the opposing, negative key is stronger. In the fifth and final paragraph, the opposing, dominant key simply floods the composition, ending the overture with a pure chord of death: "only seven thousand died of it in the army." The achieved tone is already that of tragedy.

It will be seen that each paragraph of the first chapter, that is, each movement of the overture, has a very rough and inexact correspondence to the conflict of keys in each book of the novel—each movement of the whole composition. In the second chapter, where massive development begins, both keys are again sounded quickly and almost simultaneously, first in a mountain-plain visual, then in the confrontation between the officers (the profane) inside the bordello and the priest (the sacred) trudging in the snow outside. They alternate in longer periods in the quickly following priest-baiting in the mess, and then the opposing key, still in its muted aspect, is entered as Henry returns from leave remembering his purely carnal adventures. There is a full shift to home key when Frederic and Catherine meet, and a corresponding shift to opposing key when he is wounded at the front.

The home key prevails as the love affair blossoms through most of

8. Ernest Hemingway, *A Farewell to Arms* (New York: Scribner's, 1955), 3–4; Baker, *Hemingway: The Writer as Artist*, 94–96. Baker sees the first paragraph as preview of the work.

Book II, the opposing key manifesting itself in only the briefest and most elusive phrases until the full shift to it at the end, when Henry loses his leave and must go back to the front. Book III is the reverse of Book II, in that the composition is solidly placed in the opposing key, with phrases in the home key simply ghosting at its edges. It is devoted to the Caporetto retreat and Frederic Henry's near execution and escape, with the love affair entering only in his consciousness. Book IV is roughly balanced between the two, with quicker shifts back and forth. Frederic returning to Milan is still escaping, still caught in the opposing key; the reunion at Stresa is a return to home key; the escape by boat to Switzerland represents in a sense fusion of the keys, for the lovers are fleeing necessity and yet are together; and safe arrival sees this book end firmly in home key. In Book V, the idyll on the mountainside is the strongest rendering in the entire novel of home key, and then the quick and accelerating alternation between keys begins in the hospital. Hope and fear alternate with increasing swiftness, and tension climbs very rapidly as Catherine's condition becomes serious, then grave, then fatal. Her death and Henry's desolation after it leave the dominant, opposition key in total control as the novel ends. Thus musical form has fused with and greatly concentrated the force of narrative and poem, to achieve the tragic spirit in an almost unbearable intensity of presentation.

There are many voices and phrases in each key: that is, the thrust of each is advanced by many different elements inside it. These include, obviously, image as symbol and metaphor, characters who are partial incarnations of aspects of theme, scenes which illustrate conceptions and present issues, and interior monologues that directly suggest or define meanings, as well as the main action itself. These are all contained in a flow of rushing novelistic narrative, for despite the complexities of the novel, and its mode as poem, it always glows with the joy of the storyteller telling.

The progression of images, developed as a series of steadily intensifying phrases in each key, is certainly as evident as any other element in the development. Wherever one ranks the book in the Hemingway canon, most would probably consider it his imagistic triumph; it has already been observed that the purity and concentration of image has a great responsibility for its ambience as poem. Schneider observes perceptively that the images develop the book as a musical key is developed, though he does not consider a sonata-allegro key conflict.[9] Each key has a king image, so to speak, with others arranged in a descending hierarchy. And there are, of course, occasional one-time concentrations in each pattern. Baker has made a compelling case for the mountain as king image in one force, and the plain as the top of the hierarchy in the other; he sees the rains as an "obbligato" sweeping the whole work. The view here is that the rain, even though it is coordinating symbol for the totality, belongs properly to the negative key and is the king image there—stronger even than the plain, where all the bad things happen. Such hierarchical assignments are finally subjective, of course; certainly there is a more precise balance in the mountain-plain, rain-snow polarities, and Frederic's own interior journeys are always between the significances of mountain and plain. Yet in frequency and strength, the rain does appear to dominate and tonalize the negative key and overpowers the whole work only because that key finally triumphs.

As the keys prevision their conflict and its outcome in the first chapter, so do the principal images of the novel foreshadow their development inside the keys. The result is that the chapter is a reversed-telescope view of the novel to come.[10] The beginning is a general symbolic overview of the whole—but the relationship between the two is even closer and more intricate than that. For each paragraph of the chapter is the rough equivalent and forecast of the corresponding book in the novel, in both tone and implied action. Consequently, this first chapter functions, if roughly, as both overture *and* blueprint. And it can be argued that it is, quite by itself, one of the best of the Imagist poems, so dense and so suffused with theme are the patterns of its images. Their function has been intimated in the description of the alternation of the keys. But they demand a much fuller exegesis in their own right.

The images in the first paragraph do double work: they not only connotatively suggest Book I but are in a sense the metaphor of the whole novel. As noted, the very first perception is the view of the mountain, the idea of the good, rising at a distance beyond the plain,

---

9. Schneider, "Hemingway's *A Farewell to Arms*: The Novel as Pure Poetry," 253.
10. Lillian Ross, "How Do You Like It Now, Gentlemen?" *New Yorker*, May 13, 1950, pp. 36–62. Hemingway cites Bach's counterpoint as a model for the first chapter, Ross says.

the quotidian reality and the place of pain, and across the river, the division between those realities. The imagistic rendering of the river produces the suggestion of achieved beauty and happiness—which is immediately shattered by the passing of the troops. The soldiers are not only a visual emblem of the forces of war, but also of necessity, or fate. Thus, in an instant vision, happiness is destroyed by the forces of tragic necessity or doom—a presentation of the shape of the whole novel, and a nearly perfect execution of Pound's definition of the image. Simultaneously, the same image suggests with equal force the smaller content of Book I: Henry's semipastoral life in Gorizia is to disintegrate under the advent of real war.

The second paragraph, matching Book II, suggests the consummation of the love affair between Frederic and Catherine in a temporary reprieve from war. The consummation and its emotional fruitfulness is metaphorized by "the plain was rich with crops, there were many orchards of fruit trees." With this temporal (though temporary) fulfillment the attractiveness of the purely ideational good diminishes: "the mountains were brown and bare." The war still continues and necessity-doom threatens in a distant counterpoint, but premonitions of disaster are not yet felt: "at night we could see the flashes from the artillery. In the dark it was like summer lightning, but the nights were cool and there was not the feeling of a storm coming." That Frederic and Catherine are engaged in a struggle for the ultimate good, of which they are only dimly aware, is possibly suggested by "there was fighting in the mountains."

As does Book III in the novel, paragraph three brings war into dominance. In the total story, the hostile universe as war thrusts at Henry and Catherine far more directly and brutally in Book III than before. Henry loses his convalescent leave and must leave Catherine and return to the front; she has begun the pregnancy that will be her death; he is caught in the Caporetto disaster and barely escapes execution. In the paragraph, the emergence of the war, both as a naturalistic force and as an active shape of necessity, is dramatized in the sudden increase of war traffic and in sharply chosen naturalistic details. These expand into symbol. "There were big guns too that passed in the day drawn by tractors, the long barrels of the guns covered with green branches and green leafy branches and vines laid over the tractors." Here the always phallic guns unify in images of love and death, camouflaged by deceptive attractiveness. The love-death unity is extended by the image of troops, the boxes of cartridges bulging under their capes "as though they were six months gone with child." This, too, prefigures both Catherine's pregnancy and the lethal outcome of it. The rain—concomitant of necessity and the dominant symbol of the novel—leaves the "branches bare and the trunk black" and "the country wet and dead"; emotional desolation is thus forecast.

Correlating Book IV and paragraph four is more of a problem: the direct and clearly intended correspondences that mark the other paragraphs are simply not easily visible. Book IV is devoted to the continuation of Henry's escape and his finding Catherine in Stresa, where she joins him on the last leg of the escape by boat into Switzerland. Paragraph four shows the inability of the small king to check the deterioration of the military situation (the inability of God to control fate?). The parallel is tenuous indeed, but it *may* exist in that both paragraph four and Book IV show hostile elements as advancing with no force really able to check them—despite some temporary appearance of control. This is reaching mightily and can only be justified in context.

Book V sees the mountain-idyll happiness of the lovers end in Catherine's death and Henry's final isolation—"alone in the rain." In paragraph five, there is no match for the idyll; the rain brings death as cholera to portend only the final outcome. The paragraph, too, furthers the thematic suggestion that life goes on for the species, whatever happens to the individual: "But it was checked and in the end only seven thousand died of it in the army." In the book, the emphasis is far more heavily placed upon the fact of doom and destruction—of physical life for Catherine and emotional life for Henry. An unpublished earlier version shows a much closer resemblance in intent to the paragraph, but it is a flat, unimagized declaration that generic life goes on, no matter what.

Thus the chief images reveal themselves in the first chapter; they are to reappear constantly, and constantly to be intensified. In the positive key, the mountain is the primal image and becomes finally the pure concentration of that fulfillment the principals seek; it is the symbolic object of their tragic thrust. Baker has demonstrated the mountain symbology conclusively, but it is useful to trace it again in this slightly different perspective. The mountain dominates its key as no image dominates the other, and all other images in the key rank well below it in both frequency of appearance and in intensity. The lovers are always reaching for the mountain—for ever larger and larger mountains—but cannot completely possess it, or any. The closest they come is the *side* of the mountain in Switzerland, where they are surrounded by bigger and grander mountains. Yet that mountainside represents their highest attainment; they must come down from it for the catastrophe of Catherine's death and Henry's spiritual annihilation.

After its decisive appearance in the symbolic first chapter, the mountain gets a large measure of definition in the second when the priest urges Henry to visit his parents in the Abruzzi; it is a mountain area and is "cold," "clear," "dry," and "hard"—chords that become concomitants of fulfillment and of the idea of the Good through the book. It is interesting to remember that the last three words also appear as evocations of the best in one of the great documents of the theory behind the Imagist movement, T. E. Hulme's "Romanticism and Classicism."

In a well-noted rejection, Frederic does not go there, but goes instead to the cities of the plain, not to fulfillment but gratification. Back from leave, however, while driving in convoy he notes three ranges of mountains; they appear to promise ascending degrees of the romantic good, each more distant than the one before. After his wound, mountains again show significantly, in one of the imagistic epiphanies where major thematic components are brought together in one incandescence. "We backed a horse named Light For Me that finished fourth in a field of five. We leaned on the fence and watched the horses go by, their hoofs thudding as they went past, and saw the mountains off in the distance" (141). The connotations of the horse named "Light For Me" are obvious: he is the active hope of Frederic and Catherine and loses decisively, with the mountains beckoning in the background as the object of that aspiration. The thematic implication is equally clear: they will lose in their own attempt.

As Henry returns to Gorizia the second time the mist renders invisible the tops of the mountains, matching the turn away from fulfillment that the narrative is to take. The mountains do not figure importantly again until they show suddenly, and the rain stops, as the pair are escaping to Switzerland by rowboat—clear implication in the progress of the key that after a period of reverses, fulfillment is again visible and possibly at hand. In Switzerland, Henry and Catherine at last come to the good place—"cold," "clear," "hard," and "dry"—the symbolic mountain place he had rejected once in favor of bars and whores, before he met Catherine. With her, he has found it: the brown wooden house in the pine trees on the side of the mountain. From their bedroom they see "snow on the tops of the mountains" (309). The road winding up the mountain may suggest the possibility of an even higher ascension.

For though they have a handhold on their fulfillment, they do not have absolute possession of their own ultimate and they know it: far away it looms as a visible abstraction, to be perceived but neither attained nor even approached too closely. "Up the valley where the other mountains cut it off was the *Dent du Midi*. It was a high snowy mountain and it dominated the valley but it was so far away it did not make a shadow" (290).

Even the mountain they occupy does not escape the outreach of the enemy, this time objectified as an almost abstract war. The firing of heavy but unseen guns keeps the snow from falling, and snow for the moment is the essence of mountain. By checking its fall, war-as-enemy still impedes fulfillment. When the snow finally does fall, completing the mountain, Frederic and Catherine reach the highest point of their tragic quest.

Snow is the only major image that does not appear in the first chapter, even though it ranks not far below the mountain in the hierarchy of images in the positive key. And it is major not only in this novel, but like mountain, rain, plain, and river recurs throughout Hemingway. In "The Snows of Hemingway," Bern Oldsey points out that it is the most multivalent and changing of the author's symbols;[11] good here, it functions as enemy in *For Whom the Bell Tolls* and definitely ambiguously in "Homage to Switzerland." Even here snow (good) changes to slush and dirty water (bad) when the rains come. The ruining of the snow is simultaneous with the lovers' descent from the mountains, which they can no longer see on their way down. When the mountain

---

11. Bern Oldsey, "The Snows of Hemingway," *Wisconsin Studies in Contemporary Literature*, IV (Spring-Summer, 1963), 172–98.

is lost for good, the major phase of catastrophe begins (one wonders, inevitably, if Hemingway's conception of snow as an element capable of reversing its thematic value owes anything to Joyce's "The Dead").

Images of search and quest as tragic aspiration appear progressively in the positive key; most suggest not only the tragic thrust but the forces massed against it. These last often appear for no more than an instant in a sudden reversal, a lightning-fast transposition of key. One of the most extended occurs when Frederic and Catherine lie in bed and watch a bat hunting on the roof and a searchlight sweeping the sky—quest and fulfillment simultaneously objectified. But then they hear the noises of a gun crew on the next roof, the death key intruding a whispered phrase. Doom always shadows hope in that quick transposition: Henry and Catherine approach a cathedral (religion), which is sanctuary for other lovers; they pass and leave it behind in rain-mist. One of the most forceful and sadly ironic of all such images is that of the umbrella; as they escape by boat to Switzerland, they try to use the umbrella to catch the wind. They speed ahead, then it buckles and collapses. "I was astride the handle of an inside-out, ripped umbrella where I had been holding a wind-filled pulling sail" (290). A positive force—their love—is in one instant transposed into ruin and futility; such concentrated forewarnings never let us forget the inevitability of catastrophe and keep the tragic spirit of the novel ever in our consciousness.

There are several instances of delayed transposition, where incident or image serves as ironic, reverse prophecy; it may appear first in the home key in benign aspect, then later—sometimes much later—in the opposing key as correlative of menace, doom, or impending catastrophe. In home key in Book II, Henry arrives in Milan in a train berth as a wounded officer hero; a sentry outside is part of his own apparatus that is honoring him. In Book IV, he comes back to Milan *under* a car in a freight train, and a sentry then is a clear threat. When he arrives at the hospital, a barber takes him for an Austrian in a highly comic phrase; such an error is not at all funny when transposed to the negative key, for in the Caporetto retreat he is mistaken for a German and almost executed. These ironic prophecies are usually well separated from the ultimate event, but on the retreat, one such reversal quickly follows the initial phrase. As emblem of authority, Henry fires on the two disobedient sergeants, killing one as the other escapes; shortly there-after, figures of authority fire upon him as *he* escapes. A torn apart truck engine is being worked upon by Henry's mechanics in Book I, pre-sumably with success; in Book V, Catherine's cut-open body is worked upon by surgeons, but without success.

The most massive reversal takes place in character-centered scenes. These involve Rinaldi as apotheosis of the skeptical and the profane, and the priest as the configuration of the sacred. Early, before and dur-ing his first leave, Henry opts almost unhesitatingly for the Rinaldi values; after his wounding there are carefully balanced scenes between himself and each of the other two in which his commitment to Rinaldi continues but may be less firm. After his second return, a similar pair of scenes shows he has reversed his allegiances. The larger transposition is completed, a final if not really necessary definition of the hope that will be tragic.

Rinaldi is the chief single visible configuration opposed to romantic love: he derides and negates it, however benevolent his intentions to-ward Henry. He is certainly a benign figure in himself, and Warren sees him as part of the positive force.[12] But as declared adversary of romantic love, is he not of necessity located in the negative key, just as the priest is located in the positive? There, he is the only "good" and benevolent voice, supplying an interesting variant in, but not breaking the real unity of, the black tone of the negative key. It is not a gratui-tous circumstance that he contracts syphilis.

The voices of Rinaldi and the priest may be seen as fusing, perhaps, in Count Greffi, a declared skeptic who nevertheless pronounces ro-mantic love not only authentic but an authentic religious feeling. It may not be too fanciful, even, to see Count Greffi as surrogate at last transposing Rinaldi to the positive key.

The negative, the opposing and dominant key, of course, finally be-comes the concentration of those forces that will destroy the lovers and complete the tragedy. It has strong aspects of tragic necessity, and of fate; but it is more than those: it represents that force in the universe which makes tragedy as Frye describes it. That force is as uncaring as it is lethal; again, it is abstractly indifferent but operationally hostile.

12. Warren, Introduction to *A Farewell to Arms*, xxxiv.

Which image most powerfully projects the perception of the universe as destroyer, as the great abstract antagonist of formal tragedy? The plain? The rain? The war itself? Virtually all who have described the novel's architecture see the rain as the coordinating symbol, but there is a complicated relationship between the three elements, and fixing a hierarchy among them is a little like ranking apples, oranges, and lemons. Plain, war, and rain—though they fuse in a single sweep—are not of exactly the same symbolic substance. The plain polarizes logically with the mountain, most vividly on the sacred-profane axis but also, and more importantly to the tragic architecture, in a contrast between fulfillment and catastrophe: it is a powerful configuration of both emotion and philosophy, a state of being. War, with all its highly individuated specifics, is the visible hostile *force* of the opposing key, the active element. Meanings are given both by action and context. On the other hand, the rain is given its quality as enveloping doom entirely by imagination, by the author's use of it; other writers have made it life-giving. But it seems, as pure image, to become the essence of the other two and more: finally, it equates totally with an abstract destructiveness at the core of life. This, and the fact that it is used with increasing frequency and concentration, and that it sounds the final tragic chord of the novel, would appear to make it the king image in the *key* development. Phrases of the war and plain are sounded earlier, however. Gorizia and the Villa Rossa are on the plain, and there the war manifests itself; it is not until the end of Book II that the rain appears significantly, pointing to approaching menace and equating itself with it. It does not reveal itself as the image of catastrophe until catastrophe arrives, but it makes threats of that impending event with ever-increasing power.

Baker has demonstrated a close pairing of the rain and the plain;[13] it is useful, as with the mountain, again to look at the development of the rain as the chief image in the dominant key. The rain makes a powerful end to the first chapter but does not appear again significantly until well into the second book: as it drums on the roof, Catherine sees herself dead in it. The night before Henry loses his leave, it comes down again. And the night he leaves for the front he does so in a deluge of rain, which provides some of the most pictorially effective

13. Baker, *Hemingway: The Writer as Artist*, 101–109.

imagery in the novel: the lovers leaving the cathedral behind; horse and carriage, instruments of separation, sharply outlined in the rain; and a powerful extended image in two carabinieri (military policemen) visible through the rain illumined by the light from the station. It has a powerful concentration, with the active elements of the hostile universe seen against the abstraction of its impersonal totality. More, it foreshadows directly a disaster to come. This is emphasized by a variation: as Catherine drives away in the carriage, she leans out and points at the carabiniere—a metaphorical and symbolic warning.

When Frederic returns to Gorizia, heavy mist warns of impending rain, and a high-running river of recent heavy rains. The menace is fulfilled as heavy rain falls on the retreat from Caporetto that follows a military disaster. When Henry and his cars stop at the old headquarters in Gorizia, he lies in Rinaldi's bed and lets "sleep take me" while rain falls outside; he is thus enveloped by three concomitants of the negative or the profane: Rinaldi, the rain, and sleep, a state that suggests Nada.[14]

All the disasters of the retreat take place in the rain: the killing of Aymo by his own troops, the arrest of Henry, the execution of other officers. The rain continues as Henry escapes by his neobaptismal plunge into the river and continues even after he finds a shaky sanctuary in the guns under the canvas of a flatcar. It is falling even when he rejoins Catherine in bed in Stresa, and when the barman brings news of Henry's impending arrest he is dripping from the rain. The rain becomes spasmodic as Catherine and Henry begin their escape by boat and halts as they reach a safe part of the lake and safety. A fine, "falsely" cheerful rain greets them in Switzerland.

It stops completely as they enter the high good country of the mountains and is not to begin again until they must descend to the plain for what will be Catherine's death. It marks the end of fulfillment precisely. Later, in the hospital, it begins as Catherine is wheeled into the operating theater for a Caesarean and thenceforth envelops all the action until her death. Then, in the final image, Henry walks back to the hotel in the rain.

The development of the rain is more systematic and sustained than

14. Warren, Introduction to *A Farewell to Arms*, xxii-xxiii.

other image patterns. Concomitantly, the plain is the place of all dis-asters—though also the beginning of the love affair. And war images—soldiers, guns, gunfire, vehicles—shuttle constantly through the book, assuming a more and more hostile configuration. The rain joins and focuses these, plus sleep, into the unity of the opposing key that is ultimately the death key.

Certain passages define or strongly suggest the primary theme of the novel. Best known of these may be Henry's recollection of ants on the end of a log in a campfire, recalling the lines from *Lear* so powerfully. He idly throws water on the log but it steams, rather than aids the ants, and he makes no move to save them. The often-perceived impli-cation: the power in the universe is as indifferent to men as men are to insects. Slightly less advertised is the incident of the dog searching a garbage can vainly; waiting for news of Catherine, Henry tells him, "There isn't anything, dog" (315). Much earlier comes an almost hu-morous refraction of theme in the comments of the British major at the officers' club in Milan: "He said we were all cooked but we were all right as long as we did not know it. We were all cooked. The thing was not to recognize it. . . . It was all balls. . . . They all squabbled about divisions and only killed them when they got them. . . . We were all cooked. . . . 'Good-by,' he said. Then cheerily, 'Every sort of luck!' There was a great contrast between his world pessimism and personal cheeriness" (133–34). Thus the tragedy itself is shaped in the rich and variously developed battle of the keys, which becomes increasingly un-equal. Frederic and Catherine confront a hostile universe and fight it for their happiness. They never have a chance. In the end it not only crushes but inundates them. And the impact of their loss is so over-whelming that it elevates them, beyond any reasonable doubt, well above the pathetic and into one of the purest tragic atmospheres that fiction knows.

The images that dominate the development of the keys have close rela-tionships—deliberate and fortuitous—to other arts. What has been said about Hemingway's debts to Impressionist and post-Impressionist painting, and notably to Cézanne, in *The Sun Also Rises* may simply be reaffirmed here. What is comparatively new in the control of the images is a fascinating correspondence to certain directorial techniques in film. Since we have no record of a serious Hemingway interest in the film as an art form, we can only assume that he has not deliberately made use of its strategies. This is not to say that the correspondences are accidental; they are, rather, inherent. The good motion picture director is always working with the doctrine of the image whether he knows it or not: he is always seeking the shot, the business, the quick scene that will fix and illuminate his own truths. Camera movement, however, is not a completely built-in parallel. A tradition of the craft is that the camera moves, however swiftly, in reasonably ordered sequences: when it shifts its aim from far to near, it does so by stages—long shot to medium to close. In *A Farewell to Arms*, Hemingway makes impressive shifts in scene and image that are in this traditional sequence, and he even manages to make these sweeps part of his apparatus of tragedy: their progression has an inevitability that is a subliminal preparation for the tragic emotion.

This total strategy is brilliantly effective in a whole sequence of such shifts at the beginning of Chapter 2; it gives visual objectification to the key conflict, suggests the larger thematic issues, presents aspects of most major symbols except rain, and, not the least importantly, gives a stunning view of the immediate physical world of the novel. The first sequence opens with a long shot juxtaposing mountain and plain, the basic opposition caught once more in an instant; the fictional camera moves to a medium view of the house and garden in Gorizia, rendered so romantically that it suggests romantic possibility. Medium close to close, a simple montage of images evokes war, a threat but temporarily quiescent: hospitals, artillery, bawdy houses, a damaged bridge, a smashed tunnel. The series culminates in a close-up of the little, ugly king, with his symbolic identity as quintessence and monarch of Nothing just perceptible. At the end of the series, as at the end of the novel, Nada is dominant.

The next linked series commences with a long shot of the stumps and broken trunks of a shell-ruined forest, followed by a quick cut to another long shot of a cloud coming over the mountain. The cloud approaches to medium distance, then close—close enough to surround the narrator and reveal itself as snow. As the narrator watches the snow fall across the wind, the camera moves slowly outward again, to fix the stumps thrusting from the snow in a long shot; then it cuts to medium or medium-close views of snow on the guns and footprints making paths to the latrines. The snow is always ambiguous, but it takes on its aspect of promise at the end of sequence—which is violated by the guns as war emblems and defiled by the latrine paths as aspects of the profane.

The third series in the sequence begins with a medium-long or medium view of the snow falling, the point-of-view camera clearly located inside the whore house and at its window, then cuts to a medium shot of the priest moving down the street in the ruined snow, and ends in a close-up of the priest smiling at the officers through the window—and passing on. Thus the entire sequence ends as it began, in the clash of keys. Mountain and plain contrast starts it; priest and whore house confrontation finishes it. We are shown exactly where we are, physically and thematically, and the confrontation continues with the priest-baiting in the mess, and with Henry making his first declaration for the profane as he leaves the priest for the bawdy house. The scene is presented in quick cuts, all in close shots and close-ups.

Could such an apparent, and effective, use of film technique be unintentional? Of course: we have the example of Flaubert. After all, the camera is a special kind of eye and it moves as the eye moves. Still, even though the record is blank on the matter, it would be extraordinary if one as aware as Hemingway, as deeply caught up in the artistic currents of Paris in the twenties, should be oblivious to the work of the great European film pioneers of the decade.

The admired Caporetto retreat might appear to owe much of its swiftness and compression to cinema-like quick cuts, however intuitively they were made. But its real debt is to an established fictional principle —the alternation of scene and summary—and it is as dramatic an example as we have of how valuable a precise utilization of that principle can be. Hemingway achieves that speed and compression by a rapid alternation between these elements, a decisive, sentence-by-sentence shuttle from one to the other. He will *show* images of battle in one or two sentences, then succinctly *sum up* events of a period of time in one or two more, then cut back to show battle images again. Often he divides a single sentence into the two elements. The tactic is simple—but its simplicity is the simplicity of genius; one need only compare, for example, Stendhal's Waterloo account to see just how good the Caporetto retreat is.[15]

In *The Sun Also Rises*, secondary themes fuse so closely with the primary, tragic theme that they join it in a unified, if complex, system— one tight statement. The enemy and the defenses against it are made indivisible. In *A Farewell to Arms*, the accent in the tragic theme is so heavily placed on the finality and inevitability of catastrophe that defenses are insignificant and pathetic. Consequently, the unity between the big and the small conceptions is less tight; no primitive, functional system of practical philosophy is taught. Most secondary themes complement rather than complete the first, even though at least one is closely bound to it.

Indeed, very lightly developed in this novel are certain conceptions that not only operate in *The Sun Also Rises* but have become ritualistically identified with and anticipated of Hemingway. These are: an unstated but implicitly understood *forma* of behavior—yes, that code— observed by all who attain significance and not perceived by those who fail of significance; the idea of the well-worn moment of truth coming to all and resulting in instant moral triumph or failure; the system of consciously chosen, deliberately pursued consolations as life's only gifts.

This may explain, in small part, why some readers who do not respond to Hemingway's rigid formulations elsewhere like this book. Henry never comes to that bracketed instant of pass-fail that most other Hemingway characters do: he has disasters large and small to meet, and he meets them well enough, but his subliminal intent is to survive, one way or another. He never conceives of himself as confronting a *moral* crisis—and indeed, he does not. He is wounded seriously and accepts it stoically, but there is not much else he can do. When he faces execution, he escapes by spontaneous and resolute action—but no moral decision is necessary or involved. His subsequent decision not to return to

15. Reynolds, *Hemingway's First War*, 6–15. Hemingway was not present at the retreat from Caporetto, Reynolds reminds us, but relied heavily on formal research for the materials of both this sequence and much of the rest of the book. Hemingway was not even in Italy during the period recreated in the novel. "Not only had (he) not experienced the military engagements in which Henry took part, but he had not seen the terrain of Books One and Three.... From books, maps and first hand sources, he recreated the Austro Italian Front of 1915–17. This recreation may explain, in part, his great admiration for *The Red Badge of Courage*, whose author was even further away."

the army (and doubtless be *really* executed) is completely sensible and not in the least a betrayal of trust, but it is a matter of survival and not of significant choice. When Catherine dies, he simply experiences the full force of catastrophe. No punctilious system of manners is consistently stipulated, and consequently there is no sword of rejection held blade up between those who behave properly and those who do not. To be sure, gaiety is still associated with competence and the domination of one's metier—the good surgeon versus the bad surgeons in Milan—and Catherine Barkley pointedly prefers British understatement to Italian flamboyance: "We have heroes too, darling, but . . . they're much quieter" (124). But the idea of a formalistic test of manners forcibly applied to all, as in *The Sun Also Rises*, simply does not operate.

And the compensatory values so programmatically formulated in the earlier book are advanced casually, if at all, in this one. Henry drinks wines with gusto and some knowledge, he does not dislike food, he and Catherine enjoy the races, and he has a reflection or two about sculpture early in the book and about painting later. But his approach to the pleasures is totally casual and quite unlike Jake's studious ritualism. Henry has no meditated and achieved rewards of solace: his entire commitment is to the love affair with Catherine. This is, naturally, the heart of the novel's second-most important idea—that romantic love is itself a religious sacrament. It runs powerfully through the book and is given explicit definition early by the priest and late by Count Greffi. It is finally a redemptive action by the protagonist, even though it may be diminished by being taken away before he comes to full awareness of catastrophe and so cannot be considered a real transcendence. Nor does it alter the finality of doom.

These other themes from *The Sun Also Rises* do appear and are so deeply felt that they are to continue as a consistent part of the Hemingway attitude.

(1) Pleasure and pain coexist in the human experience. The chief demonstration is in the drama itself: the pleasure of the love affair is joined to the pain of Catherine's death. But it is refracted in incident, too, as when Catherine's life ebbs and the nurses exult in their opportunity to see a Caesarean. The officers enjoy baiting the priest, who is

presumably wounded by the baiting, and in the retrospective, the fire that warms Henry destroys the ants. Many bits of action echo the idea.

(2) Incongruity and irony are at the core of existence.[16] Henry is wounded not while in action but while eating cheese, and Aymo is killed by his own troops. The reverse prophecies, cited as key transpositions, are pure examples of incongruity and irony: Henry fires on the escaping sergeant and shortly is fired on himself; he is comically mistaken for an Austrian, then almost dies because he is seriously mistaken for a German; his first train ride into Milan is as a hero, his second as a fugitive. Rinaldi prattles at length to Henry about his "love" for Miss Barkley, then sees himself instantly excluded when those two meet. The saddest incongruity of all is the execution of the officers in the Caporetto retreat, when they are themselves victims of a total, incongruous disorder.

(3) Those who achieve a triumph of metier are aristocrats; those who do not are nonaristocrats. The balanced scenes between the bad doctors and the good doctors are the most deliberate exemplification of the idea. But it has a highly effective exception in the case of Ettore, the American-Italian who is an authentic hero—and an absolute boor. In Count Greffi, noble by birth, qualities of the natural aristocrat find their supreme demonstration: he is brave, courteous, and wise.

(4) Friendship is one of the most enduring and valuable of life's commodities. Rinaldi, though the skeptic voice of the opposition, is staunchly loyal to Henry even after Henry "goes over" by falling in love with Catherine. Until that displacement, their friendship is the chief comfort in Henry's life. And lesser, almost incidental friendships significantly affect his progress. When he is wounded, his friends carry him to safety. In the Milan hospital, Gage the nurse tells him "I'm a friend" (110) and does what she can to smooth the difficulties for him and Catherine. The most casual friends do or offer him services: the barman at the coffee counter in the station offers him help after he becomes a fugitive, Simmons the singer gives him civilian clothes, Count Greffi gives him insight, the barman at the hotel in Stresa warns him of

16. E. M. Halliday, "Hemingway's Narrative Perspective," reprinted in Carlos Baker (ed.), *Ernest Hemingway: Critiques of Four Major Novels* (New York: Scribner's, 1962), 174–80.

his impending arrest and helps him escape. In this novel, contrasting with the earlier one, friendship develops more spontaneously and is less a point in a carefully prepared agenda of action.

(5) Life goes on. Next to his attitude that life is tragic, this is the most enduring constant in the Hemingway canon. Yet here it is, surprisingly, presented with at least apparent ambiguity. The last line of the first chapter, "and in the end only seven thousand died of it in the army," is clear enough. Clear enough, too, are lines from the first version of the last chapter, which one can only conclude was a kind of memo from the author to himself: "It never stops. It only stops for you. . . . The rest goes on and you go on with it."[17] But in the final version, where meaning is compacted so incomparably into image, the final view of Henry alone in the rain after Catherine's death has a powerful connotation not of continuance but of termination. Henry's real life, we feel, is as destroyed as Catherine's.

It is this note of doom—of catastrophe unleavened and untranscended—toward which all systems of the book have been converging and upon which they decisively end. The novel *is* a great study in doom. Also, defying some of the most cherished views of what tragedy ought to be, it is one of fiction's purest tragedies. It is easy to sympathize with those who consider *A Farewell to Arms* the author's greatest novel.

17. Baker (ed.), *Hemingway: Critique of Four Major Novels*, 75.

4

Men Without Women and *Winner Take Nothing:* Classic Tragedy, Miniaturization, and Bank Shots

Men without Women and *Winner Take Nothing* have a strong aspect of twinhood: it is always a mild shock to be reminded that they were not only published six years apart but that they belong, in a sense, to different periods of Hemingway's creativity. The stories in each appear to be written by a man definitely past his own youth—but *Men Without Women* was published in 1927, only a few months after *The Sun Also Rises*, and *Winner Take Nothing* came in 1933. And what some might consider to be the most impressive, the largest, story in either was actually the first of all to be written. This was "The Undefeated," composed in 1924, even before *In Our Time* was published. It is a story of Aristotelian flaw and catastrophe and is the only unarguably tragic story in both volumes. This is not to say that the author has abandoned either his tragic stance or the incipiently tragic design of his structures—a thrust toward fulfillment, a near or brief touching of it, and then loss through concluding catastrophe. He is still muting it, holding it short of full dimension, by ellipsis, by miniaturization of scale, and, even more notably now, by irony.[1] But he is still suggesting, most of the time, that the world will do us in because of the nature of things, or our own weaknesses, or both. Even if he withholds the tragic impact, he maintains the tragic attitude, which seems deeply rooted in his own existence.

1. E. M. Halliday, "Hemingway's Narrative Perspective," reprinted in Carlos Baker (ed.), *Ernest Hemingway: Critiques of Four Major Novels* (New York: Scribner's, 1962), 174–78.

The Tragic Art of Ernest Hemingway

Certain of the stories are reworkings of episodes in Hemingway's life; others come from events directly observed by him; still others come from anecdotes he has heard.[2] And as in *In Our Time*, catastrophes are presented variously. Some are single catastrophes, rendered directly and reacted to overtly by the protagonist who sustains them. And there are the double catastrophes like so many in the author's first book: one character sustains the principal catastrophe, which is observed by another, who sustains a shadow catastrophe of his own. In those stories in which the familiar persona Nick appears, he is sometimes observer, sometimes first protagonist; the Nick stories of the three collections, as well as some previously unpublished, have been edited by Philip Young as, naturally, *The Nick Adams Stories*.

However presented, the catastrophes in both books show Hemingway's continuing appreciation, whether aware or intuitive, that catastrophe is the most important and the most variable element in his structural scheme. He appears to delight in the different approaches he can take to it, and the different end results he can get. Thus some efforts wind up vaguely like tragedy but not approaching it very closely, while his steadily more impressive irony makes bitter comedy out of others. The irony, always evolving, may be even more effective in *Winner Take Nothing* than in *Men Without Women*. Certainly E. M. Halliday's assessment of the author as a great ironist is nowhere better upheld than by the two volumes considered together, even if they are much more important as demonstrations of his power to work diminuendo variations on his overriding preoccupation, the tragic idea.

As examples of that artistic preoccupation, the stories in both books could easily be considered collectively, though there may be some profit in looking at the contents of each separately. *Winner Take Nothing* is a shade more bitter in the early going and yet offers toward its end two stories with atypical, almost conventionally "happy" endings. But only one story in the two volumes is pure, unreduced tragedy. This first, keynote story of *Men Without Women*—"The Undefeated"—not only has the demanded magnitude, statement, and impact of authentic tragedy, but it offers also one of the noblest tragic conditions: the fatal flaw of

2. Carlos Baker, *Ernest Hemingway: A Life Story* (New York: Scribner's, 1969). Baker describes the sources of most of the stories, 26, 63, 159, 177, 178, 182–83, 194, 208, 227, 236, 238, 241, 246.

the aging matador is also the elevating quality that gives him redemption, transcendence, and heroic identity.

Manuel Garcia's determination to continue with his art—which he must scan with his life—has brought him nearer and nearer death before we meet him and almost gets him there in the story; it is his mortal flaw and supreme virtue. We understand, roughly, that the pattern here is an often-repeated one. His absolute determination has won him a shabby fight many times; he has briefly touched artistic fulfillment with brilliant performances right up to the inevitable disaster—the killing of the bull—then his shortcoming with the sword both destroys his previous excellence in the *faena* and brings him injury. In each bullfight, the kill is his immediate catastrophe; his inability to kill well constitutes a lesser, but equally fatal, flaw.

The great flaw—the noble *hubris*—and the lesser, mechanical flaw with the sword place the story clearly in the category of the tragedy of character origin, after both Aristotle and Frye. It may be a little less clear that it also touches Frye's other boundary. For his weakness with the sword is not his own fault; it is universe-inflicted. The implication is that if he had a capacity with the sword to match his other skills, he would be a great matador, as the promoter's man proclaims before his fall. But he does not and so is doomed; the universe is displaying its power at his expense, too.

Like *The Old Man and the Sea*, "The Undefeated" intersects other subspecies of tragedy. Manuel suffers from a Heilmanic division of essences: the confrontation between the dictates of common sense to give up fighting and of his passion to continue it produces the fateful, but ennobling and transcending choice. Also, there is an element of Hegelian tragedy here, for Manuel represents a "good" imperative, the absolute resolution of the artist to practice his art to his fullest and best. The other, colliding "good" imperative—to be sensible and give it up —may seem at first to have no adequate objectification. But if one looks closely he finds that Zurito, the picador, fits splendidly. Zurito helps Manolo, on the condition the Manuel will retire if he fails. At the end, the scene between the two thus emerges as the final confrontation between the two imperatives. Zurito is trying to cut his pigtail, the mark of the matador; gravely wounded, Manuel stops him. The imperative of the passion prevails, and we know it will very shortly carry Manuel to his death. More powerfully than any earlier story, this one dramatizes the famous Hemingway "double-dicho"[3]—a philosophic aphorism that means almost the same if reversed: "A man may be destroyed but not defeated." Hence, of course, the title.

Not only does the action of the story have universality, but so do lesser parts; the indifference of the critic, the ignorance of the crowd, the greed of the impressario—all function as operative enemies of the artist. Yet its universal representation is in the whole and these lesser incidents: it is hard to find a symbol, strictly speaking, in the story. The story seems completely naturalistic, as Hemingway can be on occasion; its visual imagery is among his most vivid, but its purpose is always to show what is going on, to make us see. This strategy can fix an emotion, even if it does not seek to concentrate an idea, and sometimes the emotion—as the heartbreak of failure—is so intense it becomes an abstraction. So Pound's theory of the image is still very much at work here.

The story is notable, too, for a technical advance: it offers a more sophisticated deployment of point of view than the author has shown before. With Flaubertian deliberation, the magic point-of-view camera moves from an objective distance outside, to the rim of the character's consciousness, to a deep penetration of that consciousness, and then out again and in on another—finally quick-cutting between two minds. The opening scene between Manolo and Retana the promoter is the defining and perhaps the best example. "The Undefeated" reveals Hemingway, at the age of twenty-six, as one of the masters and exemplars of control of point of view—and as a writer of full-bodied, formal tragedy.

There are at least five other stories in *Men Without Women* in which catastrophe is presented directly, rather than being played off an interior observer. These have the sound of tragedy, even if presented at too great a distance for tragic impact, and four have emotional origins in the life of the author. An intensely interesting example is "A Canary for One," which remains completely masked until the last line. The conversation between the narrator, his wife, and the officious American lady in the compartment of a French railway car seems only an exercise in ironic tedium; references to the couple's honeymoon carry simply a

3. A. E. Hotchner, *Papa Hemingway* (New York: Scribner's, 1966), 73.

hint, apparently comfortable, of past happiness. Only the concluding sentence reveals what truly has been witnessed: the end of a marriage, the death of love.[4]

In "Hills Like White Elephants," that not-so-casual conversation between two lovers in a railroad station on the edge of a barren Spanish plain is the finish of the whole story—once more, pure catastrophe for which earlier movements must be inferred. What happens—except that the man overcomes her resistance and persuades her to have an abortion—the settling of an unpleasant functional detail? What happens is that they kill love, deny their own possibility, and show themselves incapable of the affirmative, life-defining choice.

"Ten Indians" looks like a fugitive from *In Our Time*, fusing the actions of "The End of Something" and "The Three Day Blow." Love is lost as in the first, and as in the second, a transcendence is made, though by a perceptibly younger Nick.

"Now I Lay Me" is the closest approach to the drama of pure consciousness *Men Without Women* offers. It is, structurally and once more, also pure catastrophe, the final phase of a longer story, and the hope rather than the achievement of transcendence and reconciliation shines dimly but steadily through it. It is the last story in the book, and its muted suggestion of the hope of redemption and reconciliation arising from ruin both pairs and complements the strong, direct tragic thrust of the first, "The Undefeated." The first sets an ideal, the last a hope; singly and together they evoke compatible aspects of the human condition. The protagonist has lost the personal sense of immortality and become lost *in* the sense of a death always close at hand and threatening. In his consciousness, he has one foot held by death, constantly, and his task is to come out of that grip into life again: he must accept his loss of immortality without remaining possessed by it.

The temptation to dismiss "Banal Story" as an antistory written forty years before its fashion is almost overriding. Yet there is a protagonist and there is a drama; understanding of each lies in perception of the presentation and the working of consciousness. Although it is far too miniaturized and indirect to suggest the tragic spirit, the dramatic skele-

4. Mark Spilka, "Hemingway and the Death of Love in *The Sun Also Rises*," reprinted in Carlos Baker (ed.), *Hemingway and His Critics* (New York: Hill and Wang, 1961), 80–92.

ton, at least, of tragedy is there. Beginning with an awareness of the unsatisfactory nature of things, the consciousness toys with the possibility of a stasis, a triumph over this dissatisfaction, by a commitment to psychic escape—"the life of the mind." But even as it plays with this conception, it rejects it; finally, the consciousness is flooded with images of the death of Maera the matador, which wash away the rejected conception and leave a final and unalterable awareness—an awareness that death and the confrontation of death are life's most profound reality. Fulfillment comes not from fleeing but from accepting this reality; the life force can run strong only in the full, open view of death.

Another group of stories presents again the concept of the "observed" catastrophe—one sustained by a character who is ostensibly not the principal of the story, but which impinges upon the principal with an oblique but powerful effect. "In Another Country" is a notable one. The account of the cheerful Italian major who collapses emotionally at the news of his wife's sudden death has thrust, the achievement of happiness, and catastrophe and is thus skeletally tragic. But it is also an instrument that acts upon and instructs the "I" who tells the story, who one assumes is Nick. That "I" has seen hope rise and fall; he has been made aware again that the end of romantic love is death, and that any promises of happiness the universe makes are false.

"A Pursuit Race" is another portrait of the protagonist at catastrophe seen by another; his earlier flight from it is compared to the effort of a bicycle rider who loses the race if he is overtaken by the man who starts behind him. The race and the loss are directly presented by the author as a metaphor both of the protagonist's situation and of the mortal predicament. Yet there is a benign and gentle irony in the confrontation between overtaken rider and inexorable pursuer. The meeting between the circus advance man, William Campbell, and his boss in a Kansas City hospital room is not one between victim and nemesis but one between brothers, and the boss knows it, just as he knows he is simultaneously a transient figure of catastrophe to the defeated man in bed. When he discovers signs of recent drug use, he compassionately tells his friend there's a cure for it. But Campbell knows the universal design and where he is in it; there is no cure for anything, he answers.

For much too long a time "The Killers" was probably Hemingway's best known short story; some might agree that this was a fairly considerable misfortune for its author. Certainly the instant impression is that Hemingway is parodying not himself but the early prevailing academic stereotype of himself; then one remembers that "The Killers" did a very great deal to form that stereotype. The structure again is built upon the observed catastrophe; the protagonist of the longer, enveloping story is witness to the truncated and elliptically presented drama of another character whom he can only perceive externally. The observed catastrophe produces one theme, its impact on the witness, another. When the gangsters appear in the diner, tie up Nick and a coworker, and calmly prepare the murder of Ole Andreson, they are instantly seen as a manifestation of pure evil—which appears without warning and vanishes as suddenly. With total caprice, this pure evil has shown itself to Nick, almost taken his life, then released him unharmed. But when he goes to warn the primary victim, he finds that Ole Andreson has decided to accept death without further resistance or evasive action: his execution is suggested as only a final formality. Ole's observed drama ends with his acceptance of the old tragic postulate of nemesis, that he must die for a mysterious transgression. Nick's story—the envelope story—is a revelation: he is forced to understand that there is evil in the universe that cannot be explained or conquered or evaded. Thus a tragic design has been utilized in the drama of Ole. The tragic spirit is invoked but then shrouded; the tragic impact is not there, nor is it meant to be.

Irony—sometimes a dark species of it—gives the strongest flavor to four of the stories, and black comedy is as good a short description of them as any. They have the putative design of tragedy, but their tonal effect is sardonic, bitter, sometimes cynical. "An Alpine Idyll" may be the best example. Life and death are once more juxtaposed in instant unity, both by dramatic pattern and by symbol; once more the observed catastrophe is the end of love. But its end this time is not tragedy or even pathos but harsh laughter. The distance between observed and event is even greater than usual: the observer-narrator does not touch the central action but simply hears about it. The descent of himself and his friend from the "unnatural" heat of the mountain sun can be seen as an attempt to flee the life force; their secondhand encounter with the peasant Olz, through the landlord's story at table, is a reminder that they cannot escape it. Olz' unthinking mutilation of his wife's body by hanging a lantern from the open mouth of her frozen corpse reduces her to the level of an inanimate convenience: a woman loved, alive, has become dead, the equivalent of a piece of wood. The instant implication appears to be that of the transcience and perishability of, even the brutality latent in, romantic love. Yet a more subtle and more profound thrust is in the act, and it is developed by the apparatus of the rest of the story: the impulse of life is not simply to continue in the face of, but even to obliterate, death, not so much by rejecting it as by absorbing it totally and dismissing it. The residue is not tragedy or a close cousin—but comes close to gallows humor.

Some of Hemingway's most sympathetic critics have been annoyed with "Today Is Friday." The mock-tough dialogue of Roman soldiers who crucified Christ is not only self-parody; it projects all too heavily that early and ill-founded stereotype of the author and never really breaks out of its enveloping aspect of juvenility. Yet it is not a complete waste: it confronts one of the enduring tragedies directly and seeks a new and original way of perceiving and rendering its catastrophe. And structurally at least, the solution is interesting. A failure sometimes tells us more about a writer than a success, and Hemingway's fascination with the Crucifixion, a symbolic base for some of his best work, is documented here beyond any doubt.

"Che Te Dice La Patria" does not at first seem to be a story, even by fairly permissive standards. Yet a dramatic structure and a catastrophe are there and can be adduced: Italy is the protagonist; she has sought meaning in fascism, and the corruption she has actually come to is the catastrophe. "Che Te Dice La Patria" is a linked, linear rather than evolving, presentation of incidents showing that corruption. Although the catastrophe again is observed, it befalls the main character, Italy, and the witness-narrator is only the central intelligence.

"Fifty Grand" suggests, a little, the absurd play of the 1960s; irony and reversal are followed so swiftly by counter-irony and counter-reversal that their world seems inside out. Literally, victory is defeat and defeat, victory; catastrophe and transcendence displace each other so rapidly that one has a problem telling which is which. When welterweight champion Jack Brennan bets fifty thousand dollars against himself in a title defense, he has inverted the *apparent* scheme of things: to win, he has to lose. The first of the major ironies now manifests itself. Although won bet and lost fight appear to be both physical—and sordid—events on the same plane, these elements make a more profound, and subterranean, pattern. For Jack's real enemy is time, not his opponent, and it is from time that he wishes to wrest the psychic, transcendent victory. The unanticipated ordeal that Jack must survive to make his wish come true simply dramatizes more intensely the force of his will—and emphasizes the irony of his triumph-in-loss.

"A Simple Enquiry" is very nearly simplistic: the "anecdote" charge once made against Hemingway's early short fiction appears at first look to have some substance here. Still, a story is there, after all, thrown away as casually as a one-liner by a stand-up comic. The Italian major's intention, attempt to achieve it, and catastrophe are presented without signal and almost simultaneously, as he delicately makes a homosexual advance toward his orderly and is equally delicately repulsed. Are there to be consequences of embarrassment and humiliation for the major? Clearly not. His only reaction is one of irritation and frustration: did the orderly really lie to him? This story obliquely suggests one by John O'Hara, "Over the River and Through the Woods," in which an old man makes a misunderstood gesture toward a young girl and knows he has ruined his life. The O'Hara story *is* almost tragic; Hemingway's is cynically comic.

Both *Men Without Women* and *Winner Take Nothing* are story collections, not hybrids or mutated subspecies of the novel like *In Our Time*. Yet in each, some significance to the placing of first and final stories may be reasonably inferred. In the first book, as suggested, "The Undefeated" declares a kind of tragic ideal at the beginning; at the end, the more nearly life-size, "Now I Lay Me," acknowledges despair as a human universal but urges hope as the only counter against it. In the first story in *Winner Take Nothing*, the predatory violence both in the universe and in his own character is presented as the cause of man's undoing, of the universal catastrophe; in the last, "Fathers and Sons," his hope is seen as residing in the continuity of life and his forgiving acceptance of it. These first and last stories help, if only a little, to focus those in between and to give a unity to each volume; both have flickering tragic intimations but neither a real tragic effect.

"After the Storm" asserts that life promises and then takes away;

97

also it has near its center both an ironic commentary on the incongruity and the caprice of the universe, and a view that all life forms ultimately prey upon and consume one another. Both violence and incongruity are sounded at the outset and develop simply in image and event. The savage fight in the bar between the boat captain and a stranger is reasonless and absurd; the captain's flight to sea comes from a false understanding—he hears that the other man has died. His character as scavenger and predator is revealed by the attempt to loot an abandoned schooner, and what he finally finds is the result of a larger, more capricious violence by nature: the big liner is grounded in quicksand just under water. Bizarrely, this random violence and absurdity have created a stream of causation that has taken him close to a gratification of his greed; whatever he can take from a dead vessel belongs by laws of salvage to him. But the author's view of the universe as tempting enemy and maker of false promises is objectified in the way the prize tantalizes the protagonist: though everything he sees inside is his—if he can get it—he cannot break the glass of the ports and can only stare impotently through it at the riches inside. His torture is completed by his return with a crew and equipment only to discover that others have already taken the booty. For an instant, the teasing universe has promised him everything, then left him with nothing. He ends in catastrophe —but its emotion is one of bleak irony rather than tragedy.

"A Way You'll Never Be" would have been a proper preparatory for "Big Two-Hearted River": it shows Nick Adams in that shattered state from which the latter story renders him emerging. Young observes that it helps explain "River" and cites links of incident as well as sequence and psychic continuity between the stories.[5] This story is another Hemingway catastrophe dramatized, and even the catastrophe is in its latter stages. Nick has already survived the shock of impact and is just beginning to recover from it. His head wound has been severe enough to have him certified as irresponsible, and his first serious effort to return to active, competent life is not successful here. But as he leaves us he is still trying to climb the long slope upward to self-sufficiency. He is thus not only a shadowy, if less than tragic version of the hero who

5. Philip Young, *Ernest Hemingway: A Reconsideration* (State College: Pennsylvania State University Press, 1966), 50–55.

defines himself fighting catastrophe, but a psychologically authentic, sensitive, and complex one.

"The Sea Change" is another of those Hemingway stories that might be called anecdotal if one reads it carelessly. Not much *appears* to happen: a young woman discloses to her lover that she is going away for a lesbian affair; he is hurt and angry; he first repudiates, then forgives her and sends her off with his blessing. Yet the story not only has classic form but Hemingway signatory form: a protagonist pursues an intention, fails of it, and rises from failure to achieve reconciliation. What *really* happens is that a human being breaks out of self-isolation to join humanity. The story not only suggests Joyce's "The Dead" but may even owe a frank debt to it: like Gabriel of that story, the young man comes out of the catastrophe of his shattered, self-enclosed pride to attain compassion and community—his reconciliation and his victory.[6]

On a first contact, "Homage to Switzerland" may appear to be one of the author's most puzzling stories, but once two durable Hemingway devices are recognized its pattern and meaning become quickly clear. The first device is the use of fugue structure, here modified: three lines of apparently equal strength play against each other contrapuntally, as variations on theme. The second is the use of snow as a symbol that reverses meaning. The fugal lines are parallel episodes of catastrophe, all too ironic and low-keyed to be tragic, but all having intimations of the idea of tragedy. In railroad cafes in three Swiss cities, all virtually identical in aspect—warm interiors, comfortable furniture, snow falling outside—three single Americans pause for a meal. All the commonalty appears to be shared by the cafes, yet there is a cord that joins the travelers; all are responding to a deep personal misfortune in one way or another. All have sustained emotional catastrophes; all are suffering and responding. Once this is recognized, other elements can be seen as representational: the snow falling outside all three windows suggests the negative, destructive force of the universe, like the rain in *A Farewell to Arms*, but like Joyce's snow in "The Dead" it also suggests the human community; Oldsey has described the multivalence of Hemingway's snow exhaustively.[7] The two implications fuse: the common hu-

6. Joseph De Falco, *The Hero in Hemingway's Short Stories* (Pittsburgh: University of Pittsburgh Press, 1963), 176–79.

7. Bern Oldsey, "The Snows of Hemingway," *Wisconsin Studies in Contemporary Literature*, IV (Spring-Summer, 1963), 172–98.

man condition is to suffer at the hands of the hostile force. The snow thus accepted, the cafe becomes the refuge against it, a refuge of apparent warmth and companionship. But this refuge does not work by itself, and its sanctuary is deceptive. Sufferers are ultimately alone and confront pain and catastrophe alone.

It is hard to see how "One Reader Writes" can avoid sentimentality and total ludicrous failure, but it is an enlightening demonstration that the exactly right point of view and the precise tone of irony can save any piece of work. As dramatized catastrophe, it is ostentatiously pathetic: A woman writes a medical columnist about her husband who has returned to her from "military service" with " 'sifilus'." Yet the story is never in trouble, because the hidden narrator establishes himself as the point-of-view device at the beginning and sets up a distance between reader and character sufficient to maintain detachment and coolness.

"The Light of the World" recalls several of the early stories of *In Our Time* (Young properly puts it in *The Nick Adams Stories*): an adolescent sustains a revelation about the nature of life from an observed contact with another. Too, it suggests Joyce's "An Encounter" in that the adolescent is engaged with a companion in a journey of discovery when the contact is made, though the adventure here is not defined nearly so completely as a pilgrimage. Nor is the revelation such a closed one as Joyce's revelation of evil: the boys discover aspects of evil, but the real knowledge that comes to them is the knowledge of the dignity of tragic reconciliation and acceptance that they take from Alice, the 330-pound whore—even though the story itself is scaled well below tragic stature.

There are three observed catastrophes in "God Rest You Merry, Gentlemen," and the narrator witnesses them all from an even greater distance than usual. The implication of the submerged minidramas themselves is direct enough, as they echo Hemingway's recurring first theme: life is a cheat, and man must suffer. And a concomitant here is that the general consolations are sometimes not available; the great blow must be borne as best it can be.

There might be a temptation to see "God Rest You Merry, Gentlemen" as a kind of cartoon for "The Gambler, the Nun and the Radio." Each is set in a hospital which is a metaphor for the world, and each has three principals who have suffered blows or disappointments. Yet the later story is not only more fully developed and more technically complex; it runs almost directly counter to the earlier in meaning. In "God Rest You Merry, Gentlemen," the author views the human situation as virtually hopeless; in the other, he offers the possibility of dignity through commitment—even if the commitment is an illusion. The contrasting *response* of each life to the common condition is the substance of the story. Not proportioned to tragic size, it still offers the affirmation of Hemingway's later tragedies. And it is one of the author's clearest previsions of Sartre, as well as irresistibly urging itself as a primary source for Eugene O'Neill's *The Iceman Cometh.*

The content is developed through another Hemingway transference of fugal form to fiction. Although the story is rendered entirely through the consciousness of Mr. Fraser, if at a certain distance, the separation of the three character keys is distinct and highly formalized. Each shift in key—from Cayetano to Sister Cecilia to Mr. Fraser—is precise and clear.

The intensity of the catastrophes varies—Sister Cecilia's has to be adduced entirely—but the commitment, hope, illusion that keeps each going is painstakingly defined. Cayetano, the professional card shark who makes victims of others, is himself a bigger victim than they; his incongruous belief in luck has always cost him his "earnings," and now he has lost a leg. Yet broke and mutilated, his confidence in his ultimate good luck is serene and unshattered; it will carry him forward against the accumulations of his catastrophe. He *knows* one day he will win. One can only surmise what grief Sister Cecilia sustained; perhaps her only catastrophe is that she is not yet a saint. If so, it is a real if gentle one, and her passionate desire to become sanctified is the engine of her existence, propelling her against the forces that have frustrated her so far. For Mr. Fraser, the writer with the broken leg, the solace is the radio and the images it helps him visualize; it is the objectification of his creative vision, which is his weapon and consolation against catastrophe. For all three, the consolations become an instrument by which they define themselves in the battle against the indifferent and materially invincible adversary.

"Wine of Wyoming" is another Hemingway whisper of tragedy, too low-keyed for full tragic effect. At first humorous and even comic in tone, it is in its final manifestation quite sad: it projects a quest for a perfect communion of friendship that is thwarted on the edge of fulfillment. This is delicate and evanescent despite the robust tone of the story. It is, simply, Fontan's passionate preparation for the final dinner for the narrator and his wife, to be crowned by the drinking of wine he has himself made; the fact that Fontan views the dinner and the wine as apotheosis of friendship and communion sanctifying it is the focus of his desire. When the communion ritual aborts because the narrator and his wife postpone it for a day, Fontan's consumption of his sacramental wine comes into perspective as an act of self-destruction. When his desperate attempt at redemption—finding more wine—fails, the departing couple must leave without what he has envisioned as communion ritual and substance. Fontan feels himself a victim of catastrophe, destroyed in his roles as friend and as priest-guardian of the mysteries. He has fallen—in his own eyes tragically, if not in ours.

Like certain of the author's earliest stories, "A Clean Well-lighted Place" is built upon twin catastrophes. A protagonist meets one and an observed character the other, and here to an unusual degree one is the mirror of the other. The apparent principal of the observed catastrophe is the old man who attempted suicide the week before. As the two waiters watch him drinking in the sidewalk cafe, their attitudes are contrasted to their conversation. Only gradually does it become apparent that the older waiter's sympathy and understanding proceed from the fact that like the old man he, too, constantly confronts Nada and hopelessness. The intensity of that confrontation is revealed only at the very end, when he is also revealed as the primary protagonist. The directness of his interior monologue in the *bodega* after he leaves the cafe contrasts with the artful obliqueness of the earlier development and defines boldly the issue of the story—man's eternal confrontation with the void. His final reflection on insomnia is really an ironic comment on that blank awareness of Nada: "Many must have it" (24). Consisting almost entirely of a view of the nightmare world as it does, it is a species of nontheistic existentialism, and, in its emotional effect, has little of the tragic to offer.

It is hard, at first, to find even the shadow of a shape in "A Natural History of the Dead," for it has a plan unique in the Hemingway canon: most of it is that long and ironic discourse by the effaced narrator, performing a masquerade as a kind of Chautauqua lecturer. The mini-drama at the end seems anecdotal if effectively culminatory. Yet in its way it is complete: the veiled catastrophe of its protagonist is a dramatization of what the "lecture" has suggested by its heavy irony. The net is one of Hemingway's most effective examples of black comedy, though the statement is the same as that of what many consider his most elevated and moving tragedy, *A Farewell to Arms*. For irony is the saturating element. The discourse projects the difference between what the narrator pretends to say—that human life is sacred and that the universe has a high and protective regard for it—and what he actually does say—that the universe holds human life in operational contempt and has no regard for it whatever.

The quick shift from parody to literal here prepares us for the concluding drama, which has its ironies, too, and powerful ones, though they are chiefly in event. The central one of these is that, philosophically, the two disputants are on the same side. Both the medical officer with tear-gased eyes and the wounded artillery lieutenant are frustrated to the soul by the force that kills and tortures men. The lieutenant's plea that the doctor end a dying man's suffering by a drug overdose is the only response to that enemy he can make; the doctor declares the more complex course of action of not ending suffering by death but by such ease as he can give. When the doctor throws iodine in the lieutenant's eyes after the latter's insult he is, at least symbolically, trying to make him see though he temporarily blinds him; in the representational scheme, he has forcibly made the lieutenant like himself, red-eyed as from weeping at the plight and the impotence of men against their adversary. This adversary is defined by the repeated use of the word "nothing" (five times) in the concluding conversation, as the wounded man dies. When the doctor appears to taunt the lieutenant by declaring him in great pain, he is at the deeper level extending compassion and comradeship. The lieutenant will understand what the doctor has understood all along: that Nada destroys men and they are helpless before it.

As a portrait of a matador disgraced in his personal life, "The Mother of a Queen" is a negative of the Hemingway virtues. At first it appears to be relatively static; it is hard to see, even implied, a progression of thrust, achievement or near-achievement, and fall. Nevertheless, there is a ghost dramaturgy just barely discernible: the matador *is* a success of sorts in Mexico before he has a disaster in Spain, and before his shameful characteristics surface into full view.

In one perspective, "A Day's Wait" is that extreme rarity, a Hemingway story with an ending that is conventionally "happy." Its catastrophe is converted into victory on its own plane: after spending the day waiting to die, the narrator's son learns that he will live after all. Yet for the space of the day, and inside his consciousness, he has sustained an overwhelming catastrophe and triumphed over it. At nine years of age, he has met the "knowledge" that he was dying without cry or whimper. This drama of his psyche is seen in the perspective of his father's; the tension between the two is the tension of the finished work.

The thematic substance of "Fathers and Sons" is a once-only for the author; his life-goes-on concept is involved here with the continuity of life from generation to generation. The structural strategy is again the strategy of alternating, and sometimes opposing, keys. Naturalistically, the first key is that of Nick's father, and it is developed by Nick's recollection of him. The second key must be called at the outset the key of the Indians, and its development is an aggregate of Nick's memories of the Indian camp, his Indian friends, his initiation into sex by an Indian girl, and an imagistic rendering of the Indian country. The third and last key is the key of Nick's son, developed by his conversation with Nick. Through all keys, Nick is both protagonist and central intelligence, his consciousness being the real theater of action.

The father key fairly quickly establishes itself as a representation of the past, and of roots; the son key is equally visibly a representation of the future, and of continuity. It is the middle key, the key of the Indians, that must be defined satisfactorily before a schema can be seen. Not instantly, but in time, it reveals itself as the key of the life force, and then the schema is clear: Nick leaves his father (the past) to follow his own life force (in a sense, his own present), that life force in time produces his son (the future), and the future, by demanding an acknowledgment of and a link with the past, establishes a cycle and a continuity. Thus, the life force must free itself in the beginning from all context and all constraints—but in the end it seeks a return to context, and to continuity. Not only are ancestor-life force-descendant, and past-present-future now linked, but they can be seen as the general immortality of humanity, and Nick's perception of this is the revelation of the story. Also, with this muted revelation, something *approaching* the tragic design is finally apparent: Nick is revealed as having lived under the catastrophe of having lost his father by failing to be aware of his father as the base of his own continuity. His son brings him to that awareness and thus restores his father to him. However, since both catastrophe and transcendence occur on the same plane and in the same dimension—Nick's consciousness—the design is not tragic, but lies in the dramaturgy of "happy" resolution. But the tone is superbly elegiac, and the conception that life goes on is projected in larger terms than ever before.

Philip Young's ordering of the stories that *declare* Nick as their protagonist into a single volume, *The Nick Adams Stories*,[8] is valuable for several reasons. The most obvious, of course, is that all of them are in a sequence at last, and a sequence matching that of their source episodes in the author's own life—a progression from which Hemingway departed slightly in *In Our Time*. Another is that it makes available for the first time certain work that was previously unpublished. In the perspective of this study, however, the most useful contribution of the volume may be that it suggests something about Hemingway's early perception of himself as a writer. This is that he understood, however subliminally, that his deepest vision was tragic, and that he was most completely himself only when he was at least giving intimations of the tragic in his work.

This conclusion proceeds from his decisions on what not to publish; virtually all of the previously unpublished stories and fragments in the collection carry no hint, do not even suggest the potential, of tragedy. A more fundamental reason for the author's rejection of "The Last Good Country" is immediately visible, of course, for it is quite obviously a failure. It fails because the structure is inchoate: the account of the flight of Nick and his sister from really sinister game wardens disintegrates completely toward the end. However, one of the reasons it disintegrates is that it is not built upon Hemingway's characteristic and always putatively tragic narrative line of thrust / approach-to-fulfill-

---

8. Philip Young (ed.), *The Nick Adams Stories* (New York: Scribner's, 1972).

ment / catastrophe. Had he chosen to restructure it on that line, it might well have worked. On the other hand, "Summer People" is technically successful and a fair story. But it would have been a discordant note among the published stories, for it does not show Nick confronting catastrophe, either directly or as an observer, and trying to understand why catastrophe should be a condition of life. He simply seduces a friend's wife and feels smug about it, and he is never a sympathetic witness to what could have been a catastrophe for the friend. The exception in the collection is "The Indians Moved Away." As short as it is, it has that undeclared suggestion that tragedy is at the center of things, and it could easily have been published in any of the three collections.[9]

One of the questions *The Nick Adams Stories* raises is one that has been pondered frequently: what should be done about the young man of the stories who is the Hemingway persona when he is not called Nick? If he is called nothing, of course, there is no problem; such stories, like "A Very Short Story" and "Out of Season," fit right in. But suppose he is called Krebs, or George, even when the stories also drop precisely into the Nick sequence? Young has admitted only the stories in which Nick is called Nick—a reasonable position. But it would be interesting to see the stories with the name problem in the sequence, too. Perhaps it would not be *lese majeste* at this point to use them, altering the text boldly as needed, and then printing the originals in appendix.

Interesting as this and other aspects of *The Nick Adams Stories* are, however, some will always find the books' greatest interest in speculation as to why the author chose not to publish several quite fair efforts. Again, the rejection may imply that he had deep intuitions about his function and possibility as an artist—that he understood, however vaguely, that tragedy was his ultimate metier, and that he was at his best when working in it or at least toward it.

9. Matthew J. Bruccoli, review of *The Nick Adams Stories*, in *Fitzgerald-Hemingway Annual*, 1972, pp. 397–98. Bruccoli calls the story "perfect, though slight."

5

To Have and Have Not
The Hero of the Bold Choice

To Have and Have Not shows two departures from the author's earlier novels: a turn away from the symbolic toward the unadorned naturalistic, and a steady movement toward "conventional" tragedy, which is to say, Aristotelian tragedy.[1] The novel is dense with visual images, as always, but these are overwhelmingly directed toward the comparatively simple goal of making its universe concrete and palpable and with producing emotion; unlike the images of earlier books, these are infrequently representations of ideational abstractions. And of all his novels, *To Have and Have Not* is the first relatively straightforward tragedy of the fatal flaw.

To be sure, it is, like most tragedies, located somewhere between Frye's boundaries of tragedy—the one terminal demonstrating the powerlessness of the individual against the universe, the other showing him falling through his own failures. But though both conceptions are at work in the book, the stronger appears to be that of the fatal flaw, and this is the first of Hemingway's novels in which that weighting is apparent, though it has been evident in earlier short stories of the decade.

Certainly Harry Morgan is doomed in his struggle with the universe by the nature of things, but to a more significant degree he is the engineer of his own catastrophe by his mistaken apprehension of reality. Like all Hemingway protagonists, he seems fated to catastrophe at the

---

1. Jerry Brenner, "*To Have and Have Not* as Classical Tragedy: Reconsidering Hemingway's Neglected Novel," in Richard Astro and J. J. Benson (eds.), *Hemingway in Our Time* (Corvallis: Oregon State University Press, 1972), 67–86.

hands of tragic necessity, but unlike the earlier, he fights back, in pride and aloneness. His pride becomes *hubris*; his belief that he can survive alone, and even triumph alone, is a misunderstanding that ultimately kills him and precipitates catastrophe as finality.

And tragic necessity in this novel is not simply a mysterious universal force; it also partakes of economic exploitation. Harry is battered not only by the ineluctable, but by things as they are, politically and economically, in the United States in the Depression; his first betrayer is a businessman, his second, a government official. The novel consequently becomes a political statement, if an emotional one, as well as a formal tragedy. A proper question, of course, is whether this political aspect intensifies or dilutes the whole.

As happens so often in Hemingway, the book begins as many Greek tragedies begin, with the first perceptible movement toward catastrophe in the total drama of the protagonist. *Oedipus Rex* begins at the final phase of the whole myth; so with Harry. He is first encountered at the highest point he is to reach in terms of his most profound desire or intention: he has *achieved* a boat and a family and is supporting the second with the first honestly and fairly. He is living on his own terms but the shadow of catastrophe is already touching him. His struggle to reach this personal pinnacle can only be deduced, and the novel renders Harry's tumble from it, sometimes checked but never halted. It starts from a betrayal of Harry by an American businessman; it ends with Harry dying on the deck of another man's boat.

Almost at the outset, Harry suffers the blow from fate, or necessity, or X and is forced into a determining choice that, stubbornly maintained, pushes him finally to catastrophe. This begins with that crude cheating by Mr. Johnson, who charters his boat for nineteen days and then slips out of Havana by plane, owing Harry $825—a blow Harry might have averted by staying with Johnson for a few hours. It is a casual but devastating swipe, forcing Harry into his first great choice: should he let his family starve or accept dangerous and fatefully illegal employment? Determined to protect his own and to maintain his self-sufficiency at all costs, he chooses the outlaw job, transporting Chinese immigrants to the mainland. When he kills the Chinese entrepreneur and makes the immigrants walk ashore in Cuba, he has entered a tragic pattern which involves the unjust blow by the universe, *hubris* on his own part in response, and the fateful choice of alternatives.

Although Harry survives the Chinese adventure, the forces operating against him intensify. The Depression keeps him from earning a living by chartering his boat for fishing, and his choice to act outside the law rather than succumb, lose the boat, and go on relief is a Heilmanic, tragedy-developing choice. Hauling liquor, he is wounded by the Coast Guard; because of freakish bad luck—a high Federal official on a fishing trip sees him wounded and reports him—his boat is impounded and he loses the arm. Still holding stubbornly to his choice, he accepts the most dangerous job he has ever undertaken, that of carrying revolutionaries back to Cuba after they have robbed a Key West bank; he must rent a boat himself to do it. His plan to kill all of them before they kill him is the final manifestation of his *hubris*, and though it almost succeeds, it ends with Harry gasping his life out on the deck: "a man alone ain't got no bloody f—— chance."[2] Awareness has apparently come. He has learned something, at least, of the nature of the forces that have oppressed him: nothing can beat them and it was his fatal error to think he could. In his fall, the working of fate and his own character have been inextricably interlocked.

This linking of fatal flaw and the universe's implacability, as well as intimations of the ultimate catastrophe, develop episode by episode, incident by incident. By an appropriate dramatic irony, the novel begins with Harry refusing exactly the kind of mission that is to kill him at its end—carrying Cuban revolutionaries from the mainland to Cuba. The twin missions and his opposite responses to them bracket and focus his long catastrophe. When he rejects the first, he does so because he does not wish to imperil his hard-won economic security and emotional stasis: if he loses his boat, he loses his living. When he accepts the last he is making a desperate short-end gamble to win back some of that security, which has long been lost—as has the boat. The distance between the first point and the second is the distance of his descent, and it comes from both the universe and himself.

The shattering, unanticipated violence that terminates Harry's meet-

2. Ernest Hemingway, *To Have and Have Not* (New York: Scribner's, 1937).

ing with the first Cubans—not to mention the lives of the Cubans—is an opening chord that sounds the tone of the book and suggests life as a series of unsignaled explosions. The first image of the encounter is the thematic one: "As they turned out of the door to the right, I saw a closed car across the square toward them: The first thing a pane of glass went and the bullet smashed into the row of bottles on the showcase wall to the right. I heard the gun going and bop bop bop there were bottles smashing along the wall" (6).

Order is shattered without warning by a violence lying just beneath the deceptively tranquil surface of life. Both the order of Harry's life and his life itself are to be shattered by that same violence, and a further irony, by Cubans. Harry is sad and reflective after the young men who approached him are dead; is it possible he intuits subliminally the metaphorical significance of the episode to himself? And his regret at the deaths of these Cubans contrasts with his plan to kill their successors at the end, showing clearly the deep changes in his character that have been wrought in the interval.

The idea of deterioration in time is early reflected in the character of Eddy, the "rummy" mate. Considering Eddy's present worthlessness, Harry remembers when he used to be a "good man." Harry is to suffer a similar deterioration—though it will not be a loss of control or nerve but a steady sacrifice of all other principles to his vision of self-sufficiency.

Harry's concept of himself as his own ultimate authority is instantly apparent when his messenger brings him word of the flight of Mr. Johnson, with the $825 due Harry. He accepts the responsibility of the loss and the responsibility for making it good, by any means. Here, he does not blame fate but himself; he sends Frankie the dock bum out to find him profitable contraband to haul. It never occurs to him to abandon his responsibility, surrender his self-sufficiency, and return home defeated to starve or go on relief—nor to turn elsewhere. But he knows he has taken a decisive turn and is filled with foreboding, a foreboding that is instantly justified when Frankie comes in with Mr. Sing. Harry is ruthless in assessing the situation and planning the action he considers he must take to preserve himself, but even then some compassion enters his decision. He is, in this crisis, Aristotle's tragic protagonist who is neither all good nor all bad. He makes the battle commander's decision to save the most at the expense of the fewest: instead of killing the contraband Chinese as Mr. Sing delicately suggests, he kills Mr. Sing instead, breaking the entrepreneur's neck on the boat while receiving payment. Later, Eddie asks him why, and he answers, "To keep from killing twelve other Chinks" (5). The same space in his ruthlessness is revealed when he spares Eddie.

Harry's venture appears to have turned out honorably enough, in his perspective. He has more than recouped the money he was cheated out of. He has saved twelve innocent lives directly and, indirectly, has saved possibly hundreds more by killing a man who was systematically having his countrymen murdered. Although he never defines it so, he would be justified in considering Mr. Sing's killing a just and preventive execution. Yet his life has been changed and he has been changed by the incident. It has infected him in a sense, and the infection is metaphorically suggested by the bite Mr. Sing has given him.

Harry tries to reassure himself that he is unharmed and that the bite is not "poisonous," but he has been altered; he has chosen an outlaw's course to maintain his illusion that he can control his own destiny, and that course is to bring him, through a remorseless stream of causation, to his lonely death. Also he has killed, and the act of killing is to work secret but profound changes in him.

If one considers only the events of major dramatic significance, the next episode is the penultimate one in Harry's extended catastrophe. It is the next point of overt definition, too, for in its presentation it *seems* a natural and inescapable consequence of the Chinese adventure, though in point of fact it has been implied that Harry ran liquor before that. It also demonstrates again Hemingway's frequent practice of by-passing beginnings and middles and presenting only the culminating phase of an action. Not only Harry's progress since his slaying of Mr. Sing, but even the early and middle parts of this disaster are omitted: he is encountered only at its end, when, already severely wounded by the Cuban Coast Guard, he is trying to complete his escape, save his boat, and, at first, his contraband cargo of liquor.

It is interesting to note that this sequence is titled "Fall," with the obvious connotations of the word itself and the seasonal ones of har-

111

vest. The Chinese sequence is "Spring," a time of planting and beginning, and the last one is "Winter," with the implied death of the year matching Harry's own death. There is no "Summer."

Brief as it is, the episode renders again Harry's steadfast maintaining of his self-image in crisis, and it offers another confrontation of the Hemingway aristocrat with the nonaristocrat. At the outset, Harry is steering and managing his boat completely alone with his mate for the voyage, Wesley, lying wounded and useless among the sacks of liquor on the deck. Although Harry is the more seriously wounded, Wesley reviles him throughout the ordeal. Yet at the end Harry magnanimously forgives the mate: he is the Hemingway aristocrat always, if a crude version of it.

Another example of Hemingway's "aristocratic" values, and of the virtue of friendship, is Captain Willie, who refuses to take the government official, Frederic Harrison, back to Key West, after Harrison, on the deck of Captain Willie's fishing boat, has seen Harry dumping the liquor. Yet all the courage of Harry and Willie comes to nothing. Harry not only loses his arm, we learn in the next section, but his boat as well. And he does so through the working of a chance that is hostile in its operations. His pursuit by the Coast Guard and the wounding of himself and Wesley are an inherent risk in the rum-running and are in a sense logical and incorporated into the stream of causation. But the sighting of Harry by a high government official on a fishing trip is a wild and totally unpredictable accident. Harry is apparently undone by the X factor in the universe, yet, at the same time, such a disaster was waiting for him once he chose, out of *hubris*, a course of action in which very high risks were implicit. Character and chance have fused again to leave Harry in a worsened and more desperate situation, and it is in this situation that he makes his most desperate choice of all.

In the third and final portion of the novel, the confrontation of the opposing keys becomes stronger, their alternation swifter: the conflict crescendos, with a constant cutting back and forth between Harry's ever deeper confirmation in his *hubris* and an even heavier intimation of the approaching and ultimate disaster that will be its consequence. In the larger sense, the catastrophe of Harry's life has begun when the novel begins, but the culmination of it, the catastrophe of the specific span of the book, is to end this last action—and Harry's life.

In this phase, both boundary conceptions of tragedy are more intensely limned. The hostile forces are drawing steadily tighter around Harry, and, opposing them, he persists more stubbornly in his *hubris* and his error in understanding—his determination to maintain his self-sufficiency at all costs and his illusion that he can control his own destiny if he tries hard enough. His resolution and the destructive elements that must produce his catastrophe have contended from the beginning, and now the catastrophe is at hand.

The first intimation of it comes early, at the contact between Harry and Beelips Simmons, the crooked lawyer. He fills Harry with foreboding, a profound anticipation of doom to come. Harry's fascination with the fate of Beelips and his intense antipathy to the attorney create a suspicion that he sees in Beelips a negative projection of himself, and that he intuitively fears that Beelips' stupid engineering of his approaching death may be a parallel and forecast of Harry's own. With appropriate irony, Beelips confides he is not planning on living in Key West after the robbery: Harry is "scared" by the unaware self-sentencing.

After Beelips tells Harry the Coast Guard has found and repossessed his stolen boat, he embodies another fatal quality for Harry, becoming messenger and manifestation of the destructive element in the universe; because he is himself so clearly marked as its victim, he becomes its emblem. Harry viscerally identifies him that way as he warns him, "Keep your mouth off my business. . . . you're poison to anyone who ever touched you" (122). Harry knows Beelips will be smashed because he has stupidly set in motion forces he does not understand.

Is it random chance that has led to the discovery of Harry's boat? Hidden in the mangroves after he stole it back from the Coast Guard, it has been spotted by a man on a tall WPA truck who was not even looking for it. This might seem the wildest and purest bad luck, but Harry's outburst at Beelips suggests he feels it is the result of an element that is an unremovable part of a design. The feeling quickly intensifies into a presentiment, and for Harry the trip assumes the aspect of a journey into hell. But he refuses to withdraw; he confirms his choice to proceed and his commitment to his defining quality—at once his nobility and his *hubris*. And so he moves to the moment of fateful balance, where he will fulfill his self vision totally or fail it, where he will regain control of his destiny or die. For an instant he thinks he has done it by killing them all. But one of the "bodies" shoots him in the stomach and he knows he has lost.

Again, is this unpredictable bad luck or an inevitable and inescapable concomitant of his action—chance or *dike*? Here, the question is not a real one: from the beginning, it was a *probability* that Harry would be killed in a fight with four armed men; his own luck has actually been extremely good, just not quite good enough. His *hubris* has assaulted logic as well as tragic necessity, and he has come to his logical, fore-seeable end.

Has he also come to awareness? Dying, he considers, "I guess it was nuts all right. I guess I bit off too much more than I could chew" (174). But he does not wish to relinquish his conviction that he really had no choice: "Hell, I couldn't run no filling station" (175). Awareness comes, if it comes, with his dying speech to the Coast Guard petty offi-cers who board the boat: " 'A man,' Harry Morgan said . . . 'one man alone ain't got. No man alone now.' He stopped. 'No matter how a man alone ain't got no bloody fucking chance.' He shut his eyes. It had taken him a long time to get it out and it had taken him all of his life to learn it" (235).

Is this a primitive, intuitive revolutionary declaration? Or a postula-tion of a primitive, intuitive tragic sense of life? Or both? The important thing here is that Harry is not in the least a thinking man but a feeling one. He *feels* the world against him; he is deeply, emotionally aware of that operational hostility which its abstract indifference becomes. He is convinced now the universe crushes the individual, and in this perspec-tive, of course, he touches one of Frye's extremities of tragedy—that which demonstrates the pitiless power of the universe in its confronta-tion with the individual.

But for Harry, as for many men, this confrontation *appears* to be an economic one. He has been forced, he considers, into his choices and his actions because the world has deprived him of the right to make a rea-sonable living on his own reasonable terms. His resentment is profound and total but is directed at the government, business, the Depression, life itself. Indeed, Harry is the victim of tragic necessity *and* of a failed economic system: his last declaration is the cry of both tragic protagonist and belated revolutionary. In these specifics, certainly, Harry has come to awareness.

Has he come to awareness in another major dimension—that of perceiving and acknowledging his own fatal flaws, of character and of action? His admission, "I guess it was nuts . . . I shouldn't have tried it," balances with his feeling that he couldn't have done anything else. Like most protagonists of tragedy, Harry touches both its limits: he has been crushed by the universe in the nature of things, and his own character and acts have precipitated his catastrophe. But one feels in leaving him that his acknowledgment of responsibility is not complete—that finally he sees himself as undone by overwhelming mysterious powers and refuses to accept *fully* his own flaw as an equal cause. He has come to awareness, and an intense awareness—but it is not total. Nor has he truly transcended his catastrophe: he has won no absolute psychic victory in his physical defeat, other than demonstrating physical courage, which is final and unredeemed. He is a genuine tragic protagonist, but not of the highest and noblest order.

The untranscendent sadness and defeat is developed further in the coda of Marie's long interior monologue, which appears both to invoke and reverse Mollie Bloom's final monologue at the end of *Ulysses*. In contrast to Mollie's life-affirming "yes yes yes," Marie soliloquizes a turning away to the death of the heart. But even as the single lives of Harry and, in her own view, herself, have ended, life as a generic element, a universal force, goes on. The last line of the first chapter of *A Farewell to Arms*, "But it [cholera] was checked and in the end only seven thousand died of it in the army," is recalled, in implication, by the concluding images of *To Have and Have Not*: "Outside it was a lovely, cool, sub-tropical winter day, and the palm branches were sawing in the light north wind. . . . Through the window you could see the sea looking hard and new and blue in the winter light. A large white yacht was coming into the harbor and seven miles out on the horizon you could see a tanker, small and neat in profile against the blue sea, hugging the reef as she made to the westward to keep from wasting fuel against the stream" (262).

All are configurations of continuance: life is still only operationally hostile: it goes its way, they suggest, in hard, brilliant indifference, a beauty untouched by the devastation it quite incidentally causes.

Perhaps the most frequent and telling criticism of *To Have and Have Not* is that a substantial part of the novel, about one fifth, seems completely extraneous to the tragedy of Harry Morgan and is thus a dilution of it. This part includes a number of vignettes—that of the sexually disabled financier, the kept homosexual, the frustrated lady movie star, and the drunken veterans—and the fairly fully developed story of a fatuous writer. Such criticism is reasonable: these fragments are not in the strictest sense organic—that is, they do not advance the Harry Morgan narrative—and they must submit to the raised critical question.

However, they can survive it. Many of them present the "haves" in formal contrast to the have-nots, and the juxtaposed opposition shows the have-nots in an even harsher perspective. Also, the vignettes and some other flash portraits serve as counterpoint lines to the main, melodic line of Harry Morgan; parallel to Harry in certain respects, opposite to him in others, they represent a different development of a situation or a conception embodied in Harry—exactly as other characters do, say, with Jake in the fugue structure of *The Sun Also Rises.*

The sixty-year-old grain speculator is like Harry in his self-directedness, his indifference to strictures of convention, but he is different in that he is smarter and truly amoral, and thus a vastly superior predator. He cares about no one else; Harry cares deeply about his wife and family. With total clarity, he has chosen to be what Harry considers, wrongly, he has been forced to become. Without remorse, he has spent a lifetime ruining others within the law; Harry kills outside the law on two occasions only, and both times his victims are murderers—in fact, he chooses to kill one murderer with great risk rather than twelve innocents with no risk at all. Yet, finally, both are individuals committed to living their lives on their own terms—that is, to imposing their terms on the universe and thus to filling the outline of the subliminally conceived self. Sexual vitality is a weapon of the financier's as it has been Harry's; both in a sense are "peddling [their] *cojones.*" The speculator is the complete and successful version, Harry is the incomplete and unsuccessful one; they are, as it were, variations of the same theme. Yet failure and success both end in catastrophe, and the catastrophes are not incomparable: Harry meets instant death through his *hubris* and the speculator is dying a slow one, in part through *hubris* and in part simply through time, projected here as the universal agent of catastrophe. He has avoided almost all of Harry's mistakes, but has committed one careless arrogant act with the Bureau of Internal Revenue; this and the

116

erosion of time are destroying him as he is encountered in the book. Thus, all who try to conquer alone, die alone. But also, perhaps, all die alone—no matter how smart or how ruthless.

Dorothy Hollis, the aging movie star, is first a figure of pampered indulgence set against the harsh scrabble for existence of the conches. But she is also another harmony for one of Harry's themes, suggesting the ultimate aloneness of those who live for their own gratification, whatever its shape. One man worn out, another a drunk, she must turn to masturbation.

Treated as they are with heavy and even derisive irony, the rich happy family is apt at first to escape identification as positives of the principle of which the others are negatives. Yet they stand as such: "they are a happy family and all love each other" (239), apparently because they are rooted in family as community rather than totally isolated in self. They are, of course, firmly in the complex of haves—yet happy as they are presented as being, they are clearly in the author's view worth infinitely less attention than those, good or bad, committed to the realization of self.

Henry Carpenter is in a situation not unlike Harry's, whose first name is an informal version of his own, and he is used by Wallace Johnston as Harry has been used and betrayed by Mr. Johnson, another pairing. Their parallel is that both consider themselves in a desperate situation. Harry Morgan's response is to try to fight out of it by any means; Henry Carpenter's is to become first a homosexual whore and then a suicide, the latter an act he has opted for but not yet committed when encountered on board Johnston's yacht. A contrast to Harry in this respect, he also offers a different and ironically pathetic exfoliation of the have and have-not theme: "The money on which it was not worthwhile for him to live was one hundred and seventy dollars more a month than fisherman Albert Tracy had been supporting his family on at the time of his death three days before" (233).

Even more fully developed is the counterpoint line of writer Richard Gordon. Like Henry Carpenter, Richard Gordon can be seen as a negative of Harry; he is both a larger negative than Carpenter and a more neatly contrasting one. The personalities of Gordon and Harry are grouped about a comparable thrust—the desire to assert identity and to live on one's own terms. But the force behind Harry's thrust is strong and unyielding while that behind Gordon's is flabby and inconsequential. What is hard pride and determined self-sufficiency in Harry is, in Gordon, a weak and fatuous vanity. Harry is willing to and does back his choices with his life, while Gordon is unwilling or unable to make a complete commitment in carrying out any of his. He wishes to be known as a proletarian novelist but, we deduce, has never really known what it is to be a working man and has been unwilling to become one to learn truly what he writes about; "shit," the intellectual agitator says of his books. He wants to be the artist unfettered by convention in exploring all experiences for the sake of his work; in actuality, he is simply a man who cheats on his wife and does not have the decorum to keep it from her—and thus loses her.

A list of balances between the two can be drawn: Gordon's failure to win his wife's respect contrasts with Harry's overwhelming success with his, Gordon's shabby unfaithfulness contrasts with Harry's loyalty, Gordon's rejection of the idea of family with Harry's unquestioning commitment to his, Harry's sharp sense of reality—except for his one fatal misjudgment—with Gordon's consistently false perceptions, Harry's pride and strength with Gordon's vanity and weakness. Yet both have views of life that are different faces of self-gratification, and both are coagents of their own catastrophes; Harry loses life and Richard Gordon, love.

Thus, finally, all of these counterpoint characters illuminate in different perspectives certain aspects of the melody—Harry's story. The justly admired scene of the veterans, already casualties as a group, who assault and beat one another reasonlessly, is perhaps harmony—a miniaturization of the cruelty and absurdity that the book suggests is at the heart of the universe. The harmony-counterpoint apparatus is certainly weaker for having been constructed outside the central narrative, rather than being integral to it, as in *The Sun Also Rises* and *A Farewell to Arms*. Yet the novel is better with than without it.

One of the most striking aspects of the novel is the author's almost total abandonment of symbology in favor of a nearly completely naturalistic surface. The image or incident elevated to the symbolic or metaphorical level is rare indeed: the life-goes-on images of the last lines and the biting of Harry by Mr. Sing are among the very few of these. Whether this is a result of choice or of a dilution of artistic energy, only the writer could say. But the images simply as visuals do suggest an ebbing intensity; the careful compacting of pictures into emotional and thematic units, the deliberate composition of imagistic landscapes, the construction of a network of images running through the entire work that accents and focuses its themes—all of these, generally and in comparison with earlier and certain later novels, are not in evidence. Unquestionably, their absence, in the same comparison, diminishes the achievement of the book. Yet, on a lower level, the imagistic surface is a solid enough achievement: if it does not do all that was done in those earlier works, it renders the physical world of the book in remarkable vividness and exactitude. Conrad's command "to make you see" is faithfully honored.

The language is spare and stiff in most sections of the book, an accepted consequence of the point-of-view decisions. Much of the novel is in first person, in the voices of not only Harry but of Albert and Marie. The rest is in the voice of the effaced narrator, but in most of these sequences that narrator holds himself very close to the big character and permits himself little flexibility in either movement or idiom. The only exception is Chapter Twenty-four, devoted to the development of the harmony vignettes, where the effaced narrator speaks directly, fluently, and ironically.

The first section, "Spring," is rendered entirely from Harry Morgan's point of view. The second, "Fall," sees a shift to the effaced narrator, who moves on a very short line from neutral "central" position to a penetration of Harry's consciousness: the language is flat and studiously objective and even renderings from the outside position are colored by Harry's idiom. "Winter" begins with a first-person sequence—by Albert, rendering Harry through the sensibility of an acquaintance—and ends with Marie's Molly Bloomish interior monologue and the final externally rendered images of indifference and continuity. Except for Harry's monologues in Chapter Ten, the rest is in the effaced narrator's voice, moving from external positioning to consciousness penetration of varying degrees of depth, with Harry and the harmony-counterpoint characters. It is a supple strategy, and it works well enough; significant renderings are made both from outside and inside consciousness.

The character of Harry is manifestly unlike that of Nick Adams, Jake

119

Barnes, or Frederic Henry: these were introverted young men with no claim on overt toughness or flamboyant physicality—but with, rather, a surprisingly delicate sensibility—who confront as best they can a world that is too much for them. They are Young's real "code hero," having little in common with the *stereotype* of the Hemingway hero as it was once advanced by nonspecialists. Harry, however, moves a not inconsiderable distance toward that stereotype; indeed, one might be tempted to reason that the stereotype is compounded of aspects of Harry and those of the public Hemingway that the author presented in the not-always-fortunate journalism of his middle and late periods. The spurious "Hemingway hero" and Harry are flamboyantly strong and tough, indeed semisupermen in the physical sense; alone, they face lions or revolutionaries or blue water with resolve; they are determined to force their terms on the world; they are men envied, and consequently hated, by other men. The stereotype—again in contrast to the authentic—triumphs by toughness, physical superiority, and a species of insensitivity.

Here the shapes of Harry and the stereotype move apart. Harry does not triumph; he is destroyed in part by exactly those elements in his personality in which he resembles the stereotype. The author is not glorifying them, though he does manifestly respect them. It is clear that Harry does not represent what Hemingway thinks a man should be, and he is less a *persona* for the author than the protagonist of any previous Hemingway novel: he is unmistakably rendered as incarnating a deadly shortcoming.

As always, there was a literal model or models. Baker cites Joe Russell, a boat captain in Key West who ran rum during prohibition, as the chief model for Harry, and Bra Saunders, the model for the captain in "After the Storm," might also have contributed elements to the creation. It seems evident, and inevitable, that a large part of Harry's psyche came from Hemingway himself; from this point on he appears to have moved into Fitzgerald's strategy of choosing an acquaintance for the exterior shape of a protagonist, then pouring his own consciousness into the mold. Yet, ironically, Harry is less a disguised Hemingway than any other hero of the novels.

Russell did double duty: in another avatar as working owner of Sloppy Joe's Bar he was the model for Freddy Wallace, the bar owner. Baker assigns other acquaintances as prototypes for supporting characters. Among the more interesting were Harry Burns and Arnold Gingrich of *Esquire* as the combination model for Professor McWalsey; Gingrich warned Hemingway, writes Baker, that the book might be seen as libeling John Dos Passos as the source for Richard Gordon, and Grant and Jane Mason as prototypes of Tommy and Helene Bradley. But in writing the book, Baker observes, Hemingway was functioning only as novelist and was not concerned with the feelings of his friends.[3]

As tragedy, and as suggested earlier, the novel moves a fair distance from the locus between Frye's two boundaries occupied by the two previous tragic novels. Both were very close to the periphery that conceives of man as helpless before an operationally hostile universe; *To Have and Have Not* is just a little closer to the other, the view of man as the victim of his own flaws and mistakes. In the tragic perspective, the primary theme might be expressed as: "Life is tragic—but man participates in the shaping of his own catastrophe."

In *The Sun Also Rises*, the nuance of emphasis is on the possibility of dignification and transcendence through graceful acceptance of the universal catastrophe. In *A Farewell to Arms*, the stress is on the pure fact of catastrophe, on its awesome finality and the overwhelming might of the universe it represents. In *To Have and Have Not*, the weight is on the shared responsibility for the catastrophe, and thus another shift in the author's discernible world view has been made.

One criticism made frequently against the novel is that it is incomplete and confused as dialectic—which is somewhat like taking a horse to task for not being a moose. It is not concerned with dialectic. The author's obvious intention, socioeconomically, is to render in personal and emotional terms the disparity in American life and to show how that disparity, and the malfunctioning of the system that produced it, can be a force in the making of an individual tragedy. There is room for any and every kind of novelist, of course, but this rendering in terms of the totally concrete and the totally personal is the way of the "pure" artist. Whether "pure" art is the maximum objective of the novel, of course, is a matter of individual critical judgment.

That devil, consensus, would appear to rank *To Have and Have Not*

3. Carlos Baker, *Ernest Hemingway: A Life Story* (New York: Scribner's, 1969), 228, 239, 294, 295, 298. Baker discusses the possible models for characters.

both as an artistic failure and as the least or the next-to-least important of Hemingway's novels. It might be either of those last two, of course, and still be a very good book indeed; it is a failure only in comparison with the three Hemingway masterpieces that preceded it, and in the marmoreal view that all art fails in not achieving its absolute possibility. Every artist produces hierarchies of rank in his own work, and this extends to groupings of work as well as to individual works. Once accepted as belonging to a lesser category in Hemingway's output, *To Have and Have Not* is a completely honorable entry in that category. So seen, it comes through as an excellent minor novel: it has vitality, a strong pulse of language, a powerful tragic structure, thoroughly realized characters, and an excitingly visceral view of the economic and social reality of its time.

6

Stories of the Thirties
Enlarging a Tragic Pattern

As his own thirties and those of the century were drawing to an end, Hemingway had clearly refocused his earlier tragic vision. No longer was the uncaring yet destructive universe the overwhelmingly prepotent cause of Hemingway catastrophes; now the Hemingway man shared the blame equally. His descent began from his own character, even if the mysterious unknown gave momentum and shaped its termination. Apparently self-consciously, the author had moved to a point almost exactly between the boundaries, directly in the center of the tragic field. This is as clear in the stories written during or just after the composition of *To Have and Have Not* as it is in the novel itself.

There are other significant stresses—some might consider them enhancements—in the stories. In each of the period's three tragic stories that the author chose to include in his collected short fiction, that quality that leads to catastrophe also is, or is part of, the quality that defines and even elevates the protagonist to some kind of significance. In each story the protagonist is *striving* toward some kind of idealization, and in three that striving is directed not only to fulfillment but to the enlargement of the self. They have not only tried to fill the outlines of that self they have imagined, like Harry Morgan; they are in their way trying to improve it. Their striving is almost the striving of Goethe, if scaled down to literal size, and it culminates in catastrophe as it must, but the protagonists are larger for both the effort and its end.

What they do not do is take that final, deliberate step into termination and transcendence—all that is left to do for the Hemingway tragic protagonists to become, in the great traditional postulates, the ultimate tragic protagonists. But they are well on their way. Hemingway is at the threshold of his final phase as a tragic writer, and he is shortly to enter it, in *For Whom the Bell Tolls.*

The stories are thus, with Harry Morgan, at the edge of that phase, and at least two, probably three, might be put forward as effectively tragic. All have the architectural necessities, and for most readers the two African stories and "Capital of the World" would have the necessary intensity of emotional effect. In all three, the protagonist meets death as the result of his primary drive, and in two he calculatedly risks it, even if he does not reach for it in deliberate self-immolation on behalf of a passion he incarnates or lives by.

All were published in 1936; the order of writing was "Capital of the World," "The Short Happy Life of Francis Macomber," and "The Snows of Kilimanjaro."[1] There is compounded and thematic irony in the title of the first: Madrid is not only the place where Paco and the counterpoint characters meet catastrophe, but by an accretion it also becomes a configuration of catastrophe as the great universal of the world. If one were too quick, he might fall into a perception of the story as a simple anecdote of catastrophe; yet, as always, the apparent simplicity is not simple, and the "anecdote" is the center of a complex, if miniature, structural design. And, again, the tension in that design is created by several narrative lines working against one another in counterpoint, even though they are short lines: we are confronted with another literary version of the fugue.

The melodic, main line is of course Paco's. His defining thrust is his indiscriminate romanticism, fused—not really oddly—with his peasant's preoccupation with security: "He himself would like to be a good Catholic, a revolutionary, and have a steady job like this, while, at the same time, being a bullfighter."[2] It is his general romantic impulse, particularized for the moment into his desire to be a bullfighter, that prompts him to accept the challenge from Enriques the dishwasher, who emulates the bull by tying heavy sharp knives to the legs of a chair.

1. Carlos Baker, *Ernest Hemingway: A Life Story* (New York: Scribner's, 1969), 284, 286, 289, 332, 337.

2. Ernest Hemingway, "The Capital of the World," in *The Fifth Column and the First Forty-nine Stories* (New York: Scribner's, 1938), 141–42.

So Paco's death in the game comes directly from his desire to prove, to define himself, to *become* truly brave in his own eyes. It is a noble if youthful aspiration, and it is, operationally, the fatal flaw. But the death of Paco might or might not have the tragic impact alone. It is the contrapuntal network which surrounds and plays against it that enlarges and intensifies its emotional effect. And that structure, too, lifts it beyond the anecdote and gives it full fictional stature.

Against the principal catastrophe of Paco are three counter-catastrophes of matadors who have failed for one reason or another. In other lines, characters do not strive enough to be worthy of catastrophe, but are simple failures. And all the dramas are played out at the Luarca Hotel, carefully, though subtly, defined as a place of endings. Nobody leaves the Luarca for a better hotel, but when they do depart, their fall is rapid.

Just before Paco's death, the three toreros are rendered in attitudes that epiphanize their situation. The sick matador, once a promising, "even a sensational" fighter (139) is lying on the bed. The too-short matador sits in failure looking out the window. The matador who has lost his nerve tries to seduce Paco's sister, a chambermaid, but is taunted with his cowardice and rejected in humiliation. Balancing the small, definite catastrophes of the three matadors are the inconclusive failure of two priests from Galicia, still waiting to see their bishop in Madrid, and the abortive failure of Enriques, talented in the arts of the bull ring but so unable to control his fear that he can only wash the hotel's dishes.

Set against these who have experienced catastrophe or simple failure are those with limited success: because they have not sought much, they have achieved what they sought. A picador, whose work is of a limited character, lives "in a small tight world of personal efficiency, nightly alcoholic triumph, and insolence" (144). An older waiter, who wants nothing but work, has plenty of that. Against this network of mini-dramas—most catastrophic and subtragic, some so unwanting as to be safe—the catastrophe of Paco is played. It is the most decisive of all; the others have prepared us well for it.

The author has moved with deliberate swiftness from one line to aonther, always building in excitement, and as Paco accepts Enriques' challenge, he has reached the *stretto*, the area of climactic tension. Enriques ties the knives to the legs of the chair, while the author as effaced narrator shuttles, now rapidly, between the miniature narrative movements, giving a sentence or less to each. Then he returns to the main line and the full, though quick, enactment of Paco's catastrophe. All the lines project once more the author's deepest intuitive conviction that for all who aspire, life can only end in loss.

Yet of all the lines, Paco's is the only one that has the effect of tragedy. He has reached toward a larger self, he has awarely risked death in the process, and he has finally received it.

Francis Macomber begins his fictional life in deep disgrace, he climbs out of that disgrace to triumph, then he is destroyed almost at the instant of triumph—a recognizable version of a basic Hemingway pattern. Clearly he has won some kind of redemption in his death, and this ought to give him and the story tragic stature. Probably it does. The question of effect is again the decisive one: for many, perhaps most, the story is successfully tragic. It could be argued, even, that Macomber is the most impressively tragic of the four protagonists here, because he comes closest to accepting death deliberately for his new vision; indeed, it could be argued that in the total span of action, he has done just that. But it is probably more accurate to say that, like Paco, he has *risked* death awarely, which is not quite the same thing. Yet even if he has not passed into the company of the ultimate tragic heroes in the canon— Jordan, Santiago, Hudson—he becomes tragic enough. Like Sartre's Orestes, he finally acquires the necessary weight, even though he has had none at the outset.

The author's compounding of his character's initial disgrace is one of the most technically interesting components of the story. Macomber begins in Africa in a humiliating enough state: he is a wife-dominated cuckold. His cowardice before the lion's charge casts him lower still, and his wife's contemptuous betrayal with the hunter brings him to such a nadir of self-esteem and objective debasement that any reversal will have to be effective. His discovery of physical bravery and its subsequent translation into the strength to overthrow his wife thus become supremely effective. Despite the psychic and ethical narrowness of Macomber's triumph, the quality of the writing gives it the conviction of importance. Facing with exaltation a Cape buffalo about to kill him may not be a particularly profound or intelligent act on the face of it, but

Macomber *feels* it to be supremely profound. And it becomes so, in the framework. He is willing to die for the concept and he does die, thus becoming a tragic figure. The obvious judgment on his new value cannot alter the significance of his death to defend it—even if it comes, ironically, from his wife's gun rather than the buffalo's horns. What he dies for is a comparatively small thing—physical bravery flowering into masculine assertion—compared to the devotion to a priestly vocation which ennobles and destroys such Hemingway protagonists as Manuel Garcia, Santiago, and Robert Jordan. Consequently, the *size* of Macomber's tragedy is reduced correspondingly. But its *genuineness* as tragedy is not impaired.

Although its achievement as tragedy may be thus qualified, there are no qualifications about either its emotional validity or its dazzling technical victories. It is one of the author's most accomplished exercises in point-of-view control: he moves the fictional camera and voice from the locus of the effaced narrator to the rim and then to the interior of consciousness of one character, then withdraws and enters another (including the lion) the same way, returning at will to the station of the effaced narrator. The moves are made first with Flaubertian, graduated deliberation; then they become quick cuts from mind to mind as the *stretto* approaches and arrives. Although there are three full character lines in the composition—Wilson and Mrs. Macomber counterpoints to the Macomber melody—only the consciousness of Macomber and Wilson are really penetrated, as except for an early superficial observation of the two others, Mrs. Macomber is always seen from outside. Her proper identity as enigma is thus created and preserved.

Like much Hemingway work in the thirties, this story is firmly naturalistic and shows almost none of his early concentration on symbol and metaphor. Yet on the naturalistic level, the author's visual imagery is as vivid as ever, a model for the creation of sensory reality. One passage from the buffalo chase shows as well as any how sharply he makes us see—and hear, and feel:

> The car was going a wild forty-five miles an hour across the open, and as Macomber watched, the buffalo got bigger and bigger until he could see the gray, hairless, scabby look of one huge bull and how his neck was a part of his shoulders and the shiny black of his horns as he galloped a little behind the others that were strung out in that steady plunging

gait; . . . they drew up close and he could see the plunging hugeness of the bull, and the dust in his sparsely haired hide, the wide boss of horn and his outstretched, wide-nostrilled muzzle . . . and the car skidded, plowing sideways to an almost stop and Wilson was out on one side and he on the other, stumbling as his feet hit the still speeding-by of the earth, and then he was shooting at the bull as he moved away, hearing the bullets whunk into him.[3]

The complex of truth in the instant of time is not compellingly presented here or in any other single passage of the story. The truth is in the whole: that man should pay any price to enter his full potential and identity. This is the perception of some of the loftiest tragedies.

Certainly, the story has a great deal to be forgiven: it was the one that set the pattern for all those others in which the rich bitch crawls into the cot of the white hunter. One must remind oneself that it was the first, and that it created a cliché rather than followed one; it cannot be fairly censured for its imitations. Its glamor may occasionally become gaudiness, but this is probably an inescapable accompaniment of the glamorous story.

Its conversion from source to act is one of the more interesting of such conversions. Baker reports that Hemingway took the action almost whole from a story his friend and mentor, the professional hunter Philip Percival, told him over an African campfire. Percival, in turn, had it from another hunter. Yet the author supplied the refinements that made it fiction, as always. He modeled the character of Wilson chiefly on Percival himself, writes Baker, though Percival was austere in personal relations with female clients. Hemingway said he based Macomber on a "nice jerk" of a young sportsman he had known a long time: "He is just how he really was, only he is invented," Baker quotes Hemingway. Whatever that meant, the author seems to have made the internal Macomber a ruthless version of himself as he might have been at one variety of his worst. He "invented" Mrs. Macomber "complete with handles from the worst bitch I knew" and hinted at an earlier relationship with the model. As always, it is in the reconstituting from prototypes and event that the story becomes tragic art. "As far as I know,"

3. Ernest Hemingway, "The Short Happy Life of Francis Macomber," in *The Fifth Column and the First Forty-nine Stories* (New York: Scribner's, 1938), 126–27.

Percival told Baker, "no client has ever succeeded in shooting her husband as EH describes."[4]

"The Snows of Kilimanjaro" used up enough materials for four novels, Hemingway asserted. "I put all the true stuff in," he said, "the most load any story ever had to carry." And part of the load, Baker further reports, was his own fear that he would die too soon, his work unfinished and his talent unfulfilled.[5] He put much of his own life into those retrospectives of the dying writer Harry, and Harry is that persona of himself that dominated his cyclical periods of black depression.

He was able to give the story so much specific gravity because he evolved an even greater intensification of his long-established Greek tragedy method, where the story proper was the last full act, the extended catastrophe, of the *whole* story. In this one, the present time of the story is the last scene of the last act; in a manner of speaking, it is the catastrophe's catastrophe. The momentum and mass of the story are thus raised not to the second but to the third power, and a structure is created strong enough to carry that "load" of which the author boasts. This concentration is the reason for the story's shattering emotional impact.

And for its unquestionably tragic effect. In the neat formulations of the tragic idea, Harry is not as sharply focused a tragic protagonist as Macomber: he does not risk death in a single, instant/action for his belief, or his ethical essence, but he is brought down by fate and his own character, as a fused and inseparable force, over what is actually a long period of time. Yet, for most, "The Snows of Kilimanjaro" appears to produce a much larger measure of the tragic emotion than the Macomber story. The reasons, perhaps, are that great compaction and momentum; the quality of fateful anticipation—to which Coleridge attributes much of the power of Shakespeare's tragedies[6]—that shines

---

4. Baker, *Hemingway: A Life Story*, 286–91. Baker describes the source experiences of the two African stories and recounts the comments of Hemingway and Percival.

5. *Ibid.*, 286–89.

6. Donald A. Stauffer (ed.), "Summary of the Characteristics of Shakespeare's Dramas," in *Selected Poetry and Prose of Samuel Taylor Coleridge* (New York: Random House, 1951), 433–34.

through the story from the first line; and, quite simply, a tonality that can itself only be described as tragic. The instant coordinating symbol, the images, the interior monologues, all the parts create the deep emotional awareness of a heroic, if flawed, striving that can only end in death.

Although the present time of the story is devoted to the coming of death for Harry, his earlier surrender of his talent for comfort, and his attempt to come out of his corruption and achieve wholeness again are at the center of the total chronicle.

His marriage for money is both his self-betrayal and his long catastrophe; his attempt to rise again, "to train the fat off his soul," is his great intention and his striving. The fatal culmination of both, the long debasement and the struggle to rise from it, is his death—and the story.

The dramaturgy of the whole is sketched, explicitly if quickly, in the flashbacks. Harry's effort is doomed by the accidental thorn scratch, which he does not treat, and which has given him the blood poisoning and gangrene that is killing him. Thus fate and character have joined to produce the smaller, instant cause of Harry's physical death as they have joined in the longer phase of his interior destruction. Harry is destroyed both by his own moral flaw and the hostile unknown in the universe—in both long and short views.

Harry is actually caught between his own need to create and his compulsion to destroy: creation and destruction can be seen as the two opposing keys of the composition. His life has been a struggle between them, and his death is a kind of reconciliation of them. That struggle peaks and is crystallized in an interior monologue that sets forth the capitulation of his creativity to the luxury and sloth of his marriage. His relinquishment of his work and the personal negation that follows it are all manifestations of his urge to destroy—in this case, himself. But the opposite impulse finally revives sufficiently to bring him to the desperate attempt at regeneration, begun in the decision to come to Africa to start again, to become capable of work again.

Harry's own weakness has been the agent of his destruction through his moral disintegration; ironically, it is the incongruous, gratuitous jab from the universe that precipitates the beginning of his physical death. Yet it is his own carelessness that makes the accident fatal: "And now this life . . . was coming to a term because he had not used iodine two weeks ago when a thorn had scratched his knee as they moved forward trying to photograph a herd of waterbuck standing, their heads up, peering while their nostrils searched the air, their ears spread wide to hear the first noise that would send them rushing into the bush. They had bolted, too, before he got the picture."[7]

The short passage fuses major elements of the story: flaw and fate, destruction and creation. The attempt to photograph is the artist's attempt to represent life, to fix beauty; the failure of the attempt is an instant, mini-catastrophe that memorializes loss. The stab of the thorn is the hostile element at work; Harry's neglect of it is the working of his own flaw, his destructive force. It *is* a genuine Poundian image, for it projects the substance of all Harry's life: the drive to create, the failure, the fate-inflicted damage that is made lethal by his own destructive carelessness.

The infection of the flesh is a metaphor of Harry's infection of the spirit, and it has brought him to the threshold of death as the story formally begins. That passage also culminates the requisite, antecedent information—for it is not part of a myth known to the audience— needed to conclude Harry's tragedy. What we are to witness is communicated at the very beginning: the italicized, keynote image of the leopard frozen on Kilimanjaro's peak intimates death in aspiration. The lines that follow, the first of the story proper, are a direct, even brutal declaration of what is to come. Harry says on the cot, "The marvellous thing is that it's painless" (150). An instant visualization of waiting vultures, perhaps more frightening for being named only as "birds," reinforces those first words, as does an exchange of dialogue between Harry and his wife. This is capped by Harry's finally speaking the word "die" clearly and a closer view of the vultures.

The physical imagery of the story has been widely admired for its naturalistic evocations; its sensory power, however, is only the beginning of its purpose and effectiveness. Images create an intensely strong awareness of life that poignantly accents the centrality—that Harry is leaving life. They are a crucial part of the complex of tragedy. Many other imagistic passages also suggest—sometimes obliquely, sometimes fairly directly—Harry's thrust toward creation and his counter-impulse

7. Ernest Hemingway, "The Snows of Kilimanjaro," in *The Fifth Column and the First Forty-nine Stories* (New York: Scribner's, 1938), 159–60.

toward destruction; in these passages both home and opposing key contend. Thus we are made constantly more aware of his primary thrust, his flaw, and of his approaching death as catastrophe to the tragic pattern of his life.

Many of these imagistic miniatures also culminate in mini-catastrophes of their own, like that of the thorn scratch; these not only intensify subliminally our anticipation of the major catastrophe, but feed steadily our awareness of the story as tragedy. In the musical analogy, they can be seen again as the harmonic, vertical development. The permanent pairing, even the inextricability, of pleasure and pain, life and death, triumph and loss is often implied.

Most of these sections are in the retrospective passages, set off in the so-imitated italics. The first of these complete sequences offers both Harry's own strong sense of life in early lines, then ironic life-death pairings and mini-catastrophes, and finally transcendence. The sequence begins:

> *Now in his mind he saw a railway station at Karagatch and he was standing with his pack and that was the headlight of the Simplon-Orient cutting the dark now and he was leaving Thrace then after the retreat. That was one of the things he had saved to write, with, in the morning at breakfast, looking out the window and seeing snow on the mountains in Bulgaria and Nansen's secretary asking the old man if it were snow and the old man looking at it and saying, No, that's not snow. It's too early for snow. . . . But it was snow all right and he sent them on into it when he evolved exchange of populations. And it was snow they tramped along in until they died that winter.* (153–54)

The light in the dark is here, as fairly often with the author, a concomitant of quest; it is no accident that it begins the retrospective passages, just as another figure of quest, the leopard dead high on Kilimanjaro, precedes and thus begins the story itself. Harry is intensely aware of the light as image of quest and of himself as a putative part of it: he is waiting to board the train. The configuration of snow, usually a Hemingway "good" as rain is a "bad," is presented here as containing "bad" in it (as Oldsey has explored): *i.e.*, life has death in it, and catastrophe is always at hand. Snow is the chief element in successive extended images in the same long passage. Delicately and elliptically, it is offered as representation of life and beauty that has danger, or catastrophe, or death inseparably fused with it.

In one passage, the contentment of Christmas in the Gauertal is shattered by the appearance of the deserter, whom police are tracking by footprints in the snow. Although Harry saves the deserter, nothing reverses the catastrophe that overtakes the skischule proprietor, in another passage: after images of snow beauty begin the sequence, he loses everything in a week-long poker game in a blizzard. The immediately subsequent image is of an American or British military pilot machine-gunning, and killing, many Austrian officers on a "cold bright Christmas day with the mountains showing across the plain." Life and death contrast in image, and snow is thus not mentioned but implied: it would inevitably cover the peaks. Each of the snow images, despite its aspect of life, has contained disaster or death; the final one in the sequence, however, is a pure celebration of snow in its modality as life-force. This is the singing ski rush down the slope. Thus the images of death-in-life are capped by one of life triumphant—not only a celebration but a reconciliation. This sequence of snow images has not only sounded many of the tonalities and thematic chords of the story but has served also as a symbolic metaphor of the entire work, as the first paragraph has done in certain of the author's earlier stories: the promise of life repeatedly ends in catastrophe, but ultimately finds a kind of triumph.

The next extended retrospective presents the death of love as catastrophe. Harry is reminded of his former wife by a woman he follows in Paris, and he writes her a letter declaring he can never get over her. Then, when his present wife finds the previous wife's answer, that marriage is over, too. Love has died twice, and this double catastrophe is intensified further by its juxtaposition to images of soldiers killed by mistake.

In the subsequent retrospectives—all sharp and concentrated with Harry's sense of life, his thrust toward it—recur the mini-catastrophes: the barrels of his grandfather's guns lie untouched in the ashes of his log house that has burned; the proprietor of a hotel in the Black Forest hangs himself after inflation ruins him; a cheap Paris hotel recalls Verlaine's death in it; a half-witted ranch boy shoots his persecutor, helps bring his body in, and is arrested; a bomb leaves an officer's guts on barbed wire and the officer, still conscious, begs to be shot. Like the catastrophes a harmonic development, a hyena appears early in the story and punctuates it infrequently thereafter—an obvious but effective harbinger of Harry's approaching death.

Death arrives as a triumphant and transcendent vision. Is the vision an epiphany of fantasy that Harry achieves in the instant before death? Or is it something else? The ambivalence is deliberate; both possibilities are open. Whichever, the awaited plane "arrives," piloted by Compson, a more cheerful Charon, and takes Harry away.

The flight, for Harry, appears the final victory of his drive toward beauty and its creation: he experiences it in a dazzling flow of image. And his awareness culminates with the knowledge that he will at last reach the absolute he has moved intuitively toward all his life, an absolute that appears as Mount Kilimanjaro seen from the plane:

> And there was a new water that he had never known of. The zebra, small rounded backs now, and the wildebeeste, big-headed dots seeming to climb as they moved in long fingers across the plain, now scattering as the shadow came toward them. . . . and ahead old Compie's tweed back and the brown felt hat. . . . then they were over mountains with sudden depths of green-rising forest and the solid bamboo slopes, and then the heavy forest again, sculptured into peaks and hollows until they crossed, and hills sloped down and then another plain, hot now, and purple brown. . . . Then there were other mountains dark ahead. Then they began to climb and they were going to the East it seemed, and then it darkened and they were in a storm, the rain so thick it seemed like flying through a waterfall, and then they were out and Compie turned his head and grinned and pointed and there, ahead, all he could see, as wide as all the world, great, high, and unbelievably white in the sun, was the square top of Kilimanjaro. And he knew that was where he was going. (174)

That Harry's vision and his death are virtually simultaneous is made explicit by the text: the hyena's whimpering finally wakes Harry's wife, who finds him dead.

Thus Harry has finally triumphed over his own forces of negation to touch ultimate beauty, ultimate experience, but he has done so only through the act of death. In the perception of the story, one way or another, he has found transcendence. Indeed, he has earned it, by never really relinquishing his quest despite his mistakes and his sins, by continuing to strive, like Goethe's Faust, in the face of his flaw. The tragedy finally becomes universal, not simply a parable of the artist's fate but of man's. One way of putting its theme might be: life is tragic, real triumph is possible only in death but the quest must go on. The leopard is Harry, and all men.

Besides Hemingway's "black-ass" view of himself that seems the emotional spring of the story, there were specific episodes from his 1934 African trip that went into the raw mix of the actual that was to be subjected to the author's usual refining process. The air "rescue" in the story seems a virtual transcript of what happened; yet in one trifling difference lies the thematic utterance of the story.

Hemingway came down with amoebic dysentery shortly after his arrival, but hunted doggedly in spite of the severities of the disease. This, Baker writes, "made every victory a disappointment and converted every minor failure into catastrophe," a state highly conducive to the tragic view of things. After a few weeks of this, he suffered a prolapse of the lower intestine while grouse shooting. He became convinced, he said, that he had been chosen as "the one to bear our Lord Buddha" again.[8] Percival radioed for a plane from Nairobi.

Waiting for the plane, preparing for it with smudge fires, the descent of the pilot in tweeds and a felt hat, his casual demand for an immediate take-off for Nairobi via Arusha, the view from the air of Kilimanjaro and the countryside—all match apparently exactly the sharply imagized section of the story.[9] The pilot Pearson becomes Compson of the story, the euphony of his name preserved while it also just manages to suggest Charon. The plane in both cases was a Puss Moth. The only apparent difference between the departures of Hemingway and Harry is that Harry made his in death. The factual rescue has been elevated not simply into tragic, but mystic, transcendence.

Of Hemingway's stories of the Spanish civil war, only "Old Man at the Bridge" appeared in the stories collected in 1938, and this account of an old man awaiting death from an artillery bombardment because he chose to stay with his animals is only pathetic. Other Spanish war stories, not published between covers in the author's lifetime, seem today no more than elevated journalism. "The Butterfly and the Tank,"

8. Baker, *Hemingway: A Life Story*, 256.
9. *Ibid.*, 231, 250, 251.

"Night Before Battle," and the best, "The Denunciation," are exciting as personalized reporting, but well below the author's fictional standards; he wisely never expanded the collection to include them. Those three good stories he did publish show that he had entered his full maturity as an artist of the tragic, and almost all of the large conceptions of the later novels can be found in them.

7

For Whom the Bell Tolls
Choosing Catastrophe and Death

For Whom the Bell Tolls may be the most visible single movement in Hemingway's development as a tragic writer: it is the first novel in which the protagonist wins an unambiguous, spiritual triumph in his terminal catastrophe by a specific act of volition. Harry Morgan's death victory was limited and bitter; that of Robert Jordan is exalted and transcendent. So, after him, are to be the catastrophes of Santiago, Thomas Hudson, and Colonel Richard Cantwell. The graceful acceptance of *The Sun Also Rises*, the helplessness before doom of *A Farewell to Arms*, the hurting final awareness of *To Have and Have Not* have given way to something else: a positive, total action against the catastrophe and a resulting formal reconciliation to the universe that most students of tragedy have always insisted is the highest kind of happiness. The force of that response has been felt even by those not primarily interested in the formalities of tragedy, and for them "affirmation" has been a useful and honorable word in describing the emotional impact of *For Whom the Bell Tolls*.

Yet its power as a tragic work is only part of the novel's magnitude. Much else is in it. The author's knowledge of Spain, for example, is a substance that both fills and holds the parts of the novel together, so that it becomes an encyclopedia of Spanish life without suffering dilution of form or force by that fullness. And no other Hemingway novel has more diverse or convincing characterizations. Although its imagistic passages usually fall short of the elevation Ezra Pound stipulated, they are extremely fine as realistic renderings; indeed, no other Hemingway novel more thoroughly presents or evokes the literal event. If it has the unity of tragic structure, it also offers an epic variety of experience, like the great nineteenth-century novels: two out-of-narrative sequences, in which the protagonist is not involved, are, by acclamation, the best writing in the book. The musical principle of melody-counterpoint-harmony development is used massively and successfully in the work as a totality and with particular brilliance internally in the clubbing and the hilltop sequences. It is, finally, an encyclopedia for many things—not only social surfaces and topical history, but of emotional states and of fictional method; it is a studious and vast exercise in technique. It has its imperfections and its roughnesses, many of them, but they are not inappropriate to its size.

The book is engaged with one of the great political events and some of the great political issues of the time, and one of its most impressive features, three decades and more after publication, is its undogmatic fairness. Although acknowledgedly committed to the Spanish Republican cause and against fascism and the Fascist government of Spain, it is never propaganda. The author emphasizes, rather than conceals, the brutalities of the Republicans; he is compassionate toward those individual Spaniards who fought for fascism even though he manifests hate for the fascist order. He is generally a sympathetic admirer of the Communists in Spain, but is ultimately aloof from them: he shows their spots, as well as virtues, and is careful to make plain that communism and republicanism are not the same, though they are cobelligerents.

Interestingly, time seemed to diminish the status of the book in the short run; as Ray B. West, Jr., wrote, there was a tendency in the late forties and fifties to judge it as inferior to the earlier masterpieces. Now it seems restored to unequivocal major status, and in 1972 Baker called it Hemingway's best novel.[1] Several reasons can be advanced for the fluctuation in its literary market quotation. One, of course, is the swings

1. Ray B. West, Jr., "Ernest Hemingway: The Failure of Sensibility," reprinted in Ray B. West, Jr., *The Writer in the Room* (East Lansing: Michigan State University Press, 1968), 147. Alfred Kazin's comments on Hemingway grouped into "Ernest Hemingway: A Synopsis of a Career," in J. K. M. McCaffery (ed.), *Ernest Hemingway: The Man and His Work* (Cleveland and New York: World, 1950), 190–204. Kazin calls *For Whom the Bell Tolls* "among the best of Hemingway's works." Carlos Baker, *Ernest Hemingway: The Writer as Artist* (Princeton: Princeton University Press, 1972), 116.

in national political attitudes. Another may be that *For Whom the Bell Tolls* is less an approach to poetry than certain other Hemingway works —but it is more a novel in the grand tradition of the novel. Yet it is with the novel as a key Hemingway tragedy that this study is most concerned; it should be observed that its protagonist is not only the coauthor of his catastrophe as well as the target of necessity, but that its pattern cuts through several varieties of tragedy. These include the tragedy of Hegelian collision, the tragedy of choice, and that mode of Aristotelian tragedy in which the quality that destroys is also the virtue that dignifies and ennobles. The novel is not a perfect example of any, but it intersects all three.

From the moment Robert Jordan accepts his mission to blow the bridge for Golz, he enters a dramaturgic entity with the bridge: steadily he develops as the incarnation of an ethical absolute—duty to cause. As such, he is shortly in collision with the guerrilla leader Pablo, who becomes a configuration of another kind of duty—duty to one's immediate group. Maria, raped by the Fascists and living with Pablo's band, becomes the embodiment of another absolute or near-absolute: romantic love. She and Jordan make a total commitment to each other in the four days available to them, and it is difficult to see them as absolutes in collision in any perspective; however, she produces a suggestion of confrontation between love and duty within Jordan.

But the collision between Jordan and Pablo is not the fatal, catastrophe-producing opposition. That collision is between Jordan and the bridge. The bridge becomes the concentration of all the forces against him: the military power of the enemy forces, the destructive and absurd nature of war itself, and, finally, fascism as the negation of human liberty and dignity. From the beginning, Jordan as duty to human freedom is aimed straight at the bridge as an absolute of fascism, though an inanimate one. Each destroys the other: he blows the bridge and is himself killed in the action that is a consequence of the blowing of the bridge. Thus Hegel is generally observed, even if the nonhuman identity of the bridge creates a definitely special case.

The novel as tragedy of choice also evades perfect regularity. In the sense in which Bradley and Heilman propound their comparable views of tragedy, there is at the beginning no profound division in Jordan from which develops agonizing and fatal choices. He makes decisions and they are fatal, but they are made automatically; he has rejected his alternatives without even considering them, and his commitment to duty is so total that he is duty incarnate. He accepts the assignment, knowing it carries a strong probability of death, because it literally never occurs to him not to. Nor does he consider abandoning the assignment and escaping with Maria, though he could very easily do so: he has the choice between love and duty before the bridge-blowing but does not even acknowledge that he has it, since duty obliterates anything else on his scales. The apparatus for a Drydenesque heroic tragedy, with its choice between those imperatives, is there, but it never fully develops until the end, when Jordan makes a decisive choice. Yet, he has earlier choices even if he makes them unthinkingly and automatically.

The most visible exercise of choice, and it is itself ambiguous, precedes the end and climax of Jordan's catastrophe by only an instant—and may indeed be considered part of the catastrophe. This occurs after the blowing of the bridge when Jordan is hit and his leg is broken: then clearly a liability to the escape, he insists on remaining behind and delaying the pursuers with a machine gun while the others flee. His own death is thus assured.

The question is: how much choice does he really exercise? Could he have done anything else? The answer is: just possibly. He *might* have been lashed onto somebody's saddle somehow, thus seriously impeding the escape effort. It is irresistibly tempting to take advantage of the ambiguity and declare that Jordan really makes such a choice, for the tragic schema is strengthened across the board thereby. Let us, then, assume volition—but be aware we may be presuming. If the last act is a real choice, it is a dramatic choice for duty over love that arises from what may be, at last, a kind of division in Robert Jordan between those imperatives. And thus the novel may be admitted, not only into the tragedy of division and choice but even into its own subspecies, the heroic tragedy.

When the novel is assessed in Aristotelian terms, Robert Jordan's "flaw" is precisely the ethical absolute that he incarnates: devotion to duty. It is, obviously, a flaw only in the perspective of survival. Although this devotion is indeed fatal, it is his ennobling and self-defining virtue; it brings him to catastrophe, but it also is the means by which he transcends it.

Seen as choice, Jordan's final act is an act of transcendence in all the modes of tragedy the novel engages in; it is the spiritual triumph over material disaster. And in an interior monologue that lasts several pages, he affirms awareness, reconciliation, and transcendence.

> I have fought for what I believed in for a year now. If we win here we will win everywhere. The world is a fine place and worth the fighting for and I hate very much to leave it. And you had a lot of luck, he told himself, to have had such a good life. . . . You've had as good a life as any one because of these last days. . . . I wish there was some way to pass on what I've learned. . . . I'd like to talk to Karkov. That is in Madrid. Just over the hills there, and down across the plain. Down out of the gray rocks and the pines, the heather and gorse, across the yellow high plateau you see rising white and beautiful. That part is just as true as Pilar's old women drinking the blood down at the slaughterhouses. There's no one thing that's true.[2]

Thus he accepts a total order as well as the sum of the events that are his own life. Concomitantly, he appears to understand and accept the working of tragic necessity inside the order.

The pervasive idea that war is the expression of the universe's destructive element has found a crystallization earlier, immediately after Jordan's leg has been broken. He says that many such things happen in war, and Agustin answers that war is a "bitchery" (501).

The transcendence is reinforced when Jordan rejects the increasingly attractive possibility of suicide, not only to terminate pain but to avoid torture and the inevitable disclosure of information it will bring. He endures to engage in a fight with the pursuing Fascist cavalry that can only end his life, but will give his friends time. That act is rendered as a confrontation between the clashing imperatives: Jordan as duty to freedom and the Fascist officer, now a Hemingway surrogate of the bridge, as an emblem of enmity to it.

He ends his life, Young points out, as he began the important part of it: prone on the pine floor of the forest.[3] Thus the final passage is the Hemingway signature, an image that conveys the emotional truth of the novel as the author feels and perceives it. And the image is an

2. Ernest Hemingway, *For Whom the Bell Tolls* (New York: Scribner's, 1940), 502–503.

3. Philip Young, *Ernest Hemingway: A Reconsideration* (State College: Pennsylvania State University Press, 1966), 107–108.

epiphany of the fatal collision of the absolutes, culminating in a polarity upon which the entire novel is constructed. Thus all the modes of tragedy operative in the novel converge without disharmony in its thematic implication: "Life is tragic; one defines oneself by the *action* he takes *against* catastrophe."

So compacted, this appears to be precisely what *The Old Man and the Sea* has to say. Yet the statements of the books are not quite the same, each containing much more than the crystallization. One way of expressing the difference might be to say that *The Old Man and the Sea* is primarily concerned with man's most profound obligations to himself; *For Whom the Bell Tolls* is chiefly preoccupied with his obligations to other men. It is impossible to separate the two completely, of course, and again, the difference is essentially a matter of emphasis.

Much of the difference, obviously, comes from the secondary themes that reinforce the primary. In both books, in fact, certain auxiliary ideas are only slightly less important than the main one. In *For Whom the Bell Tolls*, the supporting concept that bears most heavily upon the book's tragic assertion has to do with what men owe one another. They owe everything including their lives, the book says, and man's chief duty is to do everything he can do for collective human dignity and freedom. The definitive act in the face of catastrophe should be an act in behalf of the human commonalty; it is the individual's chief obligation to sacrifice himself for the human community—and his greatest opportunity for a transcendent act. It is no step at all from this to Camus' plea for joint action against the Absurd—or to Communist discipline.

As ever in good Hemingway, it is the structure that makes this theme, the action that makes the point. Yet the idea is also given a semidirect statement in Robert Jordan's farewell soliloquy, quoted earlier. It is reasonable, indeed, to see this as the principal statement of the book, and those who do so need not be "wrong." It is only in the perspective of the whole Hemingway canon that the simple tragic declaration of the work seems its foremost.

This is the first occasion that obligation to the human community has been developed into an important theme in a Hemingway novel, though it has been dimly foreshadowed in *To Have and Have Not*. Its corollary is the view that all men share a common unity and identity, whatever their transient differences. Many of the Fascists are depicted as completely deserving of our empathy—Lieutenant Berrendo, the trooper Robert Jordan shoots, and the soldiers in the mill, for example—and Jordan even feels a strong surge of sympathy for the tank commander who causes his death. In the execution of the Fascists, those who are clubbed come off better than those who club; the raping of Maria and her friends, and even the shooting of her parents by the Fascists are not parities in brutality. The Loyalists, the good guys, and the Fascists, the bad guys, are neither better than nor worse than each other, within themselves; the difference is in what they fight for.

All humanity has its bright promise and its terrifying capacity for acts of darkness; the latter permeates and gives a somewhat different shape to an enduring Hemingway subtheme, the unity of pleasure and pain. The idea that some get pleasure from inflicting pain on others goes back to Hemingway's beginnings—*In Our Time* is full of it—but it is suffused with a new, black coloration in this book. He liked it, Pablo tells Pilar after the horror of the clubbing; the gypsy speaks with relish of blinding Pablo and selling him; Robert Jordan and Anselmo agree there are men who enjoy killing; the Fascists laugh as they abuse and rape Maria. The desire to inflict pain becomes a concomitant of the evil in man and tends to overwhelm the abstract balance of the pleasure-pain opposites with which earlier work is engaged.

Yet this, too, has its objectification in the book. Robert Jordan experiences his greatest happiness—abstract pleasure—even as he experiences the near-certitude of approaching death—abstract pain.

The happiness of the love affair is the great compensation for the inevitability of catastrophe, and we are back to another Hemingway conception: that it is only consolatory pleasures which are open to us, and which will alleviate the pain of catastrophe. Yet there is a considerable difference in the way the conception is offered here and in *The Sun Also Rises*. There, Jake programmatically pursues a whole system of consolatory pleasures as he lives within catastrophe day after day. Here, Robert Jordan is accorded the opportunity for a great consolation —from the same force that has sentenced him to the universal, and here terminal, catastrophe. Fortunately, he accepts and makes the most of it. The lesser consolations—reading, thinking, drinking, eating, learning— are glided over almost perfunctorily. The great consolation is romantic love, and the author insists that such love is real, does exist. The reader may be somewhat less convinced here than he was by *A Farewell to Arms*, and, yes, *The Sun Also Rises*, but he is convinced.

One constant Hemingway subtheme is substantially altered by the impact of the obligation conception. This is Hemingway's preoccupation with a spiritual aristocracy. In the earlier Hemingway novels, this aristocracy was essentially a matter of style, though certainly it was a style so encompassing that it became substance. Here, it is first a matter of substance, and a very simple substance: the aristocrats of *For Whom the Bell Tolls* are those who will "stay"—those who will meet their responsibilities with their lives. This, and only this, is the spiritual examination. Those who pass it acquire by that circumstance true dignity, and this dignity bestows a style that makes mere manner a little superficial. In early Hemingway, the spiritually elect enforced style to the point that it became substance; in this novel, substance begets style.

On the other hand, bad style is essentially that which indicates unsoundness. Pablo's excessive displays of self-centered cunning are presented to indicate he has become unsound, and his unsoundness is signaled to Robert Jordan at their first meeting. Yet when Pablo has fought well at the bridge, just before murdering his associates from other bands, his manner indicates his return to a species of soundness, even in the face of his wickedness. Anselmo's dependability is also disclosed early, manifesting itself through his uncomplicated dignity in repeated incidents.

The decisive virtue may be found in any context, and possessed of it any context becomes, almost automatically, good style. The pedantic clerk Fernando, the profane Agustin, the silent El Sordo, the loquacious Pilar are all totally dependable and thus are stylistically acceptable in spite of their idiosyncracies. Yet Hemingway finds it impossible, apparently, to divest himself totally of glamor of manner, and an echo of the old absorption appears from time to time. Golz, the converted Russian general, has a rough way of teasing and making jokes on deadly matters that is a highly individuated and attractive external; yet it would not be so if he did not have the internal, total dependability. Karkov's ironic surface mockery proceeds from the same interior austerity. A fusion of ironic manner and reliability is the ideal.

The worst ones are those who profess a quality of mind and spirit they do not have. Don Faustino, the failed bullfighter, disgraces himself at his death when he pretends bravery and scorn but lapses into uncontrollable fear. Passionaria, the propagandist, urges others to die for the Republic, but smuggles her son to safety in Russia. The Fascist captain commits theatrical braggadocio in the fight on the hilltop that only gets him killed by Sordo. Andre Marty, the official Communist hero, cultivates the totally unfounded appearance of military capacity—and kills his own men by the thousands.

In these cases, appearance and reality are at odds. With the good ones, with those who stay, the outer is a reflection of the inner. These aristocrats are above all dependable and direct; the code hero has entered responsible middle age.

This rich complex of detail, incident, and action inevitably postulates the epic, but in fiction, certainly, epic and tragedy need not foreclose each other. Baker aptly calls the book a "tragic epic" and contends that its very success as epic depends on the author's long-established use of synecdoche—the creation of one part to stand for the whole—and the use of a Homerically primitive setting; he sees the tragic center arising from the fact that Jordan's death creates its meaning and victory. Young sees the death as unambiguous spiritual triumph, too: "this time the hero has won," he writes, implicitly and strongly suggesting the parallels between the trauma-and-response of his theory and the catastrophe-and-transcendence culmination of tragedy. He correctly observes that this is the first but not the last death-triumph in Hemingway's novels.[4]

Chaman Nahal objects that there are three stories in the novel-as-epic that have no relation to one another: that of Jordan, Pablo and Pilar, and of the Russians in Madrid; Linda Wagner answers that the unity of the three parts—which she names as the love affair, the operations of war, and the life of Spain—make a unity that is sealed at the bridge.[5] The unity emerges as even tighter, despite the enormous mass of the novel, when one sees it functioning in Hemingway's melody-counter-

4. Baker, *Hemingway: The Writer as Artist*, 150; Young, *Hemingway: A Reconsideration*, 14.
5. Chaman Nahal, *The Narrative Pattern in Ernest Hemingway's Fiction* (Rutherford, N.J.: Fairleigh Dickinson, 1971), 132; Linda Wagner, "The Marinating of *For Whom the Bell Tolls*," reprinted in Linda W. Wagner (ed.), *Hemingway: Five Decades of Literary Criticism* (East Lansing: Michigan State University Press, 1974), 210–11.

point-harmony design. Jordan's line is naturally the melody, with the other characters forming counterpoint lines; Pablo, Pilar, Golz, and Karkov *do* impinge upon him strongly. The incidents and images of life in Spain weave a harmony among these lines that is Hemingway's richest and most diverse "vertical development." This line-key tension, the mass of the work, and its natural division into five sequential narrative segments make its correspondent musical form, very roughly, the symphony. The story parts: (1) the bestowal of mission, (2) the commencement of mission and intimation of the love affair, (3) the flowering of the love affair, (4) the intensified opposition to the mission and the gathering doom, (5) the successful completion of the mission and the triumph-in-death of the hero.

This symphonic resonance is in that special perspective only. In literary tradition, as several have pointed out, the story indeed has many qualities of the epic—the hero who moves through a sequence of adventures and is exalted by his own death, the numerous cast of supporting players, the background of war and intense conflict, the doomed love affair, the many lesser stories. Those who call it an epic are right enough—and one remembers wryly Hemingway's pronouncement that all bad writers are in love with the epic. But even more importantly, it is tragedy, both on its own terms and in the progression of the author's work.

Like other longer works of Hemingway's middle period, about 1931–1949, *For Whom the Bell Tolls* suggests a limited retreat from his earlier absorption with symbol, muted and often indiscernible in the naturalistic surface though it may be. He is, at the least, as intent on the image as ever, but he seems more committed to employing it as his chief weapon in a realistic rendering, in showing everything exactly "the way it was," as he brings it to the tragic singleness of impact. He is concentrating totally on making palpable the passing instant in terms of the way its manifestations look, sound, smell, and feel, and in terms of the emotional responses these specifics produce. He appears to regard, at least intuitively, an attempt at a symbolic network as a deflection of energy from the primary task; thus *For Whom the Bell Tolls* is one of the least symbolic of all his novels.

Yet, for those who wish it, a rudimentary but reasonable symbolic schema can be advanced. The cave of the guerrillas suggests the womb in construction, obviously, and the implication may be that Pablo's band, as representatives of the rest of us, must come out of the womb of comfort and safety and withdrawal to take decisive action for human commonalty. The activating agent is commitment to duty—Robert Jordan, who must accept death in the course of that commitment. In this perspective, as distinguished from its Hegelian function as an absolute emblem of fascism, the bridge might be seen as a link between the present and the corruption of the past; hence it must be destroyed. This is probably overinterpreting, yet it has some plausibility.

Items in other perspectives possibly have more substance. The fulfillment of Jordan's life—his love affair and his transcendence of catastrophe and death—takes place in the mountains, Hemingway's recurring coefficient of the most intense reality and the most heightened awareness. An occasional miniature appears, like the gray horse on which Robert Jordan is riding when he receives what will be his death wound; each of the three men who ride it is killed in turn, and it is not hard to see it as the pale rider's pale horse, a component of death. Nevertheless, the novel is probably best approached as an intense naturalistic effort. As such, it has many formidable achievements, several of which surpass in intensity the totality of the novel. One interesting part of the visual presentation is a careful attention to portraiture, seldom present in earlier novels; do we know what Mike Campbell or Bill or Rinaldi or the priest looks like? Here most of the characters—Golz, Pablo, Anselmo, Pilar—are depicted with care as soon as they appear. Pilar will serve as example: "Robert Jordan saw a woman of about fifty almost as big as Pablo, almost as wide as she was tall, in black peasant skirt and waist, with heavy wool socks on heavy legs, black rope-soled shoes and a brown face like a model for a granite monument. She had big but nice looking hands and her thick curly black hair was twisted into a knot on her neck" (34).

The Impressionist/neo-Impressionist principle of quick, heavy stress on primary elements is still maintained, but the painter's-eye lingers a little longer, the elements surrender to a little more detail. It would be pleasant to find a conscious debt, say, to Velasquez, but I think this would be fanciful, as would any debt to a Hemingway favorite, Juan Gris. The established forms of imagism-impressionism in Hemingway are still functioning.

In the visual presentations of the passing moment, of what might be called a low level of action, there is also more detail, more utilization of the casual movement or action that would have been telescoped out of existence in the earlier novels. The attempt, obviously, is to create literal reality by showing as much as can be shown; the reliance on the dominant image alone has been modified. One passage, for instance, does nothing more than make palpable the components of Jordan's explosives (250), but the relatively insignificant sequence helps invest the blowing of the bridge with intense literal reality by making real the instruments that will effect it. The sudden appearance of Pablo while the others are discussing his execution receives its proper emotional emphasis from such literal but careful imagizing. The intensity of the imagizing is increased as Jordan sustains his fatal injury, even if it does not project a conception beyond itself.

The two great set pieces—the clubbing of the Fascists and the fight on the hilltop—have their chief source of power in the sensory image, but draw on other power sources, too. The chief of these is a familiar Hemingway resource already cited: the principles of tension and development in the sonata composition. Both sequences involve the conflict between narrative melody and counterpoint and the accompanying harmonic, or vertical, development of each; both use an instrumental orchestration of characters in this development; both demonstrate a strong but subtle control of tempo.

There is a particularly formal aspect to the clubbing sequence: Pilar is established with deliberation as point-of-view authority and narrator, and thus the author has a sensibility-chorus which can not only receive and recount impressions, but also pass judgment upon them. Certainly this is a profitable use of artistic necessity, since the events of past time must be told by a character. In describing the killing of the four *guardia civiles* by Pablo, she is playing a crude overture, a reverse-telescope forecast of what is to come. Pablo gives the guards a moment to confess their sins, makes them kneel in a row, then shoots them; shortly, he makes similar but more intense preparations for the clubbing of the village Fascists, gives them time to confess, then has them killed. The killing of the guards finishes in an extended image in which the horror of the execution is poised against and fused with the ordinariness of the day and the surroundings—which is also a beauty and an indifference. Thus the contending keys meet to define themselves.

> And I stood holding the pistol and it was heavy in my hand and I felt weak in the stomach when I looked at the guards dead there against the wall: they all as gray and as dusty as we were, but each one was now moistening with his blood the dry dirt by the wall where they lay. And as we stood there the sun rose over the far hills and shone now on the road where we stood and on the white wall of the barracks and the dust in the air was golden in that first sun and the peasant who was beside me looked at the wall of the barracks and what lay there and then looked at us, and then at the sun and said, "Vaya, a day that commences." (113)

The contrast between the chilling progress of the executions—the major key—and aspects of the ordinary—the minor key—is the basic tension of the piece, and the playing of one key against the other, in the images, chiefly visual, through which they are developed, is a powerful force in the success of the sequence. The minor, appropriately, is often barely discernible, sounding simply as a quick counter to a phrase of the major. Broadly speaking, within each key the presentation of the individual Fascists can be seen as the harmonic, vertical development: their death and their manner of meeting it is a modulation of the major—the shock, or death key—and the thin notes that fit them into the earlier life of the village are an expression of the minor—the ordinary, or life key. The quotidian just touches the shock. There are other full encounters between the keys: the arranging of the lines for the execution is compared to arrangements for a tug of war, a bicycle race, or a holy procession; water is sprayed to quell the dust, as it is on any ordinary day; and just before the executions start, the square is imagized in an ironic evocation of tranquility and ordinariness. The water fountain is made the objectification, the reference, of the quotidian as poised against the extraordinary, the killing. The sequence closes with another view of it, unchanged while so much else has been changed in so short a time, so sadly: "And there was no sound but the splashing of the water in the fountain and I sat there and I thought we have begun badly. . . . I could hear a woman crying. I went out on the balcony . . . and the crying was coming from the house of Don Guillermo. It was his wife and she was on the balcony kneeling and crying" (141).

This is an intensely concentrated configuration. It fuses the fountain, the correlative of day-by-day life in the town, with the weeping widow as a correlative of the irreversible change that violent, multiple death has made upon that life. The town may look the same, but, even though life of a sort goes on, it is changed forever. It is not too much to say that this image has caught the truth of the whole war, as well as one episode of it, and thus has become truly elevated and Poundian, suffused with the emotion of tragedy.

Like the policeman with the baton in *The Sun Also Rises* and Henry alone in the rain in *A Farewell to Arms*, it is a finishing, cumulative image that is the compaction of the emotional and ideational content of the work. Pilar's added comment simply places it in a larger totality: "that was the worst day of my life until one other day. . . . Three days later when the fascists took the town" (142).

The fight on the hilltop proceeds from the same chief strategies as the clubbing—an exact sensory imagery and a melody-harmony-counterpoint development—but a different choice is made in the point-of-view method. Pilar is a fixed authority in the other; here, the effaced narrator is authority, with resultant mobility. He renders and comments anonymously, as off-screen voice, and then moves into other sensibilities as he chooses: those of El Sordo and Joaquin on the hilltop, and of Lieutenant Berrendo among others.

In the development, the opposing emotional forces are life and death; the visibly contending physical elements are El Sordo's band of Republican guerrillas fighting haplessly for their lives on the hilltop and the regular Fascist troops besieging them. It is serviceable to consider that the guerrillas are expressions of the life key, the minor key, and that the Fascist troops are the components of the major death key. Apparent violations of this pattern may be seen as transpositions: the first wave of Fascist troops has been killed and the Fascist captain is tricked and shot by El Sordo in a big sequence. Yet the colliding emotional forces and the opposing military units are generally presented in a matched polarity, and the conflict comes from the fusing of the life-death opposition with the Republican-Fascist contention in a melody-counterpoint tension. Incident and character provide the vertical lines of harmonic development inside each.

The thrust toward life is imagized in the first paragraph:

> El Sodro was making his fight on a hilltop. He did not like this hill and when he saw it he thought it had the shape of a chancre. But he had no choice except this hill, and he had picked it as far away as he could see it and galloped for it, the automatic rifle heavy on his back, the horse laboring, barrel heaving between his thighs, the sack of grenades swinging against one side, the sack of automatic rifle pans hanging against the other, and Joaquin and Ignacio halting and firing, halting and firing to give him time to get the gun in place. (33)

Death and life images are thus fused—the ammunition that carries death is a life component for El Sordo—and all images cluster around his and the band's determination to stay alive. A moment later he kills his horse, which has saved him so far, to make a barricade. This first killing for a life-saving purpose completes the first round of fusion and opposition; more, it completes the characteristic Hemingway overture that forecasts. The horse has made it to the hilltop but is killed there; so will it be with all of them.

Their preparations for a stand are the development of the life key, but the opposing, death key is sounded almost instantly in dialogue and reflection. They know the end, as does the reader-listener. "Wipe the pap of your mother's breasts off thy lips. . . . No one of us will see the sun go down this night" (333).

The death key makes a steady but muted progress in strength, intensity, and devotion. It manifests itself briefly and then is transposed in an initial, unsuccessful attack by the Fascists; it is sounded then chiefly in the consciousness of those on the hilltop, their awareness of their own approaching death always increasing. This key is transposed when El Sordo kills the shouting Fascist captain, but then it crescendos with the arrival of the planes and the bombing and death of those on the hilltop. Meanwhile, it is countered in the minor key by the specifics of the Republicans' efforts to hold to life—most notably the simulated suicide of all five, another possible transposition, which lures the Fascist captain to his death—and in the consciousness of El Sordo. "Dying was nothing and he had no picture of it nor fear of it in his mind. But living was a field of grain blowing in the wind on the side of a hill. Living was a hawk in the sky. Living was an earthen jar of water in the dust of the threshing. . . . Living was a horse between your legs and a carbine under one leg and a hill and a valley with a stream with trees along it and the far side of the valley and the hills beyond" (336).

The death key thus builds steadily but does not surge until after the transpositional shooting of the captain. Then it mounts sharply and contends with the home key in a quick, violent climax: the planes are sighted, the defenders prepare to fire; the planes approach, the defenders begin to fire; the planes dive, Joaquin, the machine gun barrel burning his back, begins an act of contrition; he completes it, the bombs drop and explode. The climax over, the dominant key sounds alone in triumph as the planes pass over the hill three times, strafing. The minor whispers feebly, however, when Joaquin is revealed as still breathing. Lieutenant Berrendo shoots him "as quickly and as gently . . . as Sordo had shot the wounded horse" (346). The *ronde* is completed; the catastrophe and the miniature tragedy of the band get a new force from the suddenly new perspective.

In the triumphant and now unopposed sweep of the death key, Lieutenant Berrendo orders the heads of the guerrillas taken. Yet, as he says prayers for a dead comrade and walks away, he becomes for a moment a life-goes-on figure, a survivor himself. Perhaps the life and death keys are fused in his final manifestation: " 'What a bad thing war is.' Then he made the sign of the cross again and as he walked down the hill he said five Our Fathers and five Hail Marys for the repose of his dead comrade. He did not wish to stay to see his orders carried out" (347). Thus the sonata-allegro is again a broadly utilized model for a Hemingway narration. Its principles are organizing agents for the marvellously precise visual and other physical images, and for the complex and—one is sure—valid psychological insights. All contribute to memorable achieved truth. We are convinced this is not simply the way it was, but the only way it could be.

These two sequences are the peaks of the novel; its nadir is the love scenes. Possibly it is these that set up initial hostility to the book in some critics. These scenes fail because Hemingway not only breaks but reverses a principle that served him so well in earlier works: to undercut anything to do with romantic love so sharply that even the possibility of sentimentality is extinguished. It was a successful tactic not only for him, the poet of implication, but actually, in a quite different way, for his great opposites, Faulkner and Joyce, explorers of the language's fullest possibilities for definition. For Hemingway, to break it and try for the metaphorical statement of romantic emotion was honorable and courageous, but it did not work.

Yet, finally, the inflated quality of the love scenes and their consequent failure does not matter much, and the failure hurts the novel as novel scarcely at all. There is too much else in it. It is massively impressive as epic, as tragedy, as grand novel in the tradition of the masters of all languages. It is the first novel in which Hemingway takes a turn to more elevated, aggressive, "positive" tragedy, and it sets the stance and the thematic pattern that most of the important later work was to follow. It has sections that are masterpieces in or out of context; it is full of richnesses of characterization, atmosphere, and image; its exhortation to political action is remarkable for being at once didactically effective and yet not a corruption of literary or historical honesty. In sum, it has a size and an internal range of effects that no other Hemingway novel has. A book by book ranking of the author's best work is a highly personal affair at best and a fatuous enterprise at worst, but those who consider *For Whom the Bell Tolls* to be his best novel are in a well-fortified position.

The book's immediate sources obviously lie in Hemingway's journalistic adventures in the Spanish civil war, though some of its deeper strengths come from the author's long involvement with Spain.[6] Hemingway knew the Russian "diplomatic" and military bureaucracy in Madrid with reasonable intimacy; he lived in the city through many bombardments, explored all the fronts outside it and many far removed from it, and he roamed about with many different Loyalist armies and smaller military units. In these pursuits, he encountered the flesh models for his fictional characters, though many personalities of the war are mentioned by their proper names, and at least one, Andre Marty, is explored in fictional technique.[7] Koltzov of the novel was the *Izvestia*

---

6. Carlos Baker, *Ernest Hemingway: A Life Story* (New York: Scribner's, 1969), 302–30, 345–48; Wagner, "The Marinating of *For Whom the Bell Tolls*," 200–11.

7. Baker, *Hemingway: A Life Story*, 347–48.

correspondent Koltsor undisguised. The Polish general Karol Simere-zewski, who called himself General Walter, was the physical model for Golz of the novel—but one intuits that Baker suspects other general officers made contributions to the character. Maria bore the name of a nurse who was raped by Fascists, like the heroine, but the fictional Maria was accorded certain of Martha Gellhorn's more provocative physical characteristics. Robert Jordan owes aspects of background and physique to Major Robert Merriman, the Berkeley economist who served with the 15th Brigade; Baker does not recognize an after-the-movie report that Jordan was physically constructed with Gary Cooper in mind, and his subsequent discussion of the Hemingway-Cooper friendship dates its real beginning well after the completion of the novel, though before its filming.[8] Like Harry Morgan, Jordan may have been given someone else's silhouette, but he had the author's own psychic innards. Baker assigns no direct models for the characters Pablo and Pilar, nor any specific sojourn of Hemingway among the guerrillas as the basis of the creation of the guerrilla band.

Certain widely separated events may be the ultimate tribute to the novel's political fairness. Alvah Bessie, Milt Wolff, and other Americans who had participated bravely in the war under Communist discipline denounced Hemingway for "mutilating" the cause he had fought for—he had written Max Perkins earlier that he had put things in the book which no Communist knew, or knowing, could afford to believe—and he was denounced in the *Daily Worker*.[9] Nineteen years later, when Hemingway visited Franco's Spain for the first time since the civil war, fearing arrest, he was instead treated like royalty by the Spanish people, former comrades and enemies alike. They understood better than anyone else, it seems, the truth of his telling of their own tragedy.

8. *Ibid.*, 352–53.
9. *Ibid.*, 356–57, 343.

8

Across the River and Into the Trees
Shaping Death and Victory

As tragedy, *Across the River and Into the Trees* appears to break sharply from an otherwise steady progression in Hemingway's novels. Given too quick a glance, it might seem to return almost exactly to that place in the tragic field occupied by *The Sun Also Rises*, where the protagonist can only bear as well as possible the catastrophe dealt by an uncaring cosmos. Certainly the book makes some movement toward that position, and certainly the situations of Colonel Cantwell and Jake Barnes have important points in common. But on a more intense viewing it is apparent that the book never really leaves the cluster of the last novels, where the tragic pattern requires decisive choice and decisive action. Cantwell resists his catastrophe deliberately, defiantly, even as he knows it is inevitable, and he defines himself by that measured resistance. Hemingway has no more aggressive hero, not even Harry Morgan. If the colonel does not have the choice between escape and destruction that Robert Jordan, Santiago, and Thomas Hudson seem to have, he does face the choice between a somewhat longer life of ever-diminishing possibility and a shorter one with the last phase shaped exactly by himself. Although his essential tragedy is still that of the individual overpowered by the hostile omnipotence, he demonstrates, far more purposefully than does Barnes, that man may win a spiritual victory in that materially foredoomed encounter. Cantwell's decision to rush toward death and dictate all the terms of the meeting thus becomes his triumph. For Hemingway, as for so many tragic authors from Sophocles onward, death itself is never the enemy, though it may be employed as a weapon by the enemy; it can sometimes come as a friend. More importantly, it serves as a climactic opportunity for affirmation and transcendence. And this is what the colonel makes of it.

To perceive the tragic architecture of this novel, however, it is first necessary to perceive its fictional architecture. Philip Young has written that in order to understand Hemingway's last novels, it may be necessary to find a new way of looking at them;[1] this is a fundamental insight, and *Across the River and Into the Trees* is the first of the books to demand it. What, then, is the way? What are the new strategies?

Well, those strategies that are new in the canon are new only for the author; the others seem simply to be intensifications of methods and concepts he has used before. Yet, taken together, they represent an altered Hemingway aesthetic, and it is necessary to understand it before the works can be completely understood as fiction or come into their full stature as tragedy.

Perhaps the most important development is that these novels not only can be but have to be read as fable. Carlos Baker has demonstrated how *Across the River* depends totally on its fabulistic underpinning and has adduced that central fable in detail.[2] Before this book, the Hemingway novel is essentially a naturalistic narrative whose meaning is the statement it makes as a whole. Although that meaning is given weight and edge by a rich symbolism and metaphor in scene, incident, and image, and though some characters, like Rinaldi and the priest in *A Farewell to Arms*, may incarnate abstractions, the novel structure is not a carefully worked out quasi allegory, and the books are not fables. This condition changes with *Across the River*: the naturalistic narrative is and will henceforth be fused with an elaborate fable that approaches the allegorical—though not so unsubtly that the resonances of fiction are lost.

A second new aspect, and a mildly surprising one for this author, is a sudden reliance on literature as source and as shaping force. Myth, the New Testament, Dante, and some iconic works of modern fiction are all utilized as reference points and subtly acknowledged. Their chief

1. Philip Young, *Ernest Hemingway: A Reconsideration* (State College: Pennsylvania State University Press, 1966), 275–77.
2. Carlos Baker, *Ernest Hemingway: The Writer as Artist* (Princeton: Princeton University Press, 1972), 283–87.

use is to give shape and thematic illumination to the autobiographical experience which is almost always the emotional and frequently the literal substance of Hemingway's work. This invocation of literature, limited essentially to Dante and the Bible in *Across the River*, becomes overwhelming in *Islands in the Stream*.

Third, Hemingway's consistent use of musical forms in counterpoint as the structural model for fiction is even more pronounced in his later work.[3] The tension, shape, and emotional impact of the novels come chiefly from the alternation of two conflicting keys. These are comparable to home key and opposing key in the sonata form, Hemingway's most often used musical paradigm. "There is a brooding awareness of the tragic in every line," writes W. W. Seward of *Across the River and Into the Trees*.[4] This awareness is created in large measure by the constantly building tension between the novel's home key, Cantwell's determination to impose form and dignity on what is left of his life, and its opposing key, death ever drawing closer, as in certain mystery plays. The protagonist's choices and actions all proceed from that convergence, and they in turn elevate him to tragic magnitude.

Fourth, in the later works there is evident an increasing preoccupation with the Crucifixion as the great metaphor of human existence. More subdued here, that preoccupation flowers in *The Old Man and the Sea* and *Islands in the Stream*, which were planned as one work. All these considerations are crucial to an examination of *Across the River and Into the Trees*. But the old Hemingway verities are not abandoned; they are incorporated into this new aesthetic.

Cantwell is deep in his extended catastrophe at the novel's outset: he

3. Marcelline Hemingway Sanford, *At The Hemingways* (Boston: Little Brown, 1962), 123–35; Baker, *Hemingway: The Writer as Artist*, 105; Sheldon Grebstein, *Hemingway's Craft* (Carbondale: Southern Illinois University Press, 1972), 35, 69; Ernest Hemingway to Wirt Williams, December 7, 1952. The author says he thought he had the harmony and counterpoint just right in *Across the River and Into the Trees*. George Plimpton, "An Interview with Ernest Hemingway," reprinted in Carlos Baker (ed.), *Hemingway and His Critics* (New York: Hill and Wang, 1961), 28. See Introduction for specific comments.

Daniel J. Schneider, "Hemingway's *A Farewell to Arms*: The Novel as Pure Poetry," reprinted in Linda W. Wagner (ed.), *Hemingway: Five Decades of Literary Criticism* (East Lansing: Michigan State University Press, 1974), 253. Schneider describes theme in the novel as being developed through images like "phrases in a musical key."

4. W. W. Seward, *Contrasts in Modern Writers* (New York: Frederic Fell, 1963), 63.

knows that the only true happiness of his life—his love for Renata—
will be terminated shortly by his damaged heart. He chooses to com-
press the rest of his life into a last visit to her in Venice and into a duck
hunt with his friend Alvarito. The meeting with Renata is his ultimate
realization of, and farewell to, romantic love and life. The hunt becomes a final metaphor of his quest for form and beauty as well as a
symbolic enactment of his meeting with death. His biological death is
almost a postscript to an event already emotionally and artistically completed. Through that precedent ritual he has faced the enemies of spirit
incarnate in the flesh, has defeated all of them by uncompromising
resolution, and so has met death on his own terms.

This simple schema of tragedy is profoundly intensified by the fable
that underlies it. As adduced by Baker, Renata, the young contessa, is
in the fable the image of the colonel's own youth, and it is given to
him to possess it again just before death (Renata, of course, means reborn). The portrait of herself that she gives him is his memory of the
happiness of his youth. Her family emeralds—which she tries to give
him outright but which he knows he cannot keep—are the treasures of
union with the past: human continuity and romantic love. Enriched by
such gifts, he dies in perfect reconciliation.

Contiguous to this is the metaphor of the hunt, not a true fable like
the other but a rich rendering of the rites of passage. Cantwell's host,
Alvarito (a diminutive of "the pale one") is death as friend, who
thoughtfully provides the ceremony's vestments and vessels. A slain
duck and drake suggest Renata and Cantwell himself. The boatman becomes death's surly servant—perhaps the author's old friend Charon—
who first insults and then, his respect won, assists his passenger.

Most tragedies will scan according to most systems of tragedy, and
so with this one: it can be measured against Aristotelian, or Hegelian,
or Heilmanic principles. The colonel functions clearly enough as Aristotelian hero, if certain adjustments are made in the most usual perception of Aristotle's fatal flaw, his cardinal stipulation. The colonel's flaw
is an operational one; what brings him to a quick death is not a shortcoming but his greatest strength, his determination to die with dignity,
on his own terms. He thus joins an elite but not particularly small
group of tragic protagonists for whom fatal flaw and supreme virtue

are the same. In the Hemingway canon alone these would include, at the least, Robert Jordan, Thomas Hudson, and Santiago.

In Hegel's tragedy of the collision of conflicting essences, the opposing elements here are inescapable death and the will to take a kind of victory from that death. Heilman's tragedy proceeds from a fateful choice between two fundamental possibilities:[5] in that perspective, Cantwell *chooses* to make an arduous expedition and to make love to his woman, knowing that his choice for happiness will precipitate his death.

It will be remembered that Frye put forward two philosophic definitions, or boundaries of the tragic field.[6] One holds that tragedy demonstrates the omnipotence of the universe at the expense of the individual; the other says that something within man himself is always the most active agent of his destruction. Like most of Hemingway's protagonists, Cantwell is undone by the inimical cosmos. But his stubborn insistence on finishing life according to his own design makes a substantial contribution to his tragedy. Finally, both hero and story exist between Frye's great tragic limits and touch both.

In this framework, developed by the thematic flow itself, and by complexes of incident and image, certain ideas are shaped. Hemingway's central conception is that of the tragic attitude: life is shaped chiefly by an abstractly indifferent but operationally hostile fate; man cannot prevent his universal catastrophe but through unremitting awareness he can confront it with bravery and style. The following concepts are related to his primary postulate: (1) The elect (the members of "the Order") are those who perceive life's tragedy through suffering and who, by a concentration of will, achieve dignity under the burden of this knowledge. (2) Awareness must be sought and maintained deliberately; transcendence is the end product of awareness. (3) Rebirth of the spirit is possible, no matter how late. (4) Romantic love may be the agent of such a rebirth, though it ultimately causes the greatest hu-

5. Robert Bechtold Heilman, *Tragedy and Melodrama* (Seattle: University of Washington Press, 1968), 3–31.
Cleanth Brooks (ed.), *Tragic Themes in Western Literature* (New Haven: Yale University Press, 1955), 5. Brooks also maintains that the tragic hero incurs suffering "by his own decision."
6. Northrop Frye, *The Anatomy of Criticism* (Princeton: Princeton University Press, 1957), 5.

man sorrow as well as the greatest happiness. (5) Christ crucified is a metaphor of the human condition: in this perspective, all men are Christ. (Peter Lisca has ascribed a Christian substructure to the entire book.[7]) (6) Death and life are a unity.

The novel's horizontal development through opposing thematic keys is, conventionally, given body by a vertical development of harmony. This harmony comprises all those nonthematic, purely literal images, incidents, and simple items of information whose function is to make the colonel and his friends and enemies real people, and Venice and Italy real places. There are many such naturalistic passages, and it is a mistake to see every incident or image as symbolic, just as it is not to see that any passage may be suddenly charged with symbol.

The modulation between keys commences at the outset of the novel, and it instantly awakens the presentiments of tragedy. The first chapter is Hemingway's signatory prevision of the whole work: it presents the protagonist as he struggles to achieve the final ritual of transcendence, only to be blocked and almost thwarted by the boatman, as uncaring emissary of death. Here, Cantwell is not identified as anything but "the shooter," which in context suggests "the seeker." The tone of the sequence and even of the work is sounded by the passing of a flock of ducks through the dark overhead. They become a logo of freedom and, in transcending the earth-bound condition, of immortality. They are both coordinating symbol and steady refrain. In a climactic visualization, they reveal themselves against Hemingway's objectified eternity, the mountains.

Cantwell's attempt to take the ducks—to achieve his life's final possibility—is repeatedly impeded by the "big brute" of a poleman of what is ultimately revealed to be a black boat (recalling the black gondola in another work about death in Venice). The boatman, inevitably, is a suggestion of the ubiquitous Charon.[8] In the face of his constant and threatening hostility, the shooter resolutely maintains his determination to achieve a deliberate and final fulfillment. Their duel, too, is conducted against the backdrop of Hemingway's mountains, always the eternal and absolute. As the shooter helps his surly boatman pole the

7. Peter Lisca, "The Structure of Hemingway's *Across the River and Into the Trees,*" reprinted in Wagner (ed.), *Hemingway: Five Decades of Literary Criticism,* 288–305.
8. Young, *Hemingway: A Reconsideration,* 115.

black boat ahead, he reflects that they are two thirds of the way to where they are going; Cantwell is doing his part to go to death properly, with his own strength. Thus the primal conflict is established and particularized in one smaller and easier to perceive. So, too, is the line of action defined: a doomed protagonist, moving consciously toward death, fights against powerful opposition to give the last moments of his life form and beauty. Tragedy is in visible motion, even if its whole shape is not yet clear.

The second and third chapters develop in great part naturalistically what the first has dramatized fabulistically. The shooter is revealed as a fifty-year-old colonel in the United States Army with a dangerous heart condition, preparing to go to Venice to see his young mistress and, with a friend, to shoot duck. Colonel Cantwell begins the trip from the army installation at Trieste (itself a near homonym of *triste*: sad). As he is driven to Venice in his Buick, he perceives countering images of life and death, some recurring from the past, some appearing in the present; they are simultaneous in the colonel's consciousness, bombed buildings and repairs on a bridge being visible in the same instant. He remembers how he defecated a week before on the exact spot where he had been wounded thirty years before that, how he made a "monument" by adding to it the amount of money his Italian decorations had produced; home and opposing keys softly resume their contention. The "monument" underlines the fusion of his personal mortality with the idea of life's continuity: "It has merde, money, blood; look how that grass grows; and the iron's in the earth along with Gino's leg, both of Randolfo's legs, and my right kneecap."[9] He remembers the dead in the canals in the first war, bloated and swollen. These are shortly countered by what appears to be life images: a big red sail moving across the land in a canal evokes the colonel's vision of "the great, slow, pale oxen," "a fine, big mule," and "a wolf, gaited like no other animal." All of these "move . . . [his] heart" (24).

As he tunes to these ambiguous perceptions of life, Cantwell becomes aware of his driver as another foe on the path—a figure of sloth, provincialism, and dullness closed against life's heart-stirring configurations. The driver would rather sleep than hunt duck—seek illumination

9. Ernest Hemingway, *Across the River and Into the Trees* (New York: Scribner's, 1950), 18–19.

—and he would like to use a Titian for a roadhouse decoration; his hometown (hence personal) museum in Wyoming is a compendium of grossness. Like the boatman, he must be opposed; thus the colonel's apparently gratuitous impatience with him is well founded schematically, if naturalistically it seems harsh. "Did you bring any K-rations... they're liable to eat Italian food, you know" (25). Cantwell must continually battle the driver, in his persona as insensitivity, to maintain his own disciplined awareness.[10] Simultaneously, harmonic development is provided by the colonel's monologue on the history of Venice, and his meditation on military strategy.

Just before they arrive he sees twelve sails paralleling him across the fields—in effect, accompanying him into town; this clear Christian note will be steadily augmented. In Venice, "the strong cold wind from the mountains that sharpened all the outlines of the buildings so they were geometrically clear" (27–28) is an image of Poundian concentration. The mountains are projected not only as the unattainable and the absolute, but as the absolute in its aspect of the eternal; the wind that blows from them is the cold breath of eternity and it clarifies that objectification of human life and death that is Venice. As the wind sharpens the shape of physical objects perceived, so does its intimation of death sharpen Cantwell's perception of life. The first boat the colonel takes is a metaphor for himself:[11] it is an excellent, well-kept craft with a motor which, like his heart, is failing. His promise to the old owner to get him a replacement engine is not to be fulfilled, any more than he himself is to get a new heart.

The two keys alternate quickly as he passes in the boat under a series of bridges. Interpretation of most of these must be speculative: perhaps the first white bridge connotes his youth; the unfinished wooden bridge his life which is to be interrupted before a normal completion; the red bridge, romantic love for Renata; the "high-flying white bridge," his youth regrasped; the black bridge that follows, his death. Such subliminal images accumulate, intensifying the tragic tone. He reflects that two stakes in the canal, joined by chains but not in contact, are "like us"

10. Lisca, "The Structure of Hemingway's *Across the River and Into the Trees*," 297. Lisca sees the chauffeur as Charon.
11. Baker, *Hemingway: The Writer as Artist*, 277–79.

bound together but still apart.[12] In the boat he passes a black diesel craft full of lumber for firewood, and later he looks through the window of the Gritti bar at "the big black hitching post for the gondolas and the late afternoon winter light on the windswept water" (54). Simultaneously a large black barge coming up the canal is making a steady bow wave. The black post is juxtaposed against the waning light of the colonel's waning life; the steady advance of the black barge is the steady advance of death. He is already in the last act of his tragedy, and all that remains is for him to dictate its form.

The counter-key appears with the presentation of the headwaiter as the Gran Maestro of the "Order," who with the colonel has fought for an old country "triumphant in defeat" (55). The description is a clue to the secret of the Order, and it is a catchphrase only on the surface. It is in fact a self-conscious formalization of the mandate of Hemingway's self-chosen aristocracy. Here, the mandate has been reduced to the ability to regard catastrophe with irony and to continue in the face of it, an ability that may be achieved only after suffering. The creation of the "Order" is one more example of the colonel's quest for form, whether it be philosophic or aesthetic, and it has at its center his and the author's view of the permanent wound as the human condition. This is adumbrated in his encounter with Arnaldo, the glass-eyed waiter: he honors those who are faithful to an ideal of conduct and who are mutilated by holding to that faith.

There is within the colonel, too, a conflict that parallels the larger conflict of the composition—that between the destructive and creative impulses in his own nature. He acknowledges it intermittently, speaking of his "good side," then calling himself a breaker of spells and asking "Why am I always a bastard and why can I not . . . be a kind and good man as I would have wished to be" (65). He continuously fights his physical and emotional weaknesses to retain an unblurred observance of his aesthetic and a "proper" stance in his engagement with tragedy. In so doing he illuminates the underlying schematic contention.

In the now profound tension between life and death, Renata enters, Cantwell's great, if transient, fulfillment. Immediately she is defined,

---

12. Baker sees the stakes as the young and old colonel, Lisca as the colonel and Renata. *Ibid.*, 278; Lisca, "The Structure of Hemingway's *Across the River and Into the Trees*," 302.

subtly but directly, by the words that signify her representational quality—"shining . . . youth" (80). She wears a funereal black sweater. So she is the colonel's youth, enclosed in his approaching death.

Almost immediately other aspects of this relationship come into view. There are muted but recurring theologic configurations: Renata fingers the colonel's maimed hand and says she dreamed it was "our Lord's hand" (84). The figure three makes several appearances, with its obvious significance, and there is a heavy play on words in an interior monologue ending "GENERAL WHERE IS YOUR CAVALRY?" (95, read: Calvary). Their meal is a last supper, provided by a devoted disciple, the Gran Maestro. (Lisca adduces additional metaphors.)[13] The not excessive Christlike character of Cantwell underlines the concept that he is Christ only as all men are Christ: they are born to be crucified and to triumph, if they can, within that crucifixion.

In that conversation, where so many thematic elements are linked, the concept of a painting of Renata as a gift of youth idealized is also brought forward. "You can have it if you like it," she says (96), "it is very romantic. . . . while it is not truly me, it is the way you like to think of me" (97).

Various objectifications continue to suggest Renata as love and youth reborn. As they walk, the wind strikes her from behind in such a manner that she seems to be moving backward—representationally receding in time. The aspect of the emeralds as her gift of love is delicately but continually stressed; that they have been passed down from woman to woman in her family underscores them as woman's faithful love and devotion and makes her guardian and giver. But they, like the love affair itself, in view of his failing heart contain the element of death: they are "stones that come from dead people," "cold" and "square" (103) like gravestones. In a paradigm of their situation, Hemingway carves a brief, illuminating dialogue:

> When the twinge came, the Colonel said to himself, the hell with that.
> "Richard," the girl said. "Put your hand in your pocket to please me and feel them." [the emeralds]
> The Colonel did.
> "They feel wonderful," he said.

13. Lisca, "The Structure of Hemingway's *Across the River and Into the Trees*," 302.

Their elevator ride to his floor in the hotel is a metaphor of the ascending happiness that her love and youth bring him. And in the same configuration the termination of that happiness—in his death—is foreshadowed. The ascent in which the colonel handles the controls is exhilarating, "a good ride" (109), but it ends in a bump. Again, their walk down the corridor has its delicate intimations of a journey in time; putting the key into the lock is both the "rite" of reentering the precincts of youth and the symbolic consummation of love, with its attendant shadow.

Whether their sexual consummation takes place in fact is often debated. In his room, Renata has told him "I have a disappointment for you, Richard. About everything" (116). The inevitable conclusion is that she is temporarily incapacitated. Yet some subsequent, highly elliptical erotic imagery presents, at the least, a very close intimacy and strongly suggests completion. It is hard to read the passage of their love making in the black gondola and believe that they are not embracing each other completely—Cantwell thus merging with youth and love in the black envelope of death. A final exchange would seem to remove any doubt:

> "We should not make more love, I know," [says Renata].
> "I don't know. Who says it?"
> "I say it because I love you. . . . Do you think we could once more if it would not hurt you?"
> "Hurt me?" the Colonel said. "When the hell was I ever hurt?" (157)

Their conversation and their movements through Venice contain much that is purely harmonic in character—the physical details of the city and its places, the colonel's reflections on military life—in short, all nonthematic detail. But when he calls her "Daughter" and asks if she would like to run for "Queen of Heaven" (83), something of consequence is intended. Cantwell, who often invokes Dante,[14] insinuates here that she is Beatrice, a spiritual constant and support if not guide in his strange journey. That journey, already in one perspective a return to the past, is soon to become a stepping off into the future. After they have parted and he is alone in the hotel room, he places her emeralds "cold and yet warm, as they take warmth . . . from his bad hand into

14. Young, *Hemingway: A Reconsideration*, 114.

his good hand" (166). In the pocket of his pajamas, over his heart they become that great Hemingway constant, consolation in catastrophe.

The key of approaching death predominates after he wakes in the morning. It is voiced in the colonel's reflection, "I guess the cards we draw are the ones we get" (179). Later, when Renata asks him what has given him his greatest sorrow he answers "other people's orders" (210). Reminders of death crescendo. He walks into the "wild cold wind off the mountains" as he watches "black-clad people climb out of the black-painted [gondola]" (184). He is insulted by two ill-mannered youths who menace him—scavengers of death come too early —but, responding in the home key, he drives them away with fierce resolution, holds purposefully to life. His progress through the markets of Venice is chiefly harmonic, but the temporarily quiescent death key surges powerfully as he is hit by a quick heart attack in the hotel lobby. Made aware of the great nearness of his death, he leaves the green stones in the hotel safe—thus providing for the return of love to the girl, his youth to the past, the continuity of life to Venice itself.

When he meets Renata later, after three telephone calls, she is again in a black sweater. In an image recalling that of her hair blown forward to suggest reversal of time, he asks her to stop and turn her head so her hair will blow "obliquely"; thus he signifies a wish to freeze time in the present. Their breakfast, a return to the Gritti, provides the balancing harmonic development, with much literal detail. He speaks bitterly of a former wife, who sounds a great deal like a former Hemingway wife as seen by Hemingway; he jabs at Eisenhower and Truman, at war correspondents and p.r. officers. Yet the thematic keys break through as they lie together in his room upstairs. " 'That is the good thing about your going to die,' she says, 'that you can't leave me' " (211). He thinks how close life comes to death when there is ecstasy, and how her black sweater feels. "Death is a lot of shit. . . . I have seen it come. . . . it comes in bed to most people . . . like love's opposite number" (220). She asks him for anecdotes about himself, "Sad stories of the death of kings" (236). And she says, "I want you to die with the grace of a happy death" (240).

The significance of Dante as a force in the colonel's life is at least partly defined here. She says he sounds like Dante, "And for awhile he was and drew all the circles. They were as unjust as Dante's, but he drew them" (246). Cantwell is in part the designer and contriver of his own life, and therefore, like Dante, of his own hell—just as he is, in part, Christ crucified.

In an interior monologue as the girl lies sleeping, he reflects that they may never see each other again, that this may be his last day of life. He visualizes death "with its ugly face, that old Hieronymus Bosch really painted" (253). But the life key continues to sound valiantly and the colonel's monologue closes on a note of transcendent triumph, as will his life: he acknowledges again the great gift of love and restored youth accorded him, in substance and in retrospect, as he looks at the sleeping Renata and at her portrait.

After Renata awakes, they go to a jeweler's shop to buy her his farewell gift. Much is made of this: she has already chosen it, they have discussed it, he has soliloquized upon it. Its significance is thus underlined. It will be one of two small, jeweled ebony heads. He sees no significant difference, but she chooses the one on the right with the "nicer" face (259). The carving is an effigy of the colonel himself; the black signifies himself after death, the studded jewels, the happiness she has brought to him. The expression suggests what he has called his good side, his better self. It is the one she prefers to cherish, though the colonel knows the other, bad, side is an equally true representation. This is the memory he will bequeath her, and he must pay for it by a check through an intermediary, Cipriani; that is, he must call upon his stored resources to give her the memory of himself as they both wish it to be. Later, she pins the carving high on her left shoulder, carrying the colonel in death near her heart for all to see.

Walking in the wind, as always a portent, he tells her again he must return all the stones and has left them for her in the Gritti safe; he does not wish her to be forever alone without love to give elsewhere. At Harry's bar, they image a trip to the American West, where they view the highest mountain, but do not complete the fantasy by climbing it: they approach and are thus witness to the unattainable ideal but know they cannot possess it. The colonel reiterates that he is sending a check to Cipriani—an objectification of the Hemingway perdurable that one must pay for everything—and they return to the Gritti, their emotional home, for their final meal. For entree, Cantwell orders sole—a clear play on sound—and they drink with it a wine from Vesuvius, a concomitant of his erupting and thus expiring heart.

As she drinks the wine with him, Renata is herself inducted into the Order, as grand secretary, and ironically told the motto: "Love is love and fun is fun. But it is always so quiet when the goldfish die" (271). Renata is now experiencing her own catastrophe, with its pain and shock, and must nevertheless continue; she thus earns and is accorded a place in the membership of those who have learned that bitter secret.[15] The Gran Maestro is asked to "produce a few smells from your off-stage kitchen, even if the wind is against us" (273), and his role becomes clear in its entirety: it is to present those rituals, whatever they may be, that will provide such comfort and solace as is possible in the face of catastrophe. It is a priestly function; he stands clear as an apotheosis of consolation.

Afterward they take the old boat with the bad engine—that metaphor of the colonel—to the garage landing. Why can't she go on the duck shoot? she asks. He tells her she isn't invited and must not ask for an invitation, and the meaning of the hunt as an ultimate epiphany emerges more strongly. She has really asked, Why can't I die too?, and been told, It is not your time and you must not make it so.

Loyally, over Cantwell's objections, she keeps the old boat for her return trip, and he, giving in, says "I only give orders and obey orders" (277). It is another half-disguised statement of the concept so strong in the work: that the universe always defeats the individual, functioning as impersonally as a bureaucracy, and he must accept defeat with grace.

In its presentation of the duck shoot, the first chapter has been overture and preview to the work. Four short chapters near the end also deal with the shoot: they reprise, strengthen, and complete the initial representation. After this, there is only the coda of the colonel's physical death.

In the final scenes, the life and death keys crescendo in conflict, then fuse in ultimate reconciliation. The colonel seeks and achieves his

15. Baker, *Hemingway: The Writer as Artist*, 272. Baker sees her admitted for comparable reasons, but considers hers as only an "honorary membership" because of her youth.

epiphany even as death closes in on him; in a more muted thematic line, a series of images urges again the universality of Christ as prototype of all men, the ordeal of death as their common end, and the spiritual transcendence of it as their best hope.

The boatman, death's emissary, continues to mar Cantwell's hunt. Yet in spite of him, the colonel kills a mated pair of ducks, which again evokes the wedding of spirit he has achieved with Renata, and its ending by imminent death—an instant and total illumination. He reflects, "it is murder . . . and what isn't nowadays?" (279). He kills others lured in by the decoy female mallard, "treachery speaking to them" (280). Here the same phrase is in effect sounded in one key and transposed instantly into the other, as it was in the first chapter: in one aspect, a treacherous promise has lured Renata and himself to their catastrophe; in an opposing perspective, Renata herself has summoned their joining and presented to him both happiness and death.

The last duck he is to shoot is a single drake, "travelling to the sea," and the colonel sees him "sharp and clear and in the sky with the mountains behind him" (281). He is a vision of life free and soaring, in sight of the unattainable ideal, moving toward the unknown; he mirrors the colonel, and his death is a configuration of the colonel's death. The vision and the death are essentially simultaneous, and one triumphs in the other.

The colonel works with the pole as the boat goes in to shore, "the snow mountains" now in sight, he and the boatman "in complete coordination" (296); he and death's envoy move in understanding now, and rapidly, but still with deliberation.

Bobby the dog recovers a crippled drake, which is put into the sack with the female mallard, both to be ultimately set free. This pairing suggests the cyclical resurgence of life, preserved generically by animal instincts and, perhaps, by fidelity.

The colonel and the boatman make their peace and Cantwell offers him a drink; he has accepted death and its injustices and bears no grudge. Later it is revealed, on a naturalistic level, that the boatman's hostility comes from the fact that Allied Moroccan troops raped his wife and daughter. Ironically, the servant of death is shown to be another victim of the random destructiveness of the universe.

The Christian symbols in this final sequence begin with the drive to the lake: three shooters ride together toward the hunt—Jesus and his two companions in crucifixion. The colonel's swollen hands again suggest stigmata. His soliloquy, "You going to run as a Christian? . . . I honest to Christ don't know" (291) presents the concept directly. The boatman has killed four ducks and found three cripples—seven, the number of days in Holy Week in which Christ went to death. Cantwell looks at his line of bagged ducks and thinks that he has barely a squad, a squad being twelve, the number of disciples. As the boatman poles the boat "sharply for the shore," Cantwell shares with him a communion of wine from a flask given him by Renata.

With quest, vision, and passage done, there remains to Cantwell only the final discharge of responsibilities and the physical act of dying. His reflections are valedictory: he has sent the four ducks promised to friends at the Gritti, although he regrets they've forgot to give the hunting dog a sausage. "You have said goodby to your girl . . . you shot well and Alvarito [death] understands. That is that" (306).

Cantwell's final actions demonstrate that deliberation which is his concomitant of form. He orders Jackson to his final destination, Trieste. He writes a note directing the disposition of his guns and of the portrait, the guns memorials of his manhood and his quest, the portrait of Renata a memorial to his youth. He gets into the back seat of the Buick under his own power, shuts the door "carefully and well" (307), and dies. Later, reading the colonel's order that the portrait and guns be returned to the Gritti for their "rightful owner," Jackson thinks, "They'll return them all right, through channels" (308).

This signatory and culminating image is again that of a universe at once indifferent and, by reason of that indifference, hostile. But Cantwell triumphs over it spiritually in going forward to meet it, and in successfully creating the design of that encounter. Throughout the extended confrontation he celebrates and makes himself champion of those qualities cherished in his own life and so, of life itself. He thus transcends catastrophe, and in the transcendence defines and elevates himself to truly tragic stature.

No Hemingway novel has been as controversial as this one; none needs deep exegesis so desperately to come into its own. One of its chief architectonic tensions is that between the colloquial idiom in which much of it is couched, and the vast formality of its structure and the language of its more profound imagery. It is the first that gives a naturalistic scaffolding to the second, joining the symbolic fable to the literal event. It is in the deceptively easy idiom, too, that most of the harmonic development takes place. And it is here that the work is most vulnerable. In countering the structural formality, the author sometimes appears cute, ponderous, even narcissistic. These imperfections recede into comparative unimportance when the work is understood: they are the occasional faulty notes that necessarily mar but cannot destroy a composition of awesome plan and singular beauty. *Across the River and Into the Trees* is notably imperfect, but it is a resounding work of art.

9

The Old Man and the Sea
The Culmination

The Old Man and the Sea was started and more than half-finished during the visit of Adriana Ivancich and her mother with the Hemingways
in Cuba, in late 1950 and early 1951. Making his own life imitate his
art, not unlike the impotence he produced after *The Sun Also Rises*,
Hemingway was delighted to fancy he generated a remarkable rebirth
of creative energy from Adriana's presence. He started the novel just
after Christmas and completed it on February 23, though he still had
to revise to achieve its full "implicaciones." It was his fastest stretch of
writing on a major book: eight weeks.

As Baker details the history of composition, the author first perceived
this novel as part three of his long novel.[1] When another section was
written immediately after, he changed this part three to part four, en-
visioning it as a coda to the earlier sections. But more than a year later
he decided to pull it from the big book and publish it by itself. Many
circumstances had pushed him glacially to this decision: the intense
enthusiasm of those who read it, Leland Hayward's urging of a one-
issue publication in *Life* magazine, perhaps a desire to "show" critics
and reviewers with a book more powerful, less vulnerable, and easier
to understand than *Across the River and Into the Trees*. But doubtless
his best reason was his deep perception that the coda was so much better
than the rest of the novel that it had to stand alone. In early 1952, he
informed Scribner's of his decision and the long publishing process be-

1. Carlos Baker, *Ernest Hemingway: A Life Story* (New York: Scribner's, 1969),
488–90.

gan. As part of the tetralogy, the novella had been called "The Sea in Being"; a phrase that Hemingway and Charles Scribner used casually to describe it in letters became its final, famous title. No other novel brought Hemingway such instant acclaim from both reviewers and formalistic critics, as well as bringing—at last—Pulitzer and Nobel prizes.

The rest of the long novel, finally *Islands in the Stream*, scarcely impinges upon this severed portion; almost all insights it brings to *The Old Man and the Sea* illuminate only the chronicle of composition. Yet contrarily, the shorter book powerfully illuminates the one that it left and so reduced, and *Islands in the Stream* is immeasurably strengthened when viewed in the perspective of its lost, best part.

That part has been seen as a paradigm of the human experience; in it, certainly, are compounded and transmuted its author's deepest psychic ordeals and triumphs. Consequently, it is almost bizarre to note that the work had its *donnée* in an incident told Hemingway by a friend in 1936 and casually noted by him in an *Esquire* article.[2] The friend had seen an old Cuban fisherman beating sharks off a big fish tied alongside his skiff. His weapon was the oar of the boat.

Immediately on publication, it was perceived that the book was layered with meanings beside the naturalistic, which was itself an overpowering universal. In attendant reviews and essays in books, Baker, Breit, Schorer, and Young considered all of the cardinal interpretations.[3] These were the naturalistic tragedy, the Christian tragedy, the parable of art and artist, and even the autobiographical mode. Baker saw the realistic and Christian tragedies as almost inseparable and the dominating aspect of the book; he pointed also to the art-artist and autobiographical strands. Young felt that the triumph of the work was the triumph of classical tragedy and saw it as the ultimate fusing of Hemingway's personality and art; he too saw the art-artist implication and the autobiographical elements as closely linked and noted the Christian symbol-

2. Ernest Hemingway, "On the Blue Water," *Esquire*, V (April, 1936), 184–85.
3. Carlos Baker, "The Marvel Who Must Die" and "The Ancient Mariner," in Carlos Baker, *Ernest Hemingway: The Writer as Artist* (Princeton: Princeton University Press, 1972), 288–328; Harvey Breit, review of *The Old Man and the Sea*, in *Nation*, CLXXV (September 6, 1952), 194; Mark Schorer, "With Grace Under Pressure," *New Republic*, October 26, 1952, p. 20; Philip Young, *Ernest Hemingway: A Reconsideration* (State College: Pennsylvania State University Press, 1966), 121–33.

ogy. Breit was most impressed with the universality of the realistic tragedy, and Schorer with the work as a drama of the artistic struggle, a struggle by no means confined to the author.

Most subsequent criticism, and it has been voluminous, has proceeded essentially from those lines set down so immediately. However, the possibility that the novel is a deliberately constructed, three-tiered (and possibly four-tiered) fable perhaps should be considered. The view here is that the naturalistic, the Christian, and the art-artist modes are all constructed carefully enough to stand alone, yet are so tightly laminated that no joining shows, and that the autobiographical is intuitive. Together these are, in final aspect, an unbroken unity. And the commitment to fable that Hemingway exhibited in *Across the River and Into the Trees* is consequently even more in evidence here.

Yet the first level, the naturalistic, is not a fable at all, and its realistic strength enhances and is enhanced by the fabulistic narratives. It *is* tragedy, the most complex Hemingway has written, and all the fables built upon it are equally tragic and are tragedy cast in that same design.

For it intersects many species and variations of tragedy, the Aristotelian being only one. These include: (1) the tragedy of the fatal flaw of *hubris*, in the sense of overreaching (Aristotle); (2) the tragedy of fatally conflicting imperatives or states of being (Hegel); (3) the tragedy of the fateful choice (Heilman-Bradley); (4) the special case of Aristotelian tragedy in which fatal flaw and supreme virtue are the same. As always, the different conceptions finally merge into a unity. The novella is much less weighted toward the concept that dominated the earliest novels—that man is reasonlessly punished by a hostile universe. Santiago acknowledges himself as the author of his own ruin: he knows that he has tried to go beyond the limits of human possibility in making his choices and obeying his imperative, and he knows that he must be punished for it. His overpunishment is one of the eternals of tragedy.

His serene acknowledgment of his responsibility inevitably recalls that of Oedipus in *Oedipus at Colonus*, and though there is no evidence whatever to suggest the play as even a minor source, another vital resemblance exists. Santiago is first encountered after the fall, and some time after; he is not only in a cast-down state but an accursed one. No longer champion, eighty-four days without a fish, he is "salao"—the worst kind of unlucky. His beginning in these depths makes his rise to the pinnacle of taking the fish more thrilling, the catastrophe of its loss more heartrending—and his victory of spirit inside and after that catastrophe more life-enlarging and transcendent.

The tragic action that starts in those depths clusters about certain dominant elements. These may be seen as (1) the magnitude and implicitly ordained quality of the struggle, (2) the heroism of the protagonist in that struggle, (3) the power of the forces arrayed against him and the inevitability of catastrophe once those forces are set in maximum motion, (4) the unalterable operation of a great and harmonious order. Fate as a presence is always powerfully felt, but Santiago is never displaced as the generator of his own tragedy. In the Hemingway sonata-allegro conflict of key areas, his will is home key, and all that drives against him is the opposing key.

In the necessarily rough parallel between novel and sonata-allegro, the magnitude of Santiago's struggle, its fated quality, and the sense of order that invests it serve as a rich, dense harmony between his heroic resolve and the forces arrayed against it. Intimations of all these tragic elements appear in early passages, before the collision of keys. The power of the enemy is evoked in lines that set forth Santiago's continuing undeserved punishment. He has gone eighty-four days without a fish, but there is a careful comparing to forty days in a fishless desert, a clear link to the Eucharistic fable, and his patched sail seems the "banner of permanent defeat."[4] His is old and has old scars, and he is a failure in the eyes of his fellow fishermen; he has no food until the little boy begs some for him. But immediately posed against these manifestos of cosmic hostility are those of his own heroism: his sea-blue eyes are "cheerful and undefeated" (2); he maintains a ritual of dignity against his poverty and hunger; he insists he is still strong enough for a huge fish. When the old man says with prophetic confidence that the greatest fish come in September, he is forecasting both magnitude (the size of the fish) and order (September: life's autumn: a time of harvest).

The old man himself has perceived the working of order almost

4. "The Old Man and the Sea," in *Three Works of Ernest Hemingway* (New York: Scribner's, 1962), 1.

from the outset. He does not complain or indulge in even secret self-pity about his eighty-four days without a fish; he remembers that he has gone eighty-seven empty days once before. Both numbers are crucial to the Christian interpretation, but he simply feels such vacancies are part of a great cosmic cycle. When he wakes and prepares to go to sea, he follows a ritual that is his private order; he joins the larger order of community in carrying his mast to the harbor in the progress of all the fishermen, then rowing to sea to the accompaniment of the oars of his fellows. Now he is entering the largest order, the order of the sea and of the universe, and the novel clearly advances it as divine order. Yet already Santiago intuits he will transgress that order: he knows he is "going far out" (13).

The hooking of the fish is not only the first climax of the composition: it is a passage of definition, an objective correlative, and it has a complex, if compact, unity. The keys come to full collision for the first time. They pound each other in an almost regular alternation, and in the repeated shocks many of the tragic conceptions of the work are urgently set forth.

The old man's "yes, yes" as he feels the fish take the hook at a great depth is the signal that it has happened: the anticipated has become the reality. He has found the fish by his knowledge of the order in which he lives. He has steered intuitively by the birds and fish he sees; among the lines he has conscientiously put out at varying depths, he has been sure that one goes very deep, and that it is skillfully baited on a strong hook. And he is always aware, in his reflections, that he is "far out" (13, 21), that he is pushing the margins of that order. The awe he feels at the weight and strength of the fish is the first undisguised declaration of the magnitude of the action, a magnitude made even larger by the first major reversal of the work—the fish's taking command of the skiff and commencing to tow it. In the old man's soliloquy, he makes clear that he and the fish are incarnations of different states of being, that each is noble, and that each is dominated by a single imperative of existence. It is equally clear that the old man has made the choice that sets the tragic action in motion. He reiterates that it has been his decision to go far out, to overreach, but an equally strong, if implicit, choice is his automatic and unspoken decision not to cut the line. "His choice had been to stay in the deep dark water far out beyond all snares and treacheries. My choice was to go there to find him beyond all people. Beyond all people in the world. Now we are joined together and have been since noon. And no one to help either one of us. Perhaps I should not have been a fisherman, he thought. But that was the thing I was born for" (26).

Thus the Aristotelian *hubris* of overreaching, the Hegelian war of imperatives, the fateful choice of Heilman and Bradley are all openly in operation. So are the ideas of magnitude and order, and strongly suggested is the idea of fate, not impossibly preordination. Now the battle of the keys has been fully joined, and for a time the fish is to be the dominant voice in the opposing key: it is the old man's will and strength against his. After the fish is taken, however, he will be in effect transposed to home key, and the conflict will then be between the fused nobility of the man and the fish against all the destructive forces that attempt to negate their now shared achievement.

From this point, the key battle maintains a steady intensity, rising imperceptibly, sometimes striking minor climaxes, always developing the conceptions now revealed. The motifs of magnitude-order-imperative-resolve-ordeal make a densely textured pattern in the conflict, one in which they cannot be cleanly separated from one another. Yet an arbitrary and approximate division may be useful.

Santiago knows his ordeal has begun the moment the fish demonstrates that he, not Santiago, is in control: a continuing element in Santiago's heroism is his knowledge that he is up against a force far more powerful than himself, and his attendant resolution to fight it anyway, and to the death—his own or his adversary's—"I do not care who kills who" (31). But pain by pain his sufferings mount, and they bring the naturalistic tragedy ever closer to the Christian fable: the agony of his back braced against the line (in the New Testament reference, Jesus' back against the cross); the easing of the contact with a burlap sack (the cloak or robe); the raw rim his straw hat makes on his forehead under the scorching sun (the crown of thorns); the bleeding hands (the nail wounds); the forcing of his face into the raw dolphin (an act of communion); his hunger and thirst and the need to eat and drink to keep sufficient strength.

But he is always aware that the fish is suffering, too, that the fish is weakening from hunger, that the fish is as heroic as himself. In the ordeal he suffers and knows the fish is suffering, he sees them as fated brothers, as heroes foreordained to fight: in the Christian fable, they will emerge as twin Christs.

But the entire battle remains a demonstration that the old man knows that both the fish and himself are fulfilling their imperatives with absolute fidelity. Not only is his determination to prevail constantly affirmed: so is his growing love for the fish, and an almost mystic desire to identify, to become one with him. Thus Hegelian imperatives indeed clash as external physical entities, but they have now also taken shape inside Santiago's mind as opposing components. They're of a somewhat different shape, however, as Santiago's love for the fish struggles sadly with his determination to achieve it by the death triumph. The issue is never in doubt, but it thrusts upon Santiago a whole new complex of emotions. He is sorry for the fish even as his resolve to kill him remains steady. Because of the fish's "behavior and great dignity" (41), no one is good enough to eat him. But Santiago's fateful choices have been made, and he stays with them.

The magnitude of the struggle—dimly foreseen at the outset, exploding into shape when the fish strikes and takes command of the boat—is constantly expanding. Aristotle's "action of a certain magnitude" has been triumphantly established; the old man's daring in going out so far and winning will emerge more and more clearly as Aristotle's fatal flaw after the killing of the fish; his violation of the ordained order then is to receive its inescapable punishment.

One of the beauties of the book is that steady unfolding of the order, image by image: each thing has its place in a giant symbiosis—sometimes kind, often cruel, but decreed and immutable. One by one, before the joining, Santiago has encountered its manifestations: flying fish, birds, dolphins, in their interrelationships; the Portuguese man of war, a poisonous intimation of evil; the comic turtles with their usefulness; the schools of fish in movement. Santiago notes lovingly that they are in their proper place, so to speak—even as he is proceeding to go beyond his own place. When he is being towed by the fish, having transgressed, the harshness that is part of the order is illuminated by the little bird that rests briefly on the taut line, before it proceeds landward to encounter the predatory hawks and likely its death. The episode of the two marlin fixes not only that harshness, but seems deliberately presented as a compaction of the universal fate. In retrospect, Santiago catches and butchers the female marlin "as quickly and as kindly as possible" (27), while her mate refuses to leave the area of the boat. His commitment and fidelity, like Frederic Henry's, has brought him in the end grief and loss: the universal catastrophe, says the author, comes to all living beings. It, too, is part of the order, and the order is clearly established as the governor of the world well before Santiago comes to the killing of the fish.

Order's most intense compaction may be the stars. Santiago looks at them three times to be sure of where he is, to reassure himself of the unchangeability of things, and, finally, to identify himself in a close kinship with them, "the stars that are my brothers" (92). Inevitably, the appearance of the stars at the end of each of the three parts of *The Divine Comedy* asserts itself; though there is nothing in this work proper to support the deliberate parallel, there is an abundance of evidence in the parent novel, *Islands in the Stream*, where Dantean references are heavy. So the stars here do seem invocations of Dante, and as Dantean manifests of eternal, even divine order, they are not accidental.

The first part of the battle of imperatives ends in the killing. In that drama, the power of those commitments, the intensity of ordeal for man and fish, the magnitude of fish and event reach their greatest intensification and become most awesome when the fish jumps high out of the water as the harpoon is killing him. Both the jump and the first rush of blood are decisive incidents in the Christian fable, but they add a less explicit mystery to and thus increase the magnitude of the naturalistic tragedy; so does the circumstance of the marlin circling the boat three times, after the third sunrise, before he succumbs and takes the spear.

The fish has been a tragic protagonist, too, though an observed one, in its own Hegelian drama, and it is reasonable to consider that this secondary tragedy has had its catastrophe in the death of the fish: it has lost its fight for life. Yet the fish is to suffer mutilation even after death, and it may be equally reasonable to conclude that this mutilation

179

is the final phase of its catastrophe and so coincides with the prolonged catastrophe of Santiago. At that point, Santiago is viewing himself and his catch as one.

The dying leap of the fish has underlined the highest point in Santiago's quest and struggle: here, he has apparently won the war of imperatives and achieved the fish. It seems for a moment that he has indeed won. But he fears he has not; knowing his violation, he already has forebodings of approaching nemesis: "If sharks come, god pity him and me" (37).

The sharks do come. Now he and the fish are to be their covictims: the fish has been transposed to home key, at last in complete unity with Santiago, and the dominating image, or phrase, in the opposing key has become the sharks. In the design of one species of tragedy, they *are* nemesis; the old man's violation of order has called them up in an obvious and inevitable stream of causation. If he had not gone further to sea than his proper limits, he would not have caught a fish big enough to tow him to sea for three days; if the fish were not so big, he could have put it, butchered, inside the boat and kept it safe from sharks; if it were not big enough to pull him to sea for three days, the sharks would not have had time and space to destroy it completely. The end was in the beginning, when he first went "too far out"; the stream of blood that went a mile into the ocean and drew the shark was simply a step in an inexorable process more than well advanced. All this is the ultimate implication of the sentence, "The [first] shark was not an accident" (56). He is not: he is an inescapable part of both natural and tragic orders.

Santiago's suffering up to this point has not yet been catastrophic in this perspective; it has been, rather, a great ordeal that he must and does withstand to achieve a triumph on that same material plane. With the coming of the first shark, his true catastrophe begins in the naturalistic mode of the story—in the Christian fable, it is hard not to consider that he has completed one cycle of crucifixion and is beginning another. Even as he is battling them with mythic courage, he reflects often on his violation, his going "out too far," and is aware that this retribution is part of the order and ultimately just. He knows his fight is lost from the start; he strikes at the sharks "with resolution and complete malignancy" but with little hope. Yet even without hope, he is defining himself by the force of his struggle *against* catastrophe: he is not, like Jake, simply *enduring* bravely and gracefully. He is fighting back with all his personal resources, and his battle is the more heroic, and the more defining, because he knows it is lost from the start. Two incidents join catastrophe to crucifixion beyond doubt: when he sees approaching sharks, he makes a sound "as a man might make, involuntarily, feeling the nail go through his hands and into the wood" (60). And having broken knife and oar and striking with his unshipped tiller—the number three again—he feels something "break" in his chest and he spits out blood to mix with water, just as the blood from the fish so mixed. When the fish is devoured and destroyed, except for the head, the catastrophe is done and reconciliation may begin.

Santiago pronounces not only his understanding but his acceptance of what has happened to him when he acknowledges, "You violated your luck when you went out too far" (66). In spite of the great over-punishment it has inflicted on him, Santiago accepts the order whole and still pronounces it good. "The wind is our friend anyway, he thought. Then he added, sometimes. And the great sea with our friends and our enemies. And bed. . . . It is easy when you are beaten, he thought. . . . I never knew how easy it was. And what beat you, he thought. 'Nothing' he said aloud. 'I went out too far' " (68). He has reflected, too, that many will worry about him, that he lives in a "good town" (65). When he sees and then enters the glow of Havana—a more decisive event in the Christian fable, where he is entering blessed-ness—he is entering, here, reconciliation and acceptance.

The fish itself is destroyed, but nothing can destroy his heroic action in having taken it and endured so much with it. The greatness of this triumph is underlined by the shift to the point of view of the little boy, who understands all, the measuring of the skeleton by the other fisher-men, the conversation with the boy. Both the physical finality of the destruction and the ineradicable triumph of his act are possibly inti-mated in his final trip up the hill with his mast, his cross, in which he falls seven times. He looks back from the hill and sees by the street light the great tail and the head of the fish "with all the nakedness between" (68).

He has won the triumph of the spirit in the deed itself, though its physical substance has been destroyed. That triumph is both clarified and intensified by his plans to go out again with the boy, using renewed parts of scrapped machines as tools. He has risen from physical defeat to transcendence: we know he will always go out again as long as his body obeys him. He has already defined the core of himself and provided us with one variant of the theme of the tragedy in his pronouncement, "A man may be destroyed but not defeated" (58)—that well-known Hemingway *double-dicho* that means almost the same if it is reversed. And he has attained the final crown of the tragic hero: awareness.

The whole theme of the literal tragedy, as well as each of the other modes, is concentrated into a double final image: the skeleton of the fish, waiting to go out on the tide with the other garbage, and, shortly afterwards, the old man's dream of lions, the last line in the book. The first, so like the image of man's coffin and bull's ear in *The Sun Also Rises*, objectifies once more the impermanence of all physical beings and states. The second, the lions, suggests that deeds once done are fixed forever in memory, and not impossibly, somehow in time.[5] They are man's only real monument against defeat, and death.

The most visible fable beneath the naturalistic tragedy of the book is the Christian fable, and it seems so much a part of the first that division may be a violence. It, too, is unambiguously tragic, and it is so in the face of a continuing cogent argument that Christian tragedy is impossible.[6] Baker, Burhans, and Waldmeir have convincingly interpreted crucifixion and resurrection as the heart of this tragedy.[7]

However, the novel as Christian tragedy is a complex vision, and

---

5. Baker, in *Hemingway: The Writer as Artist*, 308–309, sees the lion as memories of Santiago's youth, functioning in a "brace-relax . . . systolic-diastolic movement" with his exertions. Young, in *Hemingway: A Reconsideration*, 127–218, says that on the "public" (presumably naturalistic) level of the story the lions are imprecise evocations of the "poetry" in Santiago and his nostalgia for his youth.

6. Lawrence Michel, "The Possibility of a Christian Tragedy," reprinted in Lawrence Michel and Richard B. Sewall (eds.), *Tragedy: Modern Essays in Criticism* (Englewood Cliffs, N.J.: Prentice-Hall, 1963), 210–33.

7. Baker, *Hemingway: The Writer as Artist*, 299–304; Clinton S. Burhans, Jr., "The Old Man and the Sea: Hemingway's Tragic Vision of Man," reprinted in Carlos Baker (ed.), *Hemingway and His Critics* (New York: Hill and Wang, 1961), 259–68; Joseph Waldmeir, "Confiteor Hominem: Hemingway's Religion of Man," reprinted in Carlos Baker (ed.), *Ernest Hemingway: Critiques of Four Major Novels* (New York: Scribner's, 1962), 144–49.

those who come to it are apt to give it final shape for themselves. The links between Santiago and Christ—literal events and things made symbolic representations of events and things in the New Testament—are as profuse as they are unmistakable. They have been deeply explored, and each reading is apt to discover new, quite real, and obviously intended correspondences. At this point, it might be enough to accept that Santiago is established as a parallel of Christ, whatever else he might be, and go on from there. A less crudely perceived function of Santiago is that he plays a double representational role. As well as Christ figure, he is also in the elaborate fable a follower of Christ, an acolyte. He is aspirant to the priesthood, to an *earned* communion with the Eucharist, and finally to a species of Christhood himself. These two roles—that of functioning Christ and of man aspiring to spiritual Christhood—ultimately fuse. As Christ figure, he repeats the ordeal of the Crucifixion; as acolyte, he invokes the apparatus and ceremony of the Catholic church in the same order, culminating with the rite of priestly ordination. Each Santiago is indispensable to the other in the final equation of meaning. He becomes at last both human and divine, and tragic in both roles in his spiritual victory over crushing physical disaster. At the end, indeed, he stands as a figure of all men, his experience the universal human experience at its highest.

This view of the double identity of Santiago may be one of two compatible explanations as to why he completed parallel periods of trial. The first is an eighty-seven-day span without a catch, mentioned as having taken place at an earlier time; the second is his present eighty-four-day stretch of similar bad luck. The eighty-seven-day period may be the sum of Jesus' forty days in the desert, the forty days of Lent, and the seven days of Holy Week. The second, eighty-four-day period needs the three days of Crucifixion to match the first: Santiago as acolyte must pass the three-day test of his "crucifixion" to become the peer of Santiago as Christ. A simpler and yet completely complementary view is that the two long periods present the view of life as an ordeal that eternally repeats itself.

Less numerous than the linking of Santiago to his role as Christ, the situations that identify him as acolyte are nonetheless convincing. It is widely noted that his name is Spanish for St. James—a *disciple*. He eats raw fish several times, communion acts a man would perform. He invokes "the great di Maggio" (6, 37) as a man would invoke a saint. As disciple, he eats food that he himself has divided—possibly but not certainly a simultaneous appearance in both roles. When the big fish pulls him down in the skiff so his face is buried in the flesh of a raw, small fish, he is performing both an act of communion, eating a representation of the Body, and the preliminary obeisance of the priest at ordination. The washing of his hands in the ocean is like the washing of the ordinate's hands with holy water so they may be fit to administer the sacrament. The climax and culmination of the development of Santiago as ordinate is focused when he lies collapsed and prone on the bed covered with newspapers, arms "out straight and the palms of his hands up" (69). The author carefully avoids saying whether they are stretched forward in the manner of the priest at ordination, or to the side in the crucifixion posture. The ambiguity must be deliberate and it points to the simultaneity of both positions: of Christ and tested priest.

There is another Christ figure in the fable—the great fish—and his symbolic identity is developed equally systematically if less fully. He and Santiago become twin Christs, and Santiago makes increasingly more of their oneness. At the end his body becomes the Host, the Eucharist, the physical substance of the faith itself. When Santiago as acolyte brings him in and later eats his flesh, he has *achieved* the Host by ordeal and by persevering in an ever-strengthening faith.

Thus Santiago as acolyte and the fish as Eucharist have merged. Santiago and the fish as twin Christs have merged in the consummation of the fish's death and joining to the skiff. Both Santiagos merge, certainly no later than the simultaneous image of crucifixion and ordination at the end. And the three identities have merged and inevitably become the Trinity, though the relationship between the parts is suggestive rather than precise.[8] It would seem that Santiago in part of his identity is Father and, in the other part, Son. The fish is the Holy Spirit.[9] Other interpretations are at least equally feasible.

One of the most important ideas in the story is that life is cyclical—and that the cycle is one of unending crucifixion ordeals.[10] It is hard not to be convinced that two cycles of crucifixion are completed by San-

8. Baker, *Hemingway: The Writer as Artist*, 299.
9. Waldmeir, "Confiteor Hominem," 145.
10. Baker, in *Hemingway: The Writer as Artist*, suggests the cyclical conception.

tiago between the time he catches the fish and when he walks back up
the hill with the mast. The first seems to end when the line—the cross
—is removed from his back, after he takes the fish and has the mystical
moment of seeing him rise in the air, followed by the more prosaic one
of bringing him alongside. But when he sees the sharks, he makes the
kind of sound a man might make "feeling the nail go through his
hands and into wood" (60)—a crucifixion *beginning*. Yet the cross already had been on his back almost three days before it was removed.
The ordeal of the sharks has to be another crucifixion, one that ends
when Santiago spits out blood and it mixes with water. Here his bleeding matches the fish's bleeding into the water from the harpoon wound
he has inflicted, and the gush of blood and water from Jesus' side when
the soldier's lance pierces it. His acknowledgment of termination—that
he is "finished" (68)—equates with Jesus' "It is accomplished," though
necessarily reversing chronology with the spear thrust.

Two crucifixions. But how many more? Certainly the fish has undergone one, completely documented symbolically right up through his
ascension—the great leap in the air. But Santiago's long dry spell before he hooks the fish, the significant eighty-four fishless days and his
attendant humiliation, may reasonably be seen as something of one. It
has, incontestably, been a trial and an ordeal for him though not a
match for the three days. And when he starts *up* the hill on his return,
carrying his mast again, the implication is powerful that he is beginning
yet another crucifixion. And the key to the cyclical concept is presented
early in the story, when it is revealed that Santiago has earlier endured
that eighty-seven-day ordeal, which he repeats in the story, and, it seems,
will go on repeating forever.

The last few pages have several culminating images that focus themes,
each a powerful example of meaning through poetic concentration, but
none more powerful than that of life as a cycle of trial by pain. The
first is that of Santiago ascending the hill with the mast. This is as
agonizing as his first trip with it was routine, and itself becomes a
minidrama of the entire crucifixion, though its more obvious reference
is to Jesus' identical task. But an image within the passage is even more
concentrated and thematic than the whole. In a pause, he looks back
and sees the skeleton of the fish still lashed to the skiff. The fictional
camera has frozen on one Christ with his cross on his shoulder, another

a maimed corpse bound to his. Beginning and end are juxtaposed: Christ starting to Golgotha, Christ dead and lashed to the cross. The image is at once an illumination of the commonalty of all living creatures, the crucifixion as the shaped pattern of life experience for all, the cyclical and unending nature of that experience. It even suggests the simultaneity of time.

The next major image in the section is one already cited—of Santiago with his arms so ambiguously extended—in which both human and divine in Christ and, by extension, in all men is declared. It is followed by the view of the fish's bones become floating garbage, with its intimation that all that is physical is doomed to physical destruction, and that only acts and the memory of acts survive. In the last image of all, the last line of the book, the lions of the dream are as lions have always been, an emblem of life at its strongest and finest, suggesting youth, great deeds, sometimes wonderful to dream about and to long *to return to*, to possess again. In this context, they make a splendid resurrection symbol, unlikely as they might seem for it. Just as, a few moments earlier, the plans of Santiago and Manolo to use part of a junk-yard Ford to make a new lance also make a fine miniature of renewal and resurrection: the ultimate triumph over mortality.

The Christian base of the tragedy has developed at length the theme that the Christ experience is the concentrated representation of all experience—and that that experience is tragic. All who follow their appointed mission with total commitment and dedication will suffer the irreversible catastrophe but will also achieve a spiritual, transcendent victory over it. And they will come through tragedy to a knowledge of their unity with the universe and know that all things are only different aspects of that unity. All is ordered; God exists; through suffering man becomes a part of him.

The art-artist fable has less urgent and unmistakable identifications than the Christian. Rather, it declares itself by the cumulative force of its connotations. And like both the naturalistic and Christian modes, it functions as tragedy by itself, though naturally all are stronger perceived as one unified tragic work than as an addition of separates.

Seen as such a separate, the art-artist drama, however, is simple and direct. The fisherman is the artist, fishing is art, and the fish the art object.[11] Santiago the archetypal fisherman becomes Santiago the archetypal artist. Even more uniquely, this fish is the great work of art, and Santiago's struggle with it is the agony of the artist attempting to achieve the masterpiece. Forces destructive of art inevitably mutilate the masterpiece and block the artist from deserved recognition. But he has already won his triumph of the self over this material catastrophe in the performance of the great artistic act, and he reinforces it in his achievement of serenity in his abiding creative vision. The act is indestructible, and transcendence is built into it.

Simultaneous with this generic mythos is an autobiographical one, which makes Santiago a projection of Hemingway himself. It is only half-developed, sometimes almost ostentatiously visible, finally almost submerged in the larger design. That it may be intuitive and unplanned simply makes it more intriguing. In this, Santiago is Hemingway, once the greatest of all in his métier but now fallen and derided; Hemingway of scrupulous craft *and* burning personal vision; Hemingway, who has not been destroyed by his economic activity—journalism—but has used it both to survive and to nourish his real work; Hemingway, who will come back from scorn and again defeat all others with a master achievement; Hemingway, who considers he has done it and sees his just prize wrested from him by a hostile reviewing establishment; Hemingway, who is still the tragic hero, serene in the knowledge of his feat and comforted by his vision. So Santiago is thus Hemingway as artist—and champion—as well as the universal artist.[12]

This pattern is absorbed by the larger generic pattern, however, and that larger one makes certain fairly distinct assertions about the process of art and working at art. These may be conveniently, if a little Teutonically, seen as grouping into a few cardinal categories.

Imperative and isolation. Both of these are first sounded in the very first line—Santiago fishes, and he fishes alone—though their import begins to emerge forcefully only when the voyage begins. At sea, he reflects repeatedly that he was "born" to be a fisherman and that he must think of no other purpose; when the fish is towing him far out to

11. Schorer, in "With Grace Under Pressure," 20, suggests the novel as a parable of the universal artist as well as an autobiographical objectification.

12. Young, *Hemingway: A Reconsideration*, 126–27, 275. Young feels the central, perhaps the exclusive element in the art-artist dimension is Hemingway's view of himself as artist.

sea, he reflects that he has no help in the challenge of the masterpiece except what comes from himself, and the surrounding sea reminds him of his aloneness. He asserts that he will prove his commitment to his work again though he has proved it many times before, and he reiterates his determination to follow the imperative—execute the masterpiece, kill the fish—until death. His affirmation is stronger after he has glimpsed the awesome shape of the masterwork.

Nor does his fidelity ebb after he has executed the great work—tied the fish alongside; it is simply directed against new challenges. He must try to protect the work against those forces that would destroy it, and possibly all art, and he reiterates that hopeless determination as he battles the sharks. These represent not only reviewers and critics here but imperception, exploitation, that whole part of the apparatus of cynicism that attaches itself to each of the arts and will destroy it if unchecked.

And the artist strong enough to obey the imperative will be strong enough to perceive an alleviation of the aloneness, though it will not be provided by other men until the task is over. It appears, rather, in an awareness of the unity of the cosmos and all living things in it, which comes gradually to the striver in the depths of his self-imposed exile for his art. Santiago acknowledges as he sees a flight of ducks against the sky that he knows "no man . . . [is] ever alone on the sea" (32); later, the physical part of his masterpiece destroyed in total catastrophe, he can embrace the very element which, in the largest sense, destroyed it: the sea itself. He affirms himself at one with the sea, the wind, the town where he lives, the destroyed masterpiece itself. And though he grieves for this ruined master work, he appears to have attained the deep, ultimate happiness of the noblest tragic hero, in his role as artist as well as in his other identities. He knows both that the great creation will always be his, and that he himself is as ultimately responsible for its destruction as he was for its execution.

Craft, method, and luck. The first two are constantly in view in Santiago's careful preparation before he goes out—his systematic check of his gear and provisions, the care he gives to the smallest tasks, from stowing his gear to baiting the hooks—and is crystallized by his careful maintenance of his lines at exact depths and positions. He keeps them more precisely than anyone else, he reflects—not impossibly the author's tribute to the author as craftsman. He has not had luck, but he prefers skill to luck.

Yet from the first Santiago acknowledges the supreme importance of that other element, luck. He is "unlucky," the boy is on a "lucky" boat, eighty-five may be a "lucky" number. Is luck the same as that psychic indefinable, inspiration? It would seem not. Santiago speaks later of having violated his luck when he went "outside too far." Yet the shark is carefully presented as an inevitability, not an accident, and the catastrophe as a pure cause-and-effect event. Perhaps he means his *hubris* destroyed the luck that would have protected him from the harshnesses of order. For luck seems to lie outside the orderly world, to be almost a caprice of the cosmos in action, as Tyche, the goddess of luck, was considered to be essentially unrelated to any other force, even the Fates, a force apart from everything, by those Greeks of the first century B.C.

Yet luck has some kind of relationship with inspiration, the text suggests. It is luck that may reward skill, in the example of the carefully maintained lines, and luck may manifest itself in inspiration, or idea, donnée, subject.

It may manifest itself there, or anywhere, but it is not the same thing. Inspiration, imagination, creativity—whatever it is named—is one of the two prime and almost equal partners in the hard labor of art. Imagination and discipline-craft are fixed as such partners in the image of the two hands and the fish they work together to bring in (Baker's Trinity image). Santiago proclaims all three brothers: masterpiece, craft, and imagination. But which hand is which? That ancient maxim, "the left hand is the dreamer," suggests the left as the delicate and unpredictable, even uncontrollable component of imagination, with the stronger and ever faithful right as discipline and skill. Santiago's denunciation of the left as "traitor" reinforces that view, and it is the right hand with which he wins the hand wrestling championship. The left might even be characterized as the unconscious and the right as the conscious.

The powerful black man Santiago beats in the "championship" wrestling contest with his right hand seems pretty obviously the devil in the Christian tragedy, but what is he here? Less clear: perhaps the despair and doubt of both self and the validity of art that assails every artist from time to time, perhaps autobiographically one writer whom Hemingway felt he had to beat and did beat to become "champion." Who? The guess here is Faulkner, but it may be a bad guess; the whole concept has to be avowed as tenuous, and all nominations consequently speculative.

The mysterious and the miraculous. There is something in the making of the superwork that lies beyond that partnership of craft and inspiration, however, and even beyond the capricious and not at all holy element of luck. This is the awesome benediction of mystery and miracle; the artist's own exertions, however wise and strenuous, can only take him so far. Then the great work is *bestowed* or it is not.

The first intimation of mystery impending appears, dim and precise yet with unmistakable connotation, as Santiago starts out in his skiff. The silence of the sea, broken only by the sound of unseen oars stroking, is an evocative context for Santiago's reflection that he is going "far out"; in addition to its hubristic declaration, it suggests the start of a voyage into the unknown, into mystery. These notes intensify, first subtly, and then directly and powerfully when the fish takes the bait. Santiago's prayer-like invocations more directly belong to the Christian story but also strongly point to the emerging aspect of the miraculous in art. The fish is "unbelievably heavy" (21), "of great weight" (22), and Santiago marvels at his size as he envisions him "moving away in the darkness" (22). The mystery of the bestowed masterpiece is constantly deepened. When Santiago is actually taken in tow by the fish, the work assumes control of its creator; for four hours he does not see it, and he thinks of the fish as "wonderful and strange" (25), of a great and mysterious age. He reflects that the fish chose to stay in "deep dark water" and that he found him "beyond all men" (26); their joining is thus hinted as a kind of miracle as well as mystery, in the art parable as in the others. These aspects are constantly strengthened by his reflections on the size and nobility of the marlin and flower in the great death leap, the Ascension image in the Christian mode. The "great strangeness" (55) he feels in remembering it and the dimmed eyesight that accompanied it, make that sight a different kind of holy vision for the artist: this is the grail of the achieved masterpiece he has always sought. It may be glimpsed and briefly possessed if it has been truly earned, but it is not permanent and it cannot be shared—not even by fellow artists who can at least understand its magnitude and the agony it represents.

The emerging oneness of artist and masterpiece. Even greater than the agony of execution is the agony of the destruction of the achieved masterpiece, for by this time, creator and work have become one. They have been "brothers" during their battle; when the fish is tied to the boat, they almost immediately become a single entity. Which is bringing the other in, he wonders; when the sharks mutilate the fish, he feels as though their teeth are ripping him. Later he tells his sorrow to the fish; by going too far out—creating too big a work—he has destroyed them both. This may be the climax of the development of their ever-tightening oneness. The thematic implication is instantly perceived: in the execution of the masterpiece, the masterpiece ultimately becomes part of the artist. What is inflicted upon it is inflicted upon him. Here, Backman says, Hemingway's fusion of active and passive, slayer and slain, finds its strongest expression.[13]

Fate of the masterpiece. The masterpiece is always maimed by the events that are subsequent to its creation: that is, it can never be completely and truly perceived by any but the artist. It never survives intact in the dignity and honor it deserves. Developed directly by the battle and its outcome, this theme is culminated by the last image of the fish: a skeleton with a tail and fin that is now floating garbage, awaiting total oblivion by the tide.

But though the masterpiece itself may be destroyed (by hostility, misunderstanding, and misrepresentation, maiming critical attacks), the achieving of it cannot be. The execution of the work of art is not only a performance but a fact: though it may not survive in space, it will survive in time and in the greatest dimension, memory. This is one of the implications of the awe of the other fishermen at the size of the fish's skeleton and their understanding of Santiago's ordeal which attended its taking.

Another is that the achievement of the work of art is understood by the elect, the brothers in the art, and it exists as example and inspiration to them. Concomitantly, the nonelect, those who do not know, in their obtuseness confuse the achievement of the work with the destruc-

13. Melvin Backman, "Hemingway: The Matador and the Crucified," reprinted in Baker (ed.), *Hemingway and His Critics*, 245–58.

tion of it: the destroyers are honored, the creator shunned. This last, bitter irony is rendered in the comment of the tourist gazing at the ruined fish: "I didn't know sharks had such handsome beautifully formed tails" (72).

But for the true artist, for him who has reached awareness in his suffering and achieving, all of this recedes into unimportance. For him, only one thing endures and is of final significance. This is his vision, from which this work and all the artist's work comes, and it is projected in the last line, "The old man was dreaming about the lions" (72).

The fate of the work, as caught in the destruction of the fish by the sharks, is one of those phases of action that inevitably seems to belong in the autobiographical parable, too. An early view had it that the fish was this very book and the sharks were the critics, an inaccurate precognition since they had not had a chance at it during its composition and liked it when they did. The better surmise probably is that they suggest the undervaluation that Hemingway felt reviewers had accorded him since *In Our Time*, as his 1927 poem "Valentine" demonstrates. The only real single possibility is *Across the River*, as Young suggested in 1966.[14] Hemingway prized it and was dismayed at what he felt was a critical failure of perception toward it. A reasonable hypothesis is that Hemingway fused the fate of *Across the River* with that of the book-in-being.

The artistic vision. The lions that are decisive symbols in the other modes of the story are equally strong as a synthesizing and culminating image in the tragedy of art. The dream of lions is a great sustaining force for the old man as he lives in failure and charitable scorn; he summons them in his most agonized hours during his ordeal of execution, and at the end they supply the final definition to this layer of tragedy as to the others. His great work as a physical entity has been destroyed. His achievement has not only been ignored and unperceived by those who do not know, but these give credit for achievement to the very ones who have destroyed it: the tourists think the remains of the fish are those of a shark, and comment on the shark's beauty. But Santiago does not care: he has achieved the sublime indifference of the artist to everything but his deepest vision of beauty and life and of his

14. Young, *Hemingway: A Reconsideration*, 275.

work in relation to them. It is unshakable and enduring and will always renew him. He is dreaming about the lions: he is warming himself with the artistic vision. One would judge that this is Hemingway's idealized self-portrait in the crucial dimension—not himself as he knew he was, but himself as he knew he ought to be, the artist as he ought to be.

Critics, criticism, and the artist. The sharks are forces of destruction in every fable of the book but they are splendidly unlimited in each. Yet, as with the lions and the other images in the complex symbology, their unclosed, larger identities also enclose quite exact lesser identities. Thus at the first level they are all the unnameable elements of a hostile universe that crush man, but they are more narrowly nemesis; in the Christian tragedy, they are all the forces against Christ, but touches link them uniquely with the Pharisees; here, they are the huge conglomerate of the forces that assault all art: exploitation, neglect, public indifference and ignorance, self-doubt, despair—and of course the reviewers and critics. That much advertised last identity is not "wrong," but it is only one part. Still, it is the most interesting part, apparently to the author and literate public as well. And certain aspects of the author's attitude toward the sharks as reviewers-critics have not been so widely observed as his hostility.

The hostility, in fact, is directed, and carefully directed, toward only the "scavenger" sharks—the reviewers who are frantic to play follow the leader. The first shark, the Mako, is accorded a scrupulous if unloving accolade: he is as beautiful as the marlin except for his jaws, he fears nothing, he is built "to feed on all the fish in the sea" (45). This authentic, super critic is the equal of the artist but is different in function, a differentiation that is underscored by the resemblance of his teeth to "cramped" human fingers (the cramping suggesting a freezing of the creative function). Exercising his admittedly "noble" purpose, he attacks bravely. But Santiago has only contempt for those scavengers who can only follow their better and bite the fish "where he had already been bitten" (61). Thus, the great critic is as great as the great artist—but those who can only follow him and each other are cowards and unworthy.

Sharks more diffusely suggest the entire critical activity: when they are dismembered, stripped, and processed, as critics break down a creative work, at the "shark factory" (3), they make a stink that permeates the bay. Yet Santiago makes a bow to the critical activity when he acknowledges taking shark liver oil regularly; it helps the eyes, as a little pure criticism helps the artist's vision.

The economic, physical sustenance of the artist. This is the most quotidian of all the considerations developed here and it becomes most interesting when the author uses it in a candid autobiographical representation of the relationship between journalism and literature. Yet careful justice is done to the more general parallel: the old man is artist, as he was Christ at the Last Supper, when the boy brings him the gift of food to strengthen him for the next day's fishing. For after his long bad luck Santiago cannot buy for himself, and without physical nourishment, the spiritual labor of art cannot be performed. The repeated rituals of eating smaller fish in the boat, more important as communion ceremonies in the Christian fable, here stress the need of continuing physical and economic sustenance for the artist in his most elevated creative endeavor. They may be more interesting, however, as a suggestion that the artist proceeds from his own lesser work to the greater, gaining strength through the smaller for the creation of the larger. And among Santiago's reflections on the fish are many with a definite economic facing. He wonders if taking the fish were a sin, though it will keep him alive and "feed many people" (59). He thinks of the money the fish will bring in the market, enough to feed him through the winter. And he declares that he did not kill the fish just to stay alive himself—his imperative to create and pride in work were infinitely stronger than economic necessity.

Yet the biggest image of the economic activity—as the sharks were of the reviewers and critics—is the turtles, and within this generic representation there is a more piquant one of Hemingway himself. More generally, turtles and anything pertaining to them are objectifications of the economic process—the turtles themselves, their eggs, "turtling," and turtle boats. Broadly speaking, the artist must resort to some activity or practice to support himself—hiring out on turtle boats that catch them or eating their eggs. Sometimes this lower activity not only keeps the artist alive but instructs and tempers him for his real work: the practice of art—catching big fish. But the turtles are both larger and infinitely more provocative when seen as objectifications of journalism and even of journalists in Hemingway's own career. When the boy tells

Santiago that Santiago's years on the turtle boats did not hurt his eyes, Hemingway is declaring that his stretches of journalism did not hurt his own artistic vision. When Santiago speaks of eating turtle eggs to keep himself strong in the winter, the author is not only speaking of the physical nourishment but of the experience that can be fashioned into art which journalism has given him; the figure recalls certain lines from the introduction to his collected short stories, "In going where you have to go, and doing what you have to do, and seeing what you have to see, you . . . blunt the instrument you write with." But the instrument can always be rewhetted, he contends. When Santiago says he feels no mysticism about turtles, Hemingway is saying he feels none about the newspaper or magazine business, as many former newsmen profess to do. He expresses friendly contempt for the ordinary journalists, the "stupid loggerheads" (18), but admiration for the excellent journalists—*i.e.*, his good friends in the ranks—by praising green turtles and hawkbills for their "elegance and speed and great value" (18).

So the book demonstrates overwhelmingly the author's turn toward fable that became markedly evident in *Across the River and Into the Trees*. And these layers of the story are constructed to the measure of many kinds of tragedy, that fuse as the levels of the work fuse. Whether one considers this novel to be Hemingway's best or not depends on what he expects from a novel. But none is more powerful as an expression of the tragic, and none should define him so finally as one of fiction's most powerful, and subtle, prophets of the tragic vision.

Certain dim resemblances between *The Old Man and the Sea* and *Oedipus at Colonus* have been noted: they are purely emotional, tonal, and—it seems safe to say—totally accidental. Like Oedipus, Santiago begins in a cast-down, even an accursed state, but he has achieved humility and serenity. The ordeal he experiences only confirms him in that humility and serenity, which carry him to an ultimate and transcendental triumph—again like Oedipus. That is all there is between the two, and there is nothing in the record to suggest nor it is suggested here that the earlier work had any influence whatever on the later. Yet, paradoxically, "A Man of the World," a short story published five years after the novel, seems to have been modeled directly if in a sardonic fashion on the play: situation matches situation, incident pairs with incident. And the biggest part of the paradox lies in the difference in tone. Instead of the note of loftiness, the story strikes one of black comedy, even of coarseness and brutality, through most of its duration. One work is larger than life, the other perhaps smaller. Still in the end it sounds something of the same theme as *The Old Man and the Sea*, though admittedly a little more that of *The Sun Also Rises*: that we define ourselves by our confrontation of catastrophe—or, better here, the existential void.

The likenesses and the polarities are sufficient, perhaps, to justify an indulgence and look at the story as a kind of satyr play to the larger tragic work—so long as one knows perfectly well he is justifying an indulgence. It seems likely that Hemingway never thought of them that way.

The strategic foundation of the story is the way its tone plays against the *Colonus* structure that is its narrative foundation. The protagonist Blindy is foul-smelling, a slot-machine cadger and drink-moocher, repulsive to all perceptions. People in the bar avoid him. The appearance of his pus-packed eyesocket, and the details of the fight in which he lost it are almost subhuman in their coarseness, a coarseness that has turned many of the author's most sympathetic critics away from the story. Yet at the end there is, simply in retrospective, the absolutely classic Aristotelian reversal: the retelling of the maiming fight with Joe Sawyer suddenly invests Blindy with dignity; he is called Blacky again; he is invited to sleep in the backroom of the bar. His crude declaration —that he has made and is making the most of his condition and his acceptance of responsibility for it—heightens the affirmation. He has won what might be seen in a suitable context as tragic triumph—but it has taken place here in a deceptively surreal world of dark comedy. The victory thus is Sartrean; here, it is not tragic but a warped, crazy-mirror reduction of the tragic idea.

The linkings to Oedipus begin early. As blind as the one time king of Thebes, Blindy declares, "I been on lots of roads. . . . And any time I may have to take off and go on some more";[15] he is obviously providing the clue link between Oedipus' unending journey, led by his daugh-

---

15. Ernest Hemingway, "A Man of the World," *Atlantic Monthly*, CC (November, 1957), 64–66.

ter-sister, on the roads of the world. When he says to the man at the slot machine, "Your night is my night" (65), he is handing us the parallel to the Delphic prophecy that Oedipus would bring luck to those who helped him. The sacred wood, a forest of sorts, at Colonus is the place of final confrontation in the play; with tongue deep, deep in cheek, surely, the author has Blindy drink the whiskey, Old Forester. As Theseus offers sanctuary to Oedipus, so Frank the bartender tells Blindy he can sleep in the back of the bar.

The decisive, thematic pairing occurs in statements made by principals near the end of each work. Oedipus proclaims that his great suffering and noble nature make him know that all is well. In the lower-than-life matching utterance, Blindy declares that he has earned his life, sorry as it may be, and he is happy with it.

This comes after the recounting of the fight with Sawyer the years before. Each has maimed the other hopelessly, and it may be one of Hemingway's more notable feats that for the moment it counts, he can make us accept the brutality as a self-defining action. In fact, Blindy asserts his *right* to his responsibility and self-definition: "Only just don't call me Blacky any more. Blindy's my name. . . . I earned it. You seen me earn it" (66). Finally, in what is almost a grotesque played by gargoyles, we see a strange version of the human triumph enacted. Blindy has met catastrophe and the existential void, and they are both his.

One of the real significances of the repelling, morbidly intriguing little story is its clear illumination of one of the really new developments in Hemingway's work after 1950: his use of literary source. It showed in *Across the River and Into the Trees*, could be perceived in the New Testament base and Dantean references to the stars in *The Old Man and the Sea*, and was to flower in *Islands in the Stream—* which was written before the story.

Apparently for the first time here, he uses the narrative structure of a literary masterwork as his own base, as other writers used pure myth. Yet the chronology of the actual writing of his last work makes plain that he was essentially picking up where he left off in what was to be published later as *Islands in the Stream*—that he was, in this respect, simply going a bit further.

10

Islands in the Stream
A Sartrean Path to Tragic Magnitude

The last three sections of Hemingway's novel about "land, sea and air" were written in what was, for him or for any good writer, a marvellously short time. Baker describes how he wrote most of the second, "The Sea When Absent" ("Cuba" in *Islands in the Stream*), in the first three weeks of December in 1950—catching fire in the stretch from Adriana's visit, he liked to believe. As noted, he then wrote *The Old Man and the Sea* between late December and February; it first bore a title he had mused over a long time, "The Sea in Being," and was intended as the last and third part of the long novel. But he took the total novel further with "The Sea Chase," which he began shortly after the completion of "The Sea in Being" and also completed rapidly, writing from March to May. He made it part three and shifted "The Sea in Being" to part four—ultimately severing it from the rest, as we know.

The time and circumstances of the composition of the first part, "The Sea When Young," are less definite. Hemingway said on occasion that this first section had been finished as early as 1947, but Baker believes that possibly he had come to confuse at least part of his unpublished novel, *The Garden of Eden*, with this one. When the other three sections were done in such rapid sequence, Hemingway wrote his publisher that "The Sea When Young" would require a heavy, almost total rewriting, which he apparently began not long after finishing "The Sea Chase."[1]

1. Carlos Baker, *Ernest Hemingway: A Life Story* (New York: Scribner's, 1969), 488–94, 497.

The greatest significance of this chronology of composition of *Islands in the Stream* is that it establishes that "At Sea" ("The Sea Chase") was written and "Bimini" ("The Sea When Young") was massively rewritten directly after the completion of *The Old Man and the Sea*— and that *The Old Man and the Sea* was first conceived as the culmination of the longer novel and the most explicit statement of its themes. Consequently, there is a special and profound link between the first and third sections and the detached fourth, as well as the close link between both books as entities. The first section previsions quite directly certain scenes and the core of action of *The Old Man and the Sea*, the third shows a parallel struggle, and both offer preparatory, lesser iterations of the crucifixion theme and of tragic definition by action. Thus *The Old Man and the Sea* relates to *Islands in the Stream* to such a degree that the longer book cannot be approached intelligently without the illumination of the shorter—once its own summation. In sum, a critical consideration of *The Old Man and the Sea* does not need *Islands in the Stream* at all—but one of *Islands in the Stream* very urgently needs *The Old Man and the Sea*.

Baker has shown how closely *Islands in the Stream* is based upon events in the author's life.[2] No other persona is so close to Hemingway the writer as Thomas Hudson the painter, down to wives, sons, experiences, work, and grief. That cited aspect of Hemingway's later work— his fusion of all kinds of literary and mythic reference into a shaping mold for emotional essence—is also more voluminously evident here than in the companion novels. The biographical substance and the agencies of design together create a work that is powerfully tragic as a whole and approaches the tragic in two of its three almost autonomous parts, achieving it in the third. It is certainly not among Hemingway's three or four greatest novels, but like *Across the River and Into the Trees*, it needs detailed explication more than any of these to come into its considerable and unique worth.

As a tragedy, the achievement of both the first two sections is limited, for in both, Hudson is almost exclusively the protagonist hammered by the universe. But in "Bimini," the catastrophe is inflicted suddenly, gratuitously, with no sense of inevitability or of a long, remorseless, and

2. Carlos Baker, *Ernest Hemingway: The Writer as Artist* (Princeton: Princeton University Press, 1972), 384–92.

undeflectable stream of causation. A strict constructionist would be within his rights in denying it tragic stature at all. Its essay of the tragic equation is simple: by concentration and discipline and good luck, Hudson has achieved harmony and happiness in both his work and his life. Then he loses it when two of his three sons are killed in an automobile accident with their mother, his divorced second wife. As a bitterly ironic commentary on the caprice of the cosmos, this is highly satisfactory; still, it will probably be less than a real tragic statement for most. "Cuba" is much more heavily invested with the tragic tone. Hudson has already learned of the death of his third son at the beginning, even though the reader has not, and is symbolically presented on a journey through Hell as a result of that knowledge. Even though the nature of that journey is not revealed for some time, it produces a powerful effect subliminally and ultimately gives the work the desired sense of the inexorability of the workings of tragic necessity. The sudden appearance of Hudson's first wife and true love, when he is at his emotional nadir, somehow manages to seem ordained rather than accidental, and the brief, Beatrice-like salvation she brings him seems at first a compassionate, if transient, gift of consolation from a benign, if lesser, cosmic force. It is snatched away both by Hudson's own flaw—he cannot get along with her for twenty-four consecutive hours—and by the universe, which sends him orders to take his subchaser to sea at once. A consistent sadness that may well be felt as tragic emotion is in the section, and one senses inevitability, not accident, at the center of the design. The determining question on the novella's existence as tragedy is the subjective one: does it finally have tragic impact?

It seems likely, again, that the first two sections were intended simply to approach the condition of tragedy, not reach it, and to make the approach in intensifying order, thus preparing for the conclusive tragedy and emotional release of the final, third section and thus of the total novel.[3] Certainly the book is stronger when read this way. For the third section is in the pattern of all the author's novels from *For Whom the Bell Tolls* forward: the protagonist defines himself by deliberate choice and action. Here, he knowingly incurs catastrophe—and death

3. John Wain, review of *Islands in the Stream*, in *London Observer Review*, October 11, 1970, p. 33. Wain sees each as tragic in itself, which makes the novel "a triple hammer blow."

—with that choice and action. In "At Sea," under the orders that ended "Cuba," his decision to pursue the survivors of a U-boat crew who have made the mistake of murdering and thus will murder again, is final, and he knows it. He makes of this chase a defining act as he holds to it. In his death from enemy bullets, he perceives the final harmony of the universe in classic tragic reconciliation, a culmination of the whole novel as well as of this part of it.

In the complex development of these simple equations, the author makes heavy, almost startling use of literary sources. Dante is one. His hell scenes are faintly parodied in Mr. Bobby's outlining of an end-of-the-world painting for Thomas Hudson, which is a metaphorical forecast for him: through the loss of love after love, Hudson moves from one circle of private hell to another until he enters the center, which is pure isolation. And Hudson invokes Dante, heavily, in a reflection that is acknowledgment and guide to that source. Possibly a heavier, if less overt, source is Joseph Conrad. The book seems deliberately constructed to the pattern of the larger, tragic Conrad novel: the protagonist has support after support stripped from him until he is in near-total emotional isolation; he is subjected to the final, absolute moral examination; he passes by affirming his moral, ethical responsibility but brings tragic catastrophe upon himself as a consequence. The structural parallel is extended further by one of circumstance: Hudson the painter has become a wartime sea captain, and his end, and the book's, is pure Conrad—at core if not in idiom. Hemingway's expressed admiration for the great British novelist has now made the ultimate gesture—a direct imitation, though a proper and completely personalized one.[4]

"Bimini"

The most explicitly acknowledged debt to Conrad is in this first novella, where "The Secret Sharer" is heavily invoked and scrupulously identified. And that section also has a development that utilizes *The Brothers Karamazov* quite directly. "Bimini" has a complexity of construction its ease of reading is apt to conceal at first. It falls into three phases: the principal, melodic line shows the achievement by Thomas Hudson, the protagonist, of the stasis and balance necessary for successful artistic creation and personal happiness; an intricate contrapuntal development

4. Baker, *Hemingway: A Life Story*, 101, 116, 135.

shows what he might have become if that balance had not been achieved; and a second counterpoint line presents his children as components of himself. The last two insist on being viewed in the perspective of other literary works, the first of these utilizing "The Secret Sharer" and taking great pains to acknowledge it, the second drawing from the Dostoievski novel and climaxing in an episode that is a prefiguration and miniature of *The Old Man and the Sea*.

The major line is developed in a manner comparatively novel in Hemingway. Like many of the author's other works, it starts at that point where the protagonist has come closest to realizing his intention, his purpose. Instead of being a development of a long catastrophe, a descent from that high point, however, "Bimini" simply presents Thomas Hudson's fulfillment at length, and the subsequent sections are devoted to the descent. This section works its effect through the tension between this line and the two counterlines. When catastrophe does come, it is as sudden as it is brief.

As the novel begins, Thomas Hudson is presented as a man already in stasis, a man who has actually achieved the mode of life he sought.[5] He has attained a rhythm of living on Bimini that has brought him to the peak of his powers as a painter; he creates with joy and without block; he is secure in both reputation and income. His serenity in his art and life is developed at length, as is his larger happiness when his three sons by two divorced wives come for an extended visit.

The "Secret Sharer" counterpoint suggests what Hudson might have been had he not achieved discipline and harmony, and another character is offered as something like a Hudson negative, in whom the destructive element has overridden other psychic components. He is Roger Davis, a writer who also paints and whose work has gone wrong because he has not managed to bring his personal forces into a balance comparable to Hudson's. He is looking for a lost part of himself and may or may not have found it as his story ends. That part is suggested, delicately, by David, Hudson's second son, with whom Roger has a special and close relationship.

The second counterpoint, the third narrative line, is the development

5. Joseph De Falco, "Hemingway's Islands and Streams: Minor Tactics for Heavy Pressure," in Richard Astro and J. J. Benson (eds.), *Hemingway In Our Time* (Corvallis: Oregon State University Press, 1973), 39–52. De Falco sees this stasis as Hudson's Eden.

of the visit of Hudson's three sons, and it is closely joined to both other lines. The sons, after the manner of those in *The Brothers Karamazov*, are on the symbolic level components of their father's psyche, and they also relate to his second self, Roger. The three lines fuse climactically in the fishing sequence that so forcefully suggests *The Old Man and the Sea*. David—the best part of Hudson, the lost part of Roger—catches a huge fish, fights him successfully all day, and brings him to the edge of the boat only to lose him when the hook is dislodged. It is consciously presented as a mini-tragedy, which roughly metaphorizes man's fate. Its obvious parallel to *The Old Man and the Sea* is emphasized by many internal references. The three movements, though distinct, are smoothly joined: each of the two minors makes its own statement, but also strengthens and illuminates the major.

Section I of "Bimini" is a prelude that, chiefly in its tonality but sometimes by passages approaching a one-for-one symbology, evokes the creative balance Thomas Hudson has achieved. It is a rich suggestion of what his life is at its highest point—not the characteristic preview of the entire work. The first line catches Hudson's situation: "The house was built on the highest part of the narrow tongue of land between the harbor and the open sea."[6] In the context of both Part I and the entire novella, certain representations emerge. The "open sea" suggests the eternal, the universe beyond personal life, and the harbor the comparative safety and smallness of a protected individual life. The "narrow tongue of land" is that dwindling space of time that separates them. That the house stands on the "highest part" implies an elevation that commands simultaneous vision of the personal and the universal, the immediate and the eternal. Thus, and in context, this first sentence connotes that Thomas Hudson has achieved a loftiness of character and perspective and is equally aware of the universe and of himself.

The second paragraph offers another image of a more individuated implication—that of the sharks. It ends: "At night the sharks had no fear and everything else feared them. But in the day they stayed out away from the clear white sand and if they did come in, you could see their shadows a long way away" (3). The sharks here are a preparation for the shark that almost catches Hudson's son David later in the novella, and they relate obviously to the sharks in *The Old Man and the*

6. Ernest Hemingway, *Islands in the Stream* (New York: Scribner's, 1970), 3.

Sea. They are here, too, the destructive elements in the universe, a category that includes many abstractions, certainly despair. The protagonist is safe from them, apparently and temporarily, but they are waiting at a certain distance, and, as configurations, they finally strike.

A reference to fine weather between storms in the hurricane months of autumn closely parallels a similar expression in *The Old Man and the Sea* and suggests the same thing: that late middle age may be both the most dangerous time and the most creative time for a man, particularly an artist. The house itself becomes a configuration of Hudson's art, or the dedication to it that is his way of life, or both; it is a sanctuary with a view of the absolute. The house is warm in the winter because it has the only fireplace on the island, in which Hudson burns driftwood. The implications of the driftwood and its burning become visible, and then not without ambiguity, only in the context of the entire novella. The driftwood is, for one thing, achieved experience, and the burning of it is the conversion of experience to art. "It was fun to burn even the pieces he was fond of" is a clue line, suggesting the exhilaration of the conversion. "He knew the sea would sculpt more" is another, declaring that life will always provide more experience which will, in its cycle, be used for art. The extended image metaphorizes the pleasure of utilization, of transmutation, rather than permanency of the achieved object. A concomitant implication is the Hemingway constant: all things pass, and life goes on.

The conception of life as recurring rhythm, in which the seasons come and go every year, is projected also by Hudson's reflections: he does not want "to miss any spring, nor summer, nor any fall or winter" (4). Yet with the idea that seasons are permanently recurring coexists the other, equally time-crusted conception that man's life divides itself into four seasons. The prelude ends: "Winter was the best of all seasons. . . . and he looked forward to it through all the rest of the year" (6). Hudson expects the best of old age.

What is suggested with subtlety through Part I is defined boldly only a little later. Hudson crystallizes his achievement of harmony in a summarizing passage:

> Learning how to settle down and how to paint with discipline had been
> hard for him because there had been a time in his life when he had

not been disciplined. He had never been truly irresponsible; but he had been undisciplined, selfish, and ruthless. He knew this now, not only because many women had told it to him; but because he had finally discovered it for himself. Then he had resolved that he would be selfish only for his painting, ruthless only for his work, and that he would discipline himself and accept the discipline. (8–9)

His completeness is immediately underlined in a dramatic double entendre: a servant asks, "don't you want nothing?" and he answers, "I don't want [need] anything" (9).

His fulfillment thus established, the first counterpoint begins with the development of the writer Roger Davis as double and negative. The Davis line is also intimately joined to the other counterpoint, the development of Hudson's sons that climaxes in the fishing sequence. And it invokes "The Secret Sharer" as it might invoke myth, with a whole system of parallels pointing to the source. Roger appears suddenly to Hudson aboard a vessel in harbor, just as does Leggett, the Jungian second self, to Conrad's captain. He does so just as abruptly if less overtly symbolically: Leggett is first seen as a headless apparition floating fishlike and phosphorescent in a night sea; Roger drops suddenly through a hatch into the cabin of a pleasure cruiser. Both Roger and Leggett have recently committed acts of violence whose consequences they are fleeing. Leggett has killed a cowardly sailor during a storm at sea—with his fists; Roger has almost killed a motion picture potentate at a party by a pool—with his fists. Shortly after his appearance, in an underlining of his incarnation of the principle of violence, Roger almost kills another singularly nasty businessman in a fight on the pier. In Conrad's story, the narrator frequently soliloquizes on Leggett's resemblance to himself. In Hemingway's, a bartender performs this function and Hudson also broods on the resemblances. After he comes out of the water, Leggett is seen in nothing but a striped "sleeping suit"; Roger is carefully described as wearing a shirt with stripes. Leggett is repeatedly called "the swimmer"; Roger is told by the girl, Audrey Bruce, that as a child, she admired him for his swimming. In "The Secret Sharer," the double loses a hat as he dives into the sea and, floating on the water, it serves as a marker for the captain—actually and symbolically. In "Bimini," a hat similarly floats on the water—though it is not left there by Roger but by another character. The incidents are too many, the parallels too close, for there to be any doubt about the author's use and acknowledgment of source.

However, in his own fable he appears to depart from that source after establishing it. Fabulistically, in "The Secret Sharer" the captain identifies Leggett as his secret, darker self, and by both acknowledging and fulfilling his responsibility to that self, he achieves wholeness and is able to function with integrated purpose—to command his ship properly. In "Bimini," Thomas Hudson has already achieved that wholeness. He sees Roger as what he would have been if he had not achieved control of the parts of self and held them in balance. Still, Hudson understands Roger for what he is, cherishes him, and has come to terms of profound intimacy with him, just as Conrad's captain has with Leggett. By accepting the second self—indiscipline, violence—as part of his whole nature, he has already been able to restrain it and achieve control and balance.

Roger also relates actively to Hudson's life at two principal points. The first involves Audrey Bruce, a girl whose resemblance to Hudson's first wife and permanent love is accented until one accepts her as a fabulistic revisitation of the wife; she even has two names. Hudson is intensely aware of her in this sense, but she becomes engaged to and departs with Roger, not himself. This can be viewed in two ways. First, the episode may be a reenactment of Hudson's loss of his wife—the then-uncurbed violence in him, Roger, having destroyed his relationship with her. Second, and simultaneously, it can be seen as offering hope to Roger, in both his modes of existence. Literally, he may simply find in a happy marriage or relationship impetus to discipline and honest work again. Fabulistically, Audrey as love may be the element to curb and bring into balance the predominating violence that is Roger.

The other counterpoint development is the visit of Hudson's three children: their arrival is the final seal on his happiness and wholeness. They are the final externalization of, the mark upon Thomas Hudson's wholeness, and it is easy to see each of them as a component of his, and the universal human psyche.

In this phase, the oldest boy, Tommy, is presented as wise and understanding to a precocious degree. The second son, David, is as compassionate, as loving, as simply good, as believability permits. The last, Andrew, is described as "wicked boy." Together, they form a unit, harmonious and disciplined, like the nature of Thomas Hudson; it is tempting to read them in the Freudian framework as superego, ego, and id. But it is better to think of them, perhaps, in terms weighted a little differently. Tom appears to be rationality, the intelligence functioning as synthesizing agent, David as the elevated, feeling, "good" part of nature, and Andrew as the reactive, animalistic, "bad" part. The first holds the second two in balance; the three make a functioning whole. One thinks, of course, not only of *The Brothers Karamazov* but also of *All the King's Men*.

The role of the three boys as psychic components in a fable does not become clear until the end of the novella. To avoid the appearance of allegory, and to keep the representational aspects of this narrative line completely subordinated to the realistic, the author reveals their representational functions only a little at a time. The first of the devices he uses to hint at these functions is a summaristic reflection on each, made by Hudson just after they arrive. What first projects Tommy as the function of intellect is the twice-repeated word, "thinking"; later, he discusses his father's intellectual friends. David is suggested as good, or love. He is presented simply as humorous, kind, and normal, and what might be definitive adjectives are almost concealed in the text.

His symbolic nature becomes notably visible in the two dramatic episodes. In the first, he is almost hit by a shark while goggle fishing in the water and is narrowly saved when Eddie, the boat's mate, kills the shark with a machine gun. The perspective of that severed part, *The Old Man and the Sea*, insists upon itself here; the shark for the moment is a configuration of pure evil, seeking its natural adversary. But it is not until the next, and larger, sequence that David's role comes into full view: he becomes a scaled-down Christ figure by a crucifixion-ordeal he undergoes in catching and losing a giant fish, like Santiago. With his identity established with some firmness here, the previously fragile, auxiliary definitions assume more solidity: he is the "better self," not simply love but the capacity to love.

The development of Tommy as a figure of intellect or reason moves directly enough. Shortly after he is introduced, a long conversation shows him as the "friend" of Joyce, Pierce, Pound, Ford, Pascin, and others. His function as supervisor, as conscience, is enunciated when he says, aboard the boat, "In a family like ours somebody has to worry"

(26), and he acts as a coordinator of detail. He tells his father, "I know you love him [David] the most and that's right because he's the best of us" (125)—a hint that he understands the relationship of the three.

Occasional lines of conversation project further Andrew's function, and an authorial double entendre from David is typical, "Oh, the devil. . . . he probably liked you like everybody does" (55). Andrew and Roger are, fabulistically, of roughly the same substance, and one kind of a link is established between them. "I'll take Mr. Davis. . . . Somebody said his stories were truly vicious. . . . You leave it to me and Mr. Davis" (71–72).

Yet the bond between Roger Davis and David is stronger, for they are not similarities but complements. At the age of twelve, Roger lost a brother, also named David, when a canoe overturned. The dead brother David is a lost part of self, and in his deepening relationship with Hudson's son David, Roger is trying to regain that lost part. He appears to do so in David's fishing-crucifixion sequence, when he attends David lovingly, gets him through the ordeal, and gives him an undisclosed consolation afterward. His own ability to love possibly restored to him, Roger is then able to enter what may be a valid relationship with Audrey Bruce.

The symbolic identity of the three boys is finally presented simultaneously, in a deceptive farce enacted in the bar. Here, the boys in their play-acting are cast in their "real" roles in the fable. When Andrew pretends to guzzle gin, he is the uncontrolled, animalistic force, the "bad"; the abstaining David is the virtuous good; Tommy as nagging conscience emerges in a clear, supervisory, rational role. The purpose of this apparent horseplay is understood when it is seen as a defining part of a fable; before, it seems so much self-indulgence. And it still may be, for though it is a highly concentrated representational miniature, it is nevertheless a dull piece of reading. It shows, and glaringly, a tendency that mars both this book and, sometimes, *Across the River and Into the Trees*: Hemingway has come to lack complete perspective on some parts of the personal experience that he uses, even when he succeeds in making what ought to be highly successful correlatives out of them. In short, even his awesome ability to organize symbolically cannot hide an occasional case of the cutes.

Nor does it hide, here, his sentimentality. This was always Hemingway's great weakness, though he almost always kept it under iron control in the fiction he allowed to go between covers. Indeed, in his first-line work, the objectification of *sentiment* into pure image or understatement is proverbially one of his greatest strengths. It is in uncollected work, especially in journalism, that he lets the sentimentality ooze over the landscape. Then, sometimes, as in *The Dangerous Summer*, he fairly wallows in it. "Bimini" is sticky with the stuff. No subjects are more perilous for the novelist than a happy life and a loving family, and Hemingway does not surmount them gloriously. Like that episode in the bar, many of his segments work splendidly as schematics but on the literal level are quite simply cloying. Whether the respectable structure and the sometimes splendid imagery of the novella ultimately dominate this great corruption is perhaps a matter of individual judgment. But certainly "Bimini" is a very seriously flawed production. The author has successfully contained his enemy in "Cuba" and "At Sea," and the opinion here is that *Islands in the Stream* seen whole easily survives those embarrassments within its first part.

The major phase of this contrapuntal development of Hudson with his sons, certainly, is David's ordeal with the fish. There, it fuses with the companion "Secret Sharer" counterpoint line of Roger Davis, provides a metaphor for the main melodic line of Thomas Hudson, and expresses the primary, tragic theme of the whole novel. Its function would have been even clearer and the final effect perhaps stronger if *The Old Man and the Sea* had remained as coda to the composition, for David's ordeal is clearly patterned to match and to forecast Santiago's and to reflect Christ's. The matching details are dense and obvious and most need not be cited here.

It might be useful to note that the three hours, actually "three hours and five minutes," David spends with the fish correspond to Santiago's three days, which proceed from the three days of the crucifixion drama and the three hours of darkness of the Crucifixion itself. But unlike Santiago's enactment of crucifixion, it suggests the tragic rather than realizes it and is probably meant to do no more.

This section also has an incident that links it to the "Secret Sharer" line: Eddy's leaping into the water after the lost, sinking fish and leaving his hat to float on the water. It will be remembered that Leggett, the secret sharer, loses the protective hat the captain has given him as he dives from the ship; as it floats on the water, it serves as marker and guide for the captain on both levels of the story. On the realistic level, it is a guide by which he can check the movement of his ship; on the symbolic, it is a marker for his psychic and ethical life.

Here, Hemingway has kept the incident of the source but rearranged it, so to speak—a normal course for fiction proceeding from a mythic base. When Eddy—and not Roger the secret sharer—leaves the hat on the water, *his* whole function demands understanding, and the hat draws into a pattern all he has said and done in the novella. The earlier high point of his action was saving David from the shark's attack by his quick response and accurate fire. His general conduct is one not simply of devotion to but responsible care for the boys, and the leap into the sea caps and at least suggests a definition for him as an abstraction. He is fidelity, or perhaps *responsible* fidelity. When he dives after the fish, he is going beyond any reasonable expectation of realistic fidelity: he becomes an apotheosis of it. So his hat on the water, the mark of his prodigious fidelity, becomes in the symbolic mode of the story a universal standard, the guide for all to steer by, to aspire to. As such, it relates significantly to Thomas Hudson's later, ultimate act: to pursue his own responsibility at the cost of his life.

When Hudson learns that David and Andrew have been killed with their mother in a car wreck in Europe, he feels he has lost part of his own life. Fabulistically he has indeed done so. And his reflections after the death of the boys prepare for the heavy use of Dante in the next novella, "Cuba." "On the eastward crossing on the *Ile de France* Thomas Hudson learned that hell was not necessarily as it was described by Dante or any of the other great hell-describers, but could be a comfortable, pleasant and well-loved ship taking you toward a country that you had always sailed for with anticipation. It had many circles and they were not fixed as in those of the great Florentine egotist" (197). So even if the deaths of David and Andrew do not make the best catastrophe, they are made completely believable by the compelling quality of Hudson's anguish, and anguish will be the dimension in which he lives from here on.

The conclusion projects the Hemingway constant: life goes on. Shattered as he is, parts of himself lost forever, Hudson calls up the strength to continue. In his stateroom on the Atlantic liner, in the predawn hours of the fourth day after the event—an ironic resurrection touch?—he reflects: "The New Yorker is . . . evidently a magazine you can read on the fourth day after something happens. Not on the first, or the second, or the third, but the fourth" (198).

"Cuba"

The eloquent invocation of Dante and Dante's hell near the end of "Bimini" has defined, broadly, what the next part of the novel will be about: Hudson is to take a journey through hell. It will not be a hell that corresponds in even approximate arrangement to Dante's, but Hudson's reflection is a clue carefully given. And Hemingway parallels certain incidents not only in the *Inferno* but in Book VI of Vergil's *Aeneid* and possibly one in Sartre's *No Exit* to establish Hudson's locus as hell; the possible use of several literary hells as sources may emphasize the universal base of Hudson's. Philosophically, of course, his is closer to Sartre's. He is trying to resist and to confront hell with what dignity he can, and his only way is by the Sartrean thrust: man must choose and act to give meaning to a painful and chaotic universe, and he is completely responsible for those decisions and acts. Hudson is to find his life stripped to the final irreducibles of this responsibility, and he states it directly and idiomatically at the end of "Cuba": "Get it straight. Your boy you lose. Love you lose. Honor has been gone a long time. Duty you do. . . . Sure and what's your duty? What I said I'd do. And all the other things you said you'd do?" (326).

The novella moves to that definition through the standard Hemingway confrontation and development of opposing keys: the dominant key is the hell that his consciousness now represents, compounded of his griefs and agonies; the home key is his effort to endure them, to survive his journey through hell and still maintain meaning and responsibility. In this confrontation, a tragic design *complete within the novella* is embryonic, for in the larger, total novel, this movement is a heavy rush toward catastrophe. Yet the design is there: to Hudson in his grief returns his first wife, the mother of his just-dead oldest son and the one woman he truly loves. Their reunion, in effect over the body of the lost son, appears to be a communion, and the possibility of happiness is visible for a moment. They reach for it, touch it, and lose

211

it: it disintegrates as it is touched, destroyed by the irreconcilable clash of their psyches as well as by the urgent orders that send Hudson to sea. In that catastrophe, he has truly lost everything—except duty, and he goes to it.

"Cuba" may have as elaborate a structure of symbol and reference as does "Bimini"; if so, I have been unable to find it. However, there are visible representations that link it to those earlier hells. When Hudson jocularly tells a warrant officer in the embassy, to which he reports, "Go to hell," the officer replies, "I'm there now" (255); this suggests the officer as a custodian of hell—his name is Hollins, perhaps for hell-in. This is immediately emphasized by encounter in the hall with a lieutenant commander named Archer, who comments on Hudson's solidity. Inevitably, the name suggests Chiron, the centaur and archer who comments on Dante's substantiality in Canto XII of *Inferno* as he directs Nessus to take the poet across the river of blood. His reference to Hudson's solidity also suggests the corporeal substantiality of Vergil compared to the spirits in *The Aeneid*, when his weight brings the ferry deep into the water. Both Dante's and Vergil's physical contrast to the spirits on their respective descents is more generally recalled. This external fixing of Hudson in hell is to be intensified and clarified by certain of his own interior declarations, which project his hell as a universal hell, a manifestation of the human condition.

So the tension of this work-within-a-work proceeds very simply from the opposition of primary forces: Hudson's grief, his hell, and his resolution to maintain responsibility in the face of that grief. As in certain Hemingway short stories, this conflict is not expressed for much of the story; it is almost exactly at midpoint of "Cuba" that young Tom's death is revealed. Until that time, the development has consisted almost entirely of incident, image, and monologue that illuminate the complexities of Hudson's character, obliquely suggest themes, and establish the *physical* universe of the novella. In this early development, too, there is another operating contrast—that between the muted ordinariness of Hudson's actions before the disclosure of his last son's death, and the swift and dramatic revelation of his consciousness as hell after that disclosure.

The long prelude of Hudson awaking with the cat in bed with him is presented apparently humorously, but it dramatically objectifies the center of his emotional situation, and in certain of its movements it suggests various themes delicately but strongly. Artfully, the immediate present of Hudson and the cat is juxtaposed against the immediate past of Hudson's just-completed mission at sea and his nineteen hours on the bridge; this retrospects into the scene in the waterfront bar where Boise as a stray kitten is accepted by Hudson at the insistence of an unnamed son. This immediately emphasizes Boise as, in part, a son substitute, as well as another kind of love figure, for he has "outlived the boy"; there is both dramatic irony and preparation for Tom's death in the phrase. At the instant, the reader identifies the dead son as one of the two killed earlier; later, he is emotionally certain it is Tom. The Boise relationship is thus crystallized: "The way he and Boise felt now, he thought, neither one wanted to outlive the other. I don't know how many people and animals have been in love before, he thought. It probably is a very comic situation. But I don't find it comic at all" (212).

In this remarkable and deceptive opening, Hudson has thus been dramatized—not described—as a man bereft of human love, forlorn, and in isolation. This condition contrasts tellingly with his achieved stasis and happiness at the outset of "Bimini," and it is, of course and more importantly, the point from which he moves through the rest of the novel in his thrust toward a new definition. His life on the Sartrean far side of despair is already well advanced; he has not yet filled the shape of the tragic protagonist, but he is moving toward it.

After this thematic prelude, that development becomes committed to filling out Hudson's palpable world: his other cats, the *fincia*, his life at sea and ashore. Boise has been the reference point for a voyage through consciousness and time so expertly steered that one is not instantly aware that it is in progress. By the time it is done, Hudson in his new manifestation stands clearly before us, in consciousness and in physical situation.

Another cat, Princessa, prompts Hudson into a Proustian recollection about his affair with a princess aboard an ocean liner. The reverie is casual, erotic, and sometimes humorous, but it culminates in one of those Hemingway reflections that evoke the tragic and then cut, ironically and sharply, away from it. This suggestion of two tragic accompaniments, the sadness in time and the insubstantiality of love, is also hinted in a conversation about two fighting cats, one of whom seems bound to be killed by the other, "Yet once they were loving brothers" (236).

Hudson's strength and solidity in the face of the eroding impact of time and event is quickly and movingly defined in his encounter with Commander Archer as Chiron, cited earlier:

> "You don't have to feel cheerful," Fred Archer said. "You've got it."
> "You mean, I've had it."
> "You've had it. And you've rehad it. And you've rehad it doubled."
> "Not in spades."
> "Spades won't be any use to you, brother. And you've still got it."
> (256)

The impact of the idiomatic conversation is, first, that Hudson has indomitable psychic strength ("You've got it") and has suffered irreparably ("You've rehad it doubled"); he is thus given further definition as the Hemingway-Sartrean hero, one who by will and act exists after total personal disaster, one who is strong enough and large enough for tragic magnitude even if he has not yet assumed it.

The encounter also prepares for the revelation of a disaster to Hudson already sustained, and Tom's death is shortly disclosed in an archetypal Hemingway indirection: as Hudson plays poker dice with Ignacio Natera Revello, a figure of banality and sentimentality, he tells of it off-handedly. His careful stoicism plays against the excess of Ignacio's sentimentality, a contrast that offers a bitter irony. It follows an unintentional double entendre by Ignacio which foreshadows the ultimate catastrophe: he says over the dice to Hudson, "I hope you die" (262).

Ignacio is another link to the earlier hells; the comment about his name, "Sounds like an Italian cruiser" (269), calls up both the Florentine Dante and the Mantuan Vergil, who are both Italians and "cruise" through hell. The view of Ignacio as such a deliberate reference is strengthened by his comment to Hudson, "your Latin is excellent" (263), which apparently points—in context—to the utilization of Vergil.

In the context of the first direct invocation of Dante, and of the first firmly drawn hell figures, other developments in the bar suggest themselves as connections to either Dante's or Vergil's hell. The joking about "Sin Houses" by Hudson's crewmen, Willie and Henry, is a fairly heavy summoning of Dante's sin circles, and though there is nothing like a topography matching Dante's, as the author has told us there will not be, several of the sins he cites are evoked here. Willie's and Henry's urgent search for whores is a manifestation of Dante's incontinence and lust, and Hudson's love for Boise the cat a more specific pairing with Dante's sodomy. Other pairings include: the heavy drinking of all in the bar—gluttony; playing power dice for drinks—gambling; the corrupt public officials as described by the politician—fraud. In "Bimini," Roger's violence suggests Dante's circle of the wrathful, and the massacre in "At Sea," his subcircle of murderers.

However, the whore with the heart of gold, Honest Lil, who sits in semidarkness at the end of the bar and who serves briefly as Hudson's confidante, seems to evoke the Sybil and her cave in the *Aeneid*, rather than any spirit in the *Inferno*. Hudson's first wife, who comes to him directly in "Cuba" and in vision in "At Sea," appears to be another Beatrice figure promising salvation—but not able to deliver it.

Such identifications and parallels are essentially tentative, and some extremely tentative. But the utilization of Dante is declared directly by Hemingway, and the utilization of Vergil seems projected: in the perspective of these firm generalities, the less firm specifics serve to insinuate, almost subliminally, Hudson's condition and place as hell. Thus the basic conflict of the composition is enhanced, deepened, and kept always to the fore; this is Hudson versus hell, Hudson versus his great grief, and this confrontation is most moving in realistic terms as it moves toward tragic impact. The literary sources simply intensify and frame it.

Hudson's Beatrice, his first wife, never named, appears in what amounts to a materialization. Through the doorway of the bar, Hudson sees an army-chauffeured car pull to the curb and his former wife step out. A movie star, she has been entertaining troops on the island and has come looking for him..

It seems that she may indeed guide him out of hell, a promise possibly objectified when she takes him from the bar to the *fincia*. In his house, through what may be Hemingway's most mature love sequence, they move to a renewal of love and even the promise of permanent reunion. But the promise disintegrates in a quarrel, and its failure is crystallized in the aborting of a communion ritual: champagne poured is never finished, and eggs prepared are never eaten. Emergency orders summon Hudson back to sea, but the pair have already been forced into an awareness of the impossibility of a permanent return to each other. She has said, "I'm tired of you already. . . . We broke up because I got tired of you. You've always loved me and you couldn't help it and you can't help it now" (324).

The undrunk champagne goes flat and the eggs go to Boise—a circumstance heavily stressed by the text. So it is thus his cat who completes Hudson's ceremony of sacrament; at the end as at the beginning, Boise is a configuration of Hudson's isolation and loss, the remnant of his love. Hudson has reached and lost again and we now feel *him* as tragic, even though the progress of his tragedy is just becoming clearly visible. He is stripped once more of all the conventional emotional supports but duty and is thus in the Conradian vacuum as he moves toward his final action. The defining passage might be profitably repeated: "What's one more beating if we get to close? . . . get it straight. Your boy you lose. Love you lose. Honor has been gone a long time. Duty you do. . . . Sure and what's your duty? What I said I'd do" (326).

"At Sea"

It is interesting to compare the whole novel before the severing of its fourth part to Beethoven's *Ninth Symphony*, in which the first three parts are orchestral and the fourth is in voices: the first three parts of the novel are Hudson's and the fourth would belong to Santiago, who has no relationship to him except in theme. But with *The Old Man and the Sea* departed, "At Sea" becomes the last full movement in this symphony. If it is not the sublime recapitulation that the lost fourth would have been, it will certainly do. It stands alone more impressively than the other two parts and simultaneously serves as culmination: sharply tragic itself, it brings the whole novel into focus as a tragic statement. Its philosophic concerns are those of creating meaning in emptiness, purpose in pain, and salvation in hell—and of demonstrating the potential tragic stature and consequent nobility of man. "At Sea" is catastrophe and transcendence to tragedy, and Hudson becomes both tragic hero asserting himself against the universe and existential man creating, with finality, his own definition in the void.

The contending keys have undergone modification since "Cuba": there, they were anguish and Hudson's determination to function in that anguish. Here, they have been deepened and intensified, and the anguish not only includes but is dominated by the approach of death; Hudson's resolution is to execute his choice in the face of his own death. His will to duty may be seen as home key, and death as opposing and dominant key—though the proposition is equally sensible when reversed. The lower part of his consciousness, full of pain and loss, remains his hell, but that hell is now part of the total complex that threatens to destroy him.

In the face of the loss of his third and last son, and the loss of his only truly loved wife a second time, and of the death he feels approaching, he maintains the resolve to perform the function he has chosen and accepted—his "duty." That performance is not simply solace but meaning and, finally, becomes tragic action.

In this, "At Sea" follows directly one pattern of the Conradian tragic novel and confirms *Islands in the Stream* in that pattern; it has acknowledged that source elaborately in "Bimini" and will do so again, less elaborately, here. The mysterious task that has summoned Hudson and his converted pleasure cruiser is to look for wreckage or survivors of a German submarine believed sunk northeast of Cuba. After he and his crew discover the nine villagers slaughtered by German bullets, Hudson understands that this mistake has committed the Germans to a death struggle, and that if he commits himself totally to his orders he and his crew have every chance of being killed; indeed, he has recurring premonitions of death. His choice is clear: to interpret his orders discreetly and by no means dishonorably and thus avoid a shooting confrontation and survive—or, to go beyond the minimal necessities of duty, to engage a superior enemy, and thus to risk all the lives in his responsibility, including his own. With complete awareness he chooses, closes with the enemy, and virtually with foreknowledge brings about his own death. His extreme commitment to duty, which defines him, is also in dramaturgic terms the fatal flaw that kills him; his unwillingness to moderate what he conceives as his true and necessary course in his collision with the universe is the signature of the largest kind of tragic hero. And in the tradition of magnitude, he feels himself somehow in the proper rhythm of the cosmos as he dies, in reconciliation. His deliberate trade-off of his life for his duty is his transcendence: his devotion is a psychic triumph over corporeal death.

Hudson in his crisis is projected by early images, the first of which may be the first paragraph, functioning characteristically as a prevision of the whole. Although its representations are so fragile as to be indistinct, and though it cannot firmly insist upon itself as metaphor or symbol at all, it nevertheless offers a dreamlike suggestion of what Hudson will face and do. "There was a long white beach with coconut palms behind it. The reef lay across the entrance to the harbor and the heavy east wind made the sea break on it so that the entrance was easy to see once you had opened it up. There was no one on the beach and the sand was so white that it hurt his eyes to look at it" (331).

"The entrance was easy to see once you had opened it up" has a faint suggestion, in total context, that when sought resolutely the course of proper action or "duty" becomes clear; the empty white sand suggests the end of that course as death and transcendence. Such implications are clearly emotionally connotative rather than ideationally exact; much firmer is the quickly subsequent image of the land crab blocking Hudson's path on the massacre island.

Hudson speaks to him. "You on the way in, boy? . . . I'm on the way out," a dramatic irony. "You still have a chance," Hudson continues. "Nobody blames you. You're having your pleasure and doing your duty." But the crab will not clear the path and Hudson shoots him, reflecting, "Poor old crab. . . . All he was practicing was his trade. But he ought to have shuffled along" (336). The image recalls and roughly duplicates that of Frederic Henry as military authority firing at the fleeing sergeants—shortly before military authority fires at him. The crab is such a reverse emblem of Hudson: he can retire with complete honor and survive, or push a confrontation to its limits and die. He chooses the second, as will Hudson.

There are intervening implications between these two passages. Hudson says of the cut of water he is about to enter, "It's about eight times as deep as it looks," an easy, if angled, reference to the experience he is beginning; he sees "the size of the shadow of his ship on the bottom," which intensifies the subliminal implication of large, profound—and possibly ultimate—events about to ensue. Hudson's crewmen wear straw hats to investigate the island, maintaining a flimsy cover that theirs is a "scientific" expedition; these are called "scientific hats" in some extended by-play, and they are another exfoliation of the hat as duty emblem as it appeared in "Bimini."

218

These images are, too, the beginnings of the development of the opposing keys: the approach of death and Hudson's fidelity to duty in the face of death. Both are dimly sounded in the first paragraph; the shadow of the ship on the bottom has its suggestion of death, the "scientific hats" are an early allegro exfoliation of the duty-fidelity thrust.

An extended and interrupted image-reverie section, cohering about Hudson's pistol, effectively celebrates the unity of duty and death, though it is equally concerned with basic human duality. As he lies on the sand, the pistol is cited twice as "between his legs" and he says to it, "How long have you been my girl? . . . Don't answer. . . . I will see that you kill something better than land crabs when the time comes" (337–38).

The pistol is thus both object and instrument of love; he is wedded to it as death and, using it as phallus, will deliver death with it. This unity of the doer and the done to is that Hemingway constant Backman explored earlier;[7] the fused identity of death dealer/death receiver is underscored in the same passage where, aware of the pistol as a weapon with which he will kill, Hudson looks at four bullets extracted from the massacre victims and "knew they were the rest of his life" (337). He intuits he is to be both slayer and slain, and the keys of death and purpose thus merge in the pistol.

As this development of merged identity or duality is resumed, it assumes an ever more sexual configuration. He dreams his first wife is "sleeping on top of him," and in their love play, "with one hand he moistened the .357 Magnum and slipped it easily and sound asleep where it should be." In the dream, she complains, "The pistol's [duty is] in the way of everything" and puts it aside. Then she asks, "Should I be you or you be me?" and tells him, "I'll be you" (343–44). The roles are reversed in consummation, and shortly he "felt the pistol *holster* [italics added] between his legs . . . and all the hollownesses in him were twice as hollow" (345). Thus he is aware of the fusion of active-passive, male-female principles within him, just as he intuits himself to be both instrument and recipient of death: pistol-penis becomes holster-vagina.

7. Melvin Backman, "Hemingway: The Matador and the Crucified," reprinted in Carlos Baker (ed.), *Hemingway and His Critics* (New York: Hill and Wang, 1961), 245–58. References from this reprinting.

The Tragic Art of Ernest Hemingway

The development of the death key is steady, including figures of death as accomplished event as well as portents of Hudson's own death to come. The massacred villagers, the executed German sailor, the land crab Hudson shoots are all heavy phrases in the development; more subtle are those lines of speculation and dialogue that create a foreboding of Hudson's end. "I know too damn well where we are" (347), he says and is told with dramatic irony by his mate, "I promise everything will go faster than you could hope" (330). A superficially comic episode serves to prefigure his death: a pig intended for Hudson has run away from a small island supply base and rushed into the sea, committing "suicide." Shortly after the report, Hudson chides himself for plunging ahead "like a riderless horse" (356), a more serious version of the pig plunging into the waves.

The time-honored use of "west" as evocation of death appears here: "CONTINUE SEARCHING CAREFULLY WESTWARD" are the coded orders Hudson receives, and later he thinks, "The hell with the east wind. . . . Blow, blow thou western wind" (413). This defiant invocation of death is softened by his instant recantation and reflection that suggests that both winds, life and death, are the same entity and that both are good.

Actual deaths recur: first the captured, wounded German, then Peters the radioman and another German who shoots him, as Hudson and his men move against a moored turtle boat that turns out to be a one-man ambush. Well before Peters and the second German are killed, Hudson has reflected on a unity that he and the enemy share, that of awaiting death like fellow prisoners on death row. His interior agonies are always on the edge of his awareness of approaching death. Navigating a difficult channel, he thinks of it as "a bad dream . . . happening with such an intensification that he felt both in command and at the same time a prisoner of it" (414): he feels himself moving toward death as a result of both fate and choice, the eternal collusion of tragedy.

The flight of flamingoes he studies at length is fairly clearly a multivalent symbol, but one of its thrusts appears directed toward death and is the first positive view of that phenomenon: it projects it delicately as part of life, a unity, and even a beautiful one: "It's not just the black on the rose pink. It is their size and that they are ugly in detail and yet perversely beautiful. They must be a very old bird from the earliest time" (420). The black meeting rose is an obvious paradigm of death fused with life, a matching extended by the "ugly . . . beautiful" *concordia discors*, and "old bird from the *earliest* [italics added] time" suggests the unchanging permanence of the flamingo in this perspective—as death.

As Hudson enters that action in which he will be fatally wounded, two more apparent references to the Conradian base are made. The first and more direct one is the use of stakes: Hudson steers by the first, marks the site of his grounding with one, and is deceived by another in the tricky channel he enters, which leads him to a second ambush; this seems to relate to those stakes beneath the water's surface, presented at the beginning of "The Secret Sharer," with which Conrad suggests the submerged personality—and human duality. The fatal stake has, of course, a clearer and more obvious reference to the cross. The second spin-off from Conrad is the ambush, in which Hudson is shot by the Germans firing from the bank: Baker cites its resemblance to the ambush by natives of the steamer in *Heart of Darkness*.[8] It also calls to mind, and reverses, the episode in *Lord Jim* in which Gentleman Brown's evil men fire from their vessel into the natives on the bank. Hudson alone is wounded by "three chickenshit bullets" (464), and the elaborately developed death key begins to crescendo. As Hudson lies wounded, he knows he is probably going to die. From this point, the surge of the dominant, death key is met by the home, duty key: the two will contend, then join in tragedy's reconciliation and unity.

The development has begun early, with definitions of Hudson as "master" (332) and "skipper" (334), both words highly charged with the concept of responsibility, and moves slowly and simply forward as he studies the tactical situation, makes decisions, and issues elementary orders; he never leaves these necessities and they are a continuous development. The land crab has already been cited as a metaphor of Hudson, and it functions as a figure of both death and of purpose; it is a point where both keys meet and thus works as an element in them both.

Such a double function is also exercised by some subsequent images, notably the pistol. When in his dream his wife complains, "The pistol's in the way of everything," she is protesting both his duty and his close-

8. Baker, *Hemingway: The Writer as Artist*, 405.

ness to death. And the four bullets from the slain villagers that are "the rest of his life"—his death—are also the clear directives of duty: he must find those who fired them. Hudson's view of himself as pounding on "like a riderless horse" is primarily an image of his duty thrust, but it simultaneously offers the tonality of death, for that is what he is moving toward, and he knows it. The gray horse in *For Whom the Bell Tolls* is recalled.

The duty key begins with presentations of the simple obligation to function and to fidelity, and it never abandons that simplicity. But it deepens and intensifies to enlarge that conception, becoming an aware approach to the existential void, a Sartrean creation of value by self-conscious choice and aware action, as well as the great self-assertion of tragedy. A semiformalization of idiom sometimes accompanies this enlargement, as in the brief exchange between Hudson and the German prisoner:

> The German said three words with great effort.
> "He says nothing is important," said Peters.
> "Tell him he is wrong." (362)

Hudson has speculated as to which is ultimate, death or betrayal of the accepted trust; the keys balance in his soliloquy, and the confrontation is to become steadily more intense.

After he is wounded by the three bullets, Hudson lies down on the deck, taking a "last look" at the "narrow, green-banked river," in which "the water was brown but clear and the tide was flowing strong" (461)—suggestions of his life flowing out. Hudson grows weaker and accepts his pain, as he accepts, apparently, the life cycle that must ultimately bring death to those who have inflicted it. Even as he is dying, he never forgets what men owe men: he orders his crew to remove the booby traps from the turtle boat. And he is steadily aware of the beat of the boat's engines—an image that will define itself fully when the work ends.

"All your life is just pointing towards it," he considers, as he feels his strength ebbing and reflects on the traditional tragic components of incongruity, and waste: Why did the Germans commit the massacre? If they had surrendered, everything would have been all right. The whole chase is a waste, unnecessary. But the largest tragic hero feels there is an order, a design, in the face of the waste and incongruity and accepts the design whole. So with Hudson: "He felt far away now and there were no problems at all. He felt the ship gathering her speed and the lovely throb of her engines against his shoulder blades which rested hard against the boards. He looked up and there was the sky that he had always loved and he looked across the great lagoon that he was quite sure, now, he would never paint and he eased his position a little to lessen the pain. The engines were around three thousand now, he thought, and they came through the deck and into him" (466).

The beat of the motors is the beat of life, of the universe; it goes into him and he accepts, as he accepts that aspect of the sky and sea to which he is witness. He is dying in reconciliation: he has done his utmost and that is his transcendence.[9]

His last exchange with Willie suggests, not at all paradoxically, that the individual is at once part of a loving fraternity, and that he must meet final tests, specifically death, with his own isolated fortitude. It concludes:

" 'Oh, shit,' Willie said. 'You never understand anybody that loves you' " (466).

The primal conflict between death and duty has generated the tension of the composition and produced its tragic structure. However, there are other patterns and variations inside the prime design, and it is interesting to note how closely they relate to the same pattern in *The Old Man and the Sea*. The unity of the universe, so powerfully developed in *The Old Man and the Sea*, is strongly imagized here. And closely related to the conception of unity is that of duality, of the identity of opposites; again, Hudson is a preparation for Santiago and his oneness with the fish. In both books, reflections on the caprice of the sea scarcely need translation to be seen as reflections on the caprice of the universe, that incongruity or X factor that is somehow present in all tragedy.

9. Baker, De Falco, Kirsch, and others have perceived Hudson's final action and moments as triumphant, though they do not call it a tragic transcendence. Baker, in *Hemingway: The Writer as Artist*, 407–408, sees it as a triumph of duty and obligation over massively hostile forces. De Falco, in "Hemingway's Islands and Streams," 50–51, describes Hudson's victory as the possible understanding that "love is a transforming agency . . . the common bond of humanity." Robert Kirsch, in his Los Angeles *Times Calendar* review, October 18, 1970, p. 46, says Hudson (with Hemingway) here comes to "his clearest understanding of the world and himself."

And though *Islands in the Stream* could scarcely be considered a Christian tragedy, it generates a surprisingly large network of Christian symbols. These at least point toward one of the great schemes of *The Old Man and the Sea*: that each man who dies or suffers greatly for his commitment has something of Christ, the great archetype of humanity, in him. These certainly foreshadow the extraordinary development of Santiago as Christ figure, but also they refer backward to David in "Bimini." The eternal cycle is clear once more.

The bullets are a visible part of the complex: Hudson is fatally wounded by three, the number of days of the Crucifixion, at the end of the work; earlier he has reflected that the four from the bodies of the slain villagers are "the rest of his life" (337). The four and the three make seven, the number of days of Holy Week, and the combining of the two figures into one sum anticipates the more extensive combination of numbers in *The Old Man and the Sea*, the twice-repeated eighty-seven days. The figure three, of various significances in the Christian apparatus, is reiterated several times: Hudson notices "three small holes" (463) in the deck canvas made by the bullets that hit him, and he reflects on the "three chickenshit bullets . . . to fuck good painting" (464). As the beat of the engines goes into him, while he lies dying, he thinks, "the engines were around three thousand now" (466). And earlier, as he has approached the ambush that will mean his death, his dinghy signals him to keep to the right of three small keys.

The wooden stake in the channel that decoys him to his death may be a representation of the cross, and his nakedness, except for a covering of the loins, a parallel to Christ's on the cross. The leap of David's fish in "Bimini" is an ascension image, and in *The Old Man and the Sea* the same image is one of the crucial instants of the work. Both "At Sea" and *The Old Man and the Sea* utilize a play on the name Peter. After his crucifixion drama, Santiago directs Manuel to give the head to Pedrico, who can use it in fish traps—a clear parallel to Peter as head of the church and its chief proselytizer. More obscure is Hudson's consideration of Peters the radioman: "It is certain that he is not up to what we have. But maybe he is up to much better things" (401). This suggests, perhaps, the well remarked early failure of the disciple Peter, and his later redemption. Why? For no visible reason, except to add to the small complex of Christ symbols and to serve as a plant, a preparation, for the more moving use of the name and the complex in *The Old Man and the Sea*.

There are invocations of Christ, made aloud by participants with, one assumes, authorial double entendre, like those made by Santiago in *The Old Man and the Sea*. Hudson speculates as he closes on the fugitives, "Christ knows what's beyond that" (418). Immediately afterward he is wounded. Willie says, " 'Jesus Christ' " (458) in addressing him and declares, overtly speaking of the destroyed turtle boat, "Christ couldn't repair her in a month the best day he was in that carpenter shop" (458–59). There are enough such invocations, incidents, and images to make a Christian complex unmistakably evident. Hudson is less than overwhelming as Christ character, yet this dimension of him enriches the novella by adding to it that solid secondary theme, that all who commit totally achieve a kind of Christhood.

It will be remembered that in the fabulistic construction of *The Old Man and the Sea*, Santiago has another archetypal role, that of artist engaged in the execution of the work of art. Since Hudson is an artist by vocation and overtly, he inevitably makes a certain preparation for Santiago in the art-artist fable; it is, however, a limited and ambiguous preparation, for there is something akin to paradox in this relationship of the two characters. Although Hudson has been a painter of total vocation—and is a partly universal figure of the artist in "Bimini"—his pursuit of the fleeing enemy simply does not suggest an art-artist representation at all, much as one would like it to. The forecasting, then, comes to this: Hudson as literal artist prepares us subliminally for Santiago as symbolic and universal artist.

So finally, though both works stand alone they share a compelling unity. That unity may not enhance *The Old Man and the Sea* at all, but an awareness of it multiplies by several times the impact of *Islands in the Stream*. As tragedies, they remain close kin in all their "implicaciones."

CONCLUSION

A Triumph in Tragedy

Nearly half a century after his first artistic explorations of it, the young man of the Michigan lake country had come a long way from his early understanding of his own life, of what had happened to *him*. That was an intense but narrow understanding: he first saw himself in combat with a superior force which he might in a limited sense "beat." The world was a tough place but he could survive in it by being just as tough—in spite of that extra burden of sensitivity and psychic vulnerability. He was by no means without the capacity to empathize, but most profoundly he was interested in himself against the world—not man against it. Understandable enough, for the centering of one's world around himself is universal, a natural law. Certainly one of the significant marks of maturity is that one can see himself as exactly representational, that in the larger sense his plight is precisely everybody's plight, that he is important no more and no less than everybody is important. As an artist, Hemingway came to this kind of maturity early, however far he may have gone from it personally in the adulation poured upon him as a culture saint. Although his first real novels were based directly upon his own experiences, and though his most passionate interest was himself via his persona protagonists, he could still see himself and them as universals. More importantly, he could see in their sufferings the sufferings of all; he could objectify his own experience totally now. Those heroes were bound to lose the unequal tragic battle with the universe and could do nothing about it except lose beautifully. But everybody else, he understood and demonstrated, was in the same fix. Finally, Jake Barnes and Frederic Henry are everybody.

They have little control over what fate does to them except to take it with style, and Henry does not get a chance to do even that in the end. But the later heroes learn to do more. They learn to fight back. This brings them no closer to "winning" than were their predecessors, but they are larger and heavier human beings for the struggle. It is the valor of the struggle, the intensity and endurance with which they invest it, that gives them their weight. The struggle is always futile in material terms, but never in those of the spirit. For it is there that they earn their victory. In short, they are tragic heroes who have moved into a larger kind of tragedy—finally the largest of all tragedies, where they willingly *choose* death in defense of their commitment rather than compromise it.

It is hard not to see parallels between Hemingway the man and his character, Colonel Cantwell, who chose to dictate the shape of the last days of his life and make them his monument rather than live a little longer. When he put the shotgun to his forehead after joining his wife in the Italian love song, did Hemingway think he was also shaping his own end to his own terms, completing his own tragedy with an act of will and transcendence? No one can know. It does seem possible and perhaps even more than possible.

Whatever took place in his consciousness that morning in Idaho, it is not unrelated to the forces within him that shaped his protagonists: they are finally refractions of their creator. And it is really he who has moved into a larger, more generous, and affirmative perception of life. For those who love tragedy, it is at its highest the greatest affirmation of all and shows the human situation and human possibility more clearly and more intensely than any other representation of either.

Hemingway declared life to be a tragedy early, both in his work and outside it, and he accepted his role as a prophet of tragedy almost from the beginning—possibly after some subterranean struggle. From that beginning, his tragic vision was to become more and more clearly ordered, his tragic conceptions to progress steadily. It would be fatally easy to see that steady progression within the boundaries of tragedy as an improvement. Certainly he moved to a more easily perceivable, a more "classic," a far more scannable kind of tragedy in the novels published after 1930. Very few have felt that *The Sun Also Rises* is tragedy at all, not even the earliest and firmest advocate of Hemingway's stature as a tragedian, and the insistence in this study that the book is authentic tragedy is a report from a very small minority. Although questioned by some, *A Farewell to Arms* has been fairly generally experienced as tragedy, unquestionably because of the unchallengeable impact of its unambiguous catastrophe. But its protagonist has not won that spiritual triumph in material disaster that many of the best critics feel is indispensable to tragedy. On the other hand, all the novels from *To Have and Have Not* forward are rich in examples of fateful decision, colliding imperatives, the fatal flaw in many variations, and an overpunishing nemesis called up by an all-too-understandable, sometimes exalted transgression. And only *To Have and Have Not* does not offer an extremely clear transcendent triumph by the protagonist. Even in that book, as well as the others, however, the protagonist stakes his very life deliberately on a course he has chosen; there and in every later book except *The Old Man and the Sea* he loses that life, and Santiago's loss is 'forcefully put forward as an equally great one. The author's path in the tragic field is easy to see: he has moved from a position almost on top of Frye's omnipotent fate boundary, where the universe punishes man unfairly simply to demonstrate its power, to one in dead center. His protagonists choose their paths are are coresponsible for their destinies even when X overpunishes them with the cruelest unfairness. They have challenged the cosmos in a confrontation they cannot win; they have won their dignity and their identity by this assertion of self; they lose their lives or an equivalent; but they take away the larger victory. They have achieved in a transcendent death or destruction that heroism Leo Gurko sees all Hemingway prototypes as seeking.[1]

Yet, is this inevitability as "improvement"? On its face it would seem to be. But how many would suggest, say, that *Islands in the Stream* or *To Have and Have Not* are "better" than *The Sun Also Rises* or *A Farewell to Arms*? The question answers itself. Whatever their irregularity as tragic works, these early novels have been felt almost universally as more intense emotional experiences and have been seen as more powerful personal statements and more accomplished examples of literary art than all but one or two other Hemingway books:

1. Leo Gurko, *Ernest Hemingway and the Pursuit of Heroism* (New York: Crowell, 1968). Gurko projects the author's great thrust as a quest for his own unique kind of heroism, one both satisfying and "sustainable."

virtually unanimous consensus places them in the very first line of the author's works. This may mean that regularity is not everything in producing the tragic impact—or it may mean, of course, that in the complexities of modern fiction, the tragic effect is not the ultimate effect.

Whichever, a steady progression by the author toward the making of highly self-conscious tragedy can be seen—starting, even, from the less-than-tragic stories of *In Our Time*. Of this progression, certain reasonably inevitable conclusions emerge. The first is that almost from the beginning of his writing career Hemingway had a powerful intuitive perception of life as tragedy, and that his first attempts to give it the shape of art were equally intuitive—and therefore original and "irregular." The second is that after he came to an awareness that his perception of life was tragic, and that formal tragedy was his natural way of ordering his experience, he acquired the systematic knowledge to construct such tragedies.

However the deep tragic attitude was developed into an extraordinary instrument of technique, it was developed, and it functioned with absolute consistency though with many modulations in getting the effect it was after. The real novels are all tragedies. So are a few of the stories. Most of the other stories and the ostensible memoirs may not be tragic themselves but they catch and refract the light of tragedy in glints and quick iridescences that give them more exciting and mysterious tones and hint at dimensions not really perceived. The body of Hemingway's work becomes one of the most compelling, and varied, achievements in tragedy that fiction has to offer. When critical vision is no longer even partially blocked by his public persona, so awesome and yet so destructive of a cool appraisal of his authentic value, another generation may decide he was one of the century's greatest makers of tragedy.

Index

Index

Index

Index

first wife of, 200, 211–12, 215–16, 219, 221–22; death of, 201, 218, 220, 221, 222, 223; and loss of love, 202, 206, 211–12, 213, 216; and visit of sons, 203, 206–10; and death of sons, 210 211, 212, 214, 216; and hell, 211, 212, 215; and Boise the cat, 212–13, 215, 216; and land crab, 218, 220–21; mentioned, 137
Hulme, T. E., 19–20, 76

Iceman Cometh, The (O'Neill), 101
Image: in "Snows of Kilimanjaro," 130, 131, 133; in *For Whom the Bell Tolls*, 141–42, 146; in *Old Man and the Sea*, 182, 185; in *Islands in the Stream*, 217–18, 219. *See also* Imagist ideals; Metaphor; Symbol
Imagist ideals: and Hemingway fiction, 17–19; and Impressionist painting, 19–20 and *n*; in *In Our Time*, 34; in *Farewell to Arms*, 73, 76; Hulme on, 76; in "Snows of Kilimanjaro," 131; in *For Whom the Bell Tolls*, 148. *See also* Pound, Ezra
Impact: as element of tragedy, 8–9; and *The Sun Also Rises*, 11, 43; and *Farewell to Arms*, 11, 68; and *Men Without Women* and *Winner Take Nothing*, 89, 95; and "Short Happy Life of Francis Macomber," 126; and "Snows of Kilimanjaro," 129; of *Islands in the Stream*, 200; in Hemingway canon, 229
Impressionist/post-Impressionist techniques: and Hemingway fiction, 17, 19–21; and Imagist poetry, 19–20; and *Farewell to Arms*, 82; and *For Whom the Bell Tolls*, 147–48
"In Another Country," in *Men Without Women*, 94
"Indian Camp," in *In Our Time*, 31–32, 33, 36
"Indians Moved Away, The," 106
In Our Time, 29–39; and tragedy, 10, 31–32, 33–34; as autobiographical, 29–30, 105; publication of, 30; interchapters in, 30, 34–35; unity of stories in, 30–31, 32–33; summary of stories in, 33–39; pleasure/pain unity in, 52, 143; mentioned, 89, 90, 93, 97, 192, 229
Irony: defined, 5–6; in *Farewell to Arms*, 15, 71, 78–79, 87, 218; in *For Whom the Bell Tolls*, 15; in *To Have and Have Not*, 15, 109, 110; in *Men With-*

out Women, 90, 94, 95–96; in *Winner Take Nothing*, 98, 100, 102–103; in "Snows of Kilimanjaro," 132; in *Across the River*, 163; in *Islands in the Stream*, 200
Islands in the Stream, 198–225; tragedy in, 14, 69, 199–200, 201, 216; musical form in, 26; literary sources for, 157, 179, 197, 201, 202, 203; Christian symbols in, 157, 224–25; and *Old Man and the Sea*, 173, 199, 202, 203, 204, 207, 216, 223, 224, 225; composition of, 198–99; autobiographical source of, 199; "Bimini" in, 199–200, 201–11, 213, 218; sons in, 200, 203, 206–10, 211, 212, 214, 216; death of Hudson in, 201, 218, 220, 221, 222, 223; sharks in, 203, 207, 210; criticism of, 208–209; Sartrean aspects of, 211, 212, 213, 216, 222; "Cuba" in, 211–16; "At Sea" in, 216–23; pistol image in, 219, 221–22; mentioned, 15, 59, 228. *See also* Hudson, Thomas
Ivancich, Adriana, 172, 198

James, Henry, 20, 27
Jaspers, Karl, 3
Joaquin, in *For Whom the Bell Tolls*, 150, 152
Jordan, Robert, in *For Whom the Bell Tolls*: as tragic protagonist, 13, 126, 139, 159; and irony, 15; choices of, 13, 139, 140, 141; and musical form, 25, 146; and duty, 127, 139–40, 141, 147; and the bridge, 139; flaw of, 140; and human community, 142; pleasure/pain unity in, 143; aristocracy of, 144; death of, 145, 146; model for, 154. *See also* Love
Joyce, James, 27, 99, 153, 207

Karkov, in *For Whom the Bell Tolls*, 144, 146
"Killers, The," in *Men Without Women*, 94–95
Killinger, John, 43
King Lear (Shakespeare), 55, 82
Krieger, Murray, 3, 10
Krutch, Joseph, 3, 9

Lair, Robert, 21
"Last Good Country, The," in *Nick Adams Stories*, 105–106
Leggett, in "Secret Sharer," 205–206

236

Index

Index

Index

Religion: in *The Sun Also Rises*, 49, 52, 56–57; in *Farewell to Arms*, 78, 81, 86. *See also* Christianity; Crucifixion

Renata, in *Across the River*: and romantic love, 158, 162, 165, 167, 169; as image of youth, 158, 163–64, 165; as Beatrice, 165; and catastrophe, 168; mentioned, 161

Republican guerrillas, in *For Whom the Bell Tolls*, 147, 150–51

"Revolutionist, The," in *In Our Time*, 30, 33, 38

Reynolds, Michael, 66–67 and *n*

Rinaldi, in *Farewell to Arms*, 65, 79, 81, 87, 147, 156

Robbe-Grillet, Alain, 46

Romanticism, 44, 47

Romeo and Juliet (Shakespeare), 1, 5, 65

Romero, Pedro, in *The Sun Also Rises*: source for, 41; and Brett, 46, 52, 60, 61; as ideal, 48; as aristocrat, 50, 51; and Robert Cohn, 52; and religion, 57; mentioned, 55

Ross, Lillian, 20

Ross, M. L., 48

Rovit, Earl, 42

Sanford, Marcelline Hemingway, 22

Santiago, in *Old Man and the Sea*: as tragic protagonist, 14, 126, 137, 159; and irony, 15; as author of his tragedy, 56, 174, 175, 176, 180, 181; choice of, 155, 176–77, 178; initial trials of, 174, 175, 183, 185, 189; struggle of, 175, 177, 179, 180; and order, 176, 178, 180, 181; imperatives of, 178, 180, 188; triumphs of, 181–82; and Christ, 183, 209, 224, 225; as disciple, 183–84; merges with fish, 184, 191, 223; as artist, 186–95, 225; and Hemingway, 187; and luck, 189; economic considerations of, 194–95; mentioned, 26, 59, 127, 209

Sartre, Jean-Paul, 10, 14, 101, 126, 211

Sartrean thrust: of *The Sun Also Rises*, 40, 42, 44–45; of *Farewell to Arms*, 68; of "Cuba," in *Islands in the Stream*, 211, 213, 214, 216, 222. *See also* Existentialism

Saunders, Bra, 120

Scheler, Max, 3

Schneider, Daniel, 66, 72–73

Schorer, Mark, 173, 174

Scribner, Charles, 172, 173

"Sea Change, The," in *Winner Take Nothing*, 99

"Secret Sharer, The" (Conrad), 201, 202, 204, 205–206, 209–10, 221

Seward, Richard, 3

Shakespeare, William, 129

"Short Happy Life of Francis Macomber, The," 11, 126–29

"Simple Enquiry, A," in *Men Without Women*, 97

"Snows of Kilimanjaro, The," 129–35; and tragedy, 11, 129, 134–35; source of, 129, 135; thorn scratch in, 130, 131, 132; opposing keys in, 130, 131; frozen leopard in, 131, 132, 135; transcendence in, 134

Snow symbology: in *Farewell to Arms*, 73, 77–78, 83–84; in "Homage to Switzerland," 99; in "Snows of Kilimanjaro," 132–33

"Soldier's Home," in *In Our Time*, 32, 33, 36

Sonata/sonata-allegro form: defined, 22, 23; in *To Have and Have Not*, 25; in *For Whom the Bell Tolls*, 25, 148, 152; in *Farewell to Arms*, 25, 70–72; in *Islands in the Stream*, 26; in *Old Man and the Sea*, 175

Sophocles, 155

Spanish civil war: as source for *For Whom the Bell Tolls*, 138, 153–54; Hemingway stories of, 135–36

Spilka, Mark, 42–43, 62

Spiritual triumph. *See* Transcendence

Stein, Gertrude, 21*n*, 27, 40, 49

Steiner, George, 9

Stendhal, 27, 85

Stewart, Donald Ogden, 27, 41

Style, 49, 50, 144–45. *See also* Aristocracy

"Summer People," in *Nick Adams Stories*, 106

Sun Also Rises, The, 40–64; as tragedy, 1, 10–11, 13–14, 40, 43, 49, 137, 227–28; imagism in, 18; mounted policeman in, 18, 46, 52, 53, 63, 150; impressionism in, 20–21, 82; fugue form in, 24, 46, 116; public reception of, 40–43; autobiographical source of, 40, 41; as final phase of total story, 44, 45; romanticism in, 44, 47; fishing trip in, 45–46, 56, 60, 62; characters contrasted in, 46–49; swimming scenes in, 46, 61–62; corollary themes of, 49–53; aris-